23 $\frac{95}{25}$

D0206144

Ibsen — a dissenting view

BY THE SAME AUTHOR

Brecht, published by Oliver & Boyd 1961
The Twentieth Century Views Kafka (editor), published by Prentice-Hall 1962

PUBLISHED BY CAMBRIDGE UNIVERSITY PRESS

Goethe the Alchemist, 1952 (out of print)
Kafka's Castle, 1956 (out of print)
An Introduction to German Poetry, 1965
(revised as *German Poetry. A Guide to Free Appreciation,* see below)
The German Tradition in Literature 1871–1945, 1965
Poems of Goethe. A Selection with Introduction and Notes, 1966 (out of print)
Goethe. A Critical Introduction, 1967
Franz Kafka, 1973
Brecht. The Dramatist, 1976
German Poetry. A Guide to Free Appreciation, 1976
(with poems recorded on cassette, 1977)

Ibsen – a dissenting view

A STUDY OF THE LAST TWELVE PLAYS

RONALD GRAY

FELLOW OF EMMANUEL COLLEGE AND
LECTURER IN GERMAN IN THE UNIVERSITY OF CAMBRIDGE

CAMBRIDGE UNIVERSITY PRESS

CAMBRIDGE

LONDON · NEW YORK · MELBOURNE

WITHDRAWN

MOUNT ST. MARY'S
COLLEGE
EMMITSBURG, MARYLAND

Published by the Syndics of the Cambridge University Press
The Pitt Building, Trumpington Street, Cambridge CB2 1RP
Bentley House, 200 Euston Road, London NW1 2DB
32 East 57th Street, New York, NY 10022, USA
296 Beaconsfield Parade, Middle Park, Melbourne 3206, Australia

© Cambridge University Press 1977

First published 1977

Printed in Great Britain
by W & J Mackay Limited, Chatham

Library of Congress Cataloguing in Publication Data
Gray, Ronald D
Ibsen, a dissenting view.
Bibliography: p. 224
Includes index.
1. Ibsen, Henrik, 1828–1906 – Criticism and interpretation. I. Title.
PT8890. G794   839.8'2'26   77-5653
ISBN 0 521 21702 4

Contents

Preface   vii

1 The earlier plays   1
2 *Pillars of Society*   26
3 *A Doll's House*   41
4 *Ghosts*   59
5 *An Enemy of the People*   84
6 *The Wild Duck*   99
7 *Rosmersholm* and *The Lady from the Sea*   114
8 *Hedda Gabler*   131
9 *The Master Builder*   149
10 Last plays   163
11 Conclusion   200
Appendix. The poetry and the prose   213

A list of critical works referred to   224
A chronological list of all the plays   226
Index   227

Preface

For the earlier plays and the last of all I have used either the version in Everymans Library (Dent) or William Archer's (Hill and Wang). It would have been brash of me to have offered a translation all my own for the last twelve, and I have allowed myself to be guided a good deal by the translations in *The Oxford Ibsen* (The Clarendon Press, 1960–77) by James McFarlane and Jens Arup. (The last three appeared while this book was in proof.) References to *The Oxford Ibsen* are given at the end of quotations for ease of comparison. However, since I was not trying to render the plays as wholes, and there were some passages where a slightly different reading was important to my argument, I have made a translation, bearing in mind the interests of bringing out some particular point, or I have slightly re-phrased for other reasons. I was generously helped in this by Janet Mawby, who saved me from several linguistic errors of my own contriving, and made many critical comments. I am also grateful to Michael Black for more than usually detailed criticisms and help.

I

The earlier plays

There is still a large body of opinion that remains unconvinced by the reputation Ibsen has gained as the greatest dramatist of the last hundred years, as the modern Aeschylus, Shakespeare or Racine. The reader who looks up the index of *Scrutiny*, for example, will find no study of even one of his plays, and only a couple of brief review-articles partly referring to him: a surprising, though evidently intentional omission by Dr Leavis and his associates from their broadly comprehensive survey of the great European and American men of letters. Lawrence, once his early enthusiasm had passed, was equally dismissive, and so were Yeats and Synge, while Eliot paid Ibsen remarkably little attention or respect. In 1956 Mary McCarthy found his work, viewed as a whole, 're-petitive and inchoate' (p. 176)★; the most recent dissent was in October 1975 by John Weightman, in *Encounter*. On the other hand, dramatists from Shaw to Osborne have admired Ibsen very much, critics continue to speak in terms of the highest praise, and a great portion of European drama would scarcely be as it is if it were not for his stimulus.

The cleavage goes deep, and is in some ways hard to compre-hend. Ibsen represents, after all, for many spectators and readers, some of the best elements in the Western liberal tradition. His intense individualism cannot be denied. He is the insistent questioner of authority, the man who took nothing on trust, who insisted that a husband may not take his wife's devotion for granted, or a father his son's, who challenged unthinking patriotism at a time when nationalism was as strong as it has ever been, and who was equally emphatic in demanding that religion should be an expression of the true, untrammelled self. No one could have

★ Page-references to critical works relate to the 'List of critical works referred to' on pp. 224–5.

been more seemingly persistent in his search for that true self than Ibsen. The dramatic excitement of his plays comes, moreover, from a profound awareness of the difficulties of the quest: in order to insist that a proper concern for one's own self was one of the supreme duties, Ibsen had to attack root and branch centuries of a contrasting tradition. Selflessness was the Christian ideal which Ibsen, like Nietzsche, thought it necessary to expose for its ultimately self-seeking motive, and the clash between the old and the new continually provided him with the stuff of drama.

More of his success comes from the fact that at a certain point in his career Ibsen made a deliberate choice. The first half of his work, up to 1873, when *Emperor and Galilean* was published, was almost all concerned with the past, and with poetry in a traditional sense of the word. In nine out of the first thirteen plays the subject-matter is either Norwegian or ancient history. In nine (not counting fragments, or his opera libretto) he wrote in verse or included verse passages. In the second half, after *Emperor and Galilean*, he never wrote verse again, and never set the action anywhere but in the Norway of his own day. He ceased even to publish poetry after his *Poems* had appeared in 1871. This concentration on the modern scene, with all the vividness of its topics and the realism of unpoetic speech, contributed to the impact he made. No dramatist before him had combined modernity and social problems with such determination.

In addition, the last twelve plays, after 1873, had for the most part an ingenuity in construction, much indebted to a form of French theatre which Ibsen disliked, but which he deliberately adapted to his own purpose. He took over the fashionable mode of Sardou, Scribe, Meilhac and Halévy, and turned it into a vehicle for his own passionate concerns. This helped him, no doubt, to gain a public from among spectators already familiar with the mode. But the public was scarcely to be gained without a precise, craftsmanlike attention to detail, a cleanness of dramatic outline. One of the claims to fame made on his behalf is the neatness of his expositions, the naturalness with which he brings characters on and off stage, the positioning of his climaxes, the bringing down of his curtains. He disciplined himself to avoid the awkwardness of monologues and asides. He rid himself of the complicated plots and sub-plots, the coincidences, which bedevilled some of his earlier work. He made his plays tell by actions rather than words: Nora slams the door on her husband; Mrs Alving holds in her own hand the poison with which she may have to end her son's life; Hedda Gabler almost visibly destroys Løvborg as she burns his manuscript in the stove.

His stage sets were exemplary in their design: the portrait of General Gabler dominates the scene in which his daughter is brought to suicide; the depressing rain is seen through the long conservatory throughout *Ghosts*, until, ironically, the sunrise floods the mountains at the end; the space off-stage is employed to conceal menacing actions – it is where Oswald is heard flirting with Regine, a fatal moment for Mrs Alving, and it is where the 'white horses' of the Rosmersholm millstream await their victim; it is where John Gabriel Borkman paces up and down, *over* the characters' heads this time, and it is where the spire stands which Solness must climb, and from which he must fall to his death.

But it was the passionate concerns which carried Ibsen through. The portrait by Edvard Munch, still a young man when Ibsen had finally achieved fame, shows the impression he was able to make towards the end of his life. The hair and beard stand out from the portrait head like pointed flames, more resembling Blake's Jehovah than a portrait of a man, and Munch had not misread Ibsen, in seeing him as seeking, and perhaps expressing, a kind of divinity. From his earliest work, there is a ferocity, a dynamism that distinguish all but the least interesting of his early plays, the pieces he wrote in pursuance of his contract to write one a year for the theatre at Bergen. In the later works, this becomes a carrying force, which not only persists through each work, but carries on a sequence from one to another. The conclusion of one play is scarcely reached before Ibsen is devising the next which will amplify or, just as often, contradict it, in a continual cycle of expansion and contraction, systole and diastole.

There is something in this passion which links Ibsen with Goethe's *Faust*, though there is no need to suppose he continually had this play in front of him. *Faust*, published between 1808 and 1832, had achieved, by the time Ibsen had reached manhood, the status of a great classic of European literature. By the middle of

the century, so Jakob Burckhardt declared, it had become the
inescapable destiny of German youth to ponder its mysteries;
commentaries had begun to pour out, Faust himself became the
ideal man, the Titan, the 'Himmelsstürmer', and no Northern
dramatist could be ignorant of all this. Whether Ibsen shared this
popular enthusiasm is less important than that it existed, and that,
with his voracious appetite for newspapers and all accounts of
what was 'in the air' at the moment, he would not have failed to
catch the drift of Goethe's play, however often he read or saw it.
He knew at least a few lines by heart, and his biographer, Halvdan
Koht, takes for granted that Faust was in his mind while con-
ceiving two of his plays. Indeed, he seems to have been familiar
with at least some vital features of Goethe's interpretation of the
old legend, perhaps even with earlier versions of it.

Goethe's treatment of Faust's quest had a good deal in common
with the account which Hegel, Goethe's younger contemporary,
gave of the so-called 'world-historical man' (*weltgeschichtlicher
Mensch*). For Hegel, who influenced Ibsen first in his youth,
through Heiberg, the Napoleons, Alexanders, Mohammeds of
history not merely conquered vast areas of the earth's territory,
but summed up in themselves the whole spirit and history of their
times. They were the embodiment of a universal Will, or rather
of a Spirit, akin to the Holy Ghost of Christian doctrine, which
gave rise to or brought about all events at all times, and with which
they identified themselves. Just as, in popular versions of modern
scientific theory, the atom is sometimes said to be a kind of universe in miniature, with planets circling round a central sun, so
the world-historical man formed a microcosmic version of the
macrocosm, and more than that, a full representation of the
macrocosm as it existed in his day and age.

Goethe does not define Faust's rôle exactly in those terms. He
does, however, make Faust say, at the moment of his pact with the
devil, that he is seeking not happiness but complete self-identification with the whole of humanity, 'the crown of mankind':

> Und was der ganzen Menschheit zugeteilt ist,
> Will ich in meinem innern Selbst geniessen,
> Mit meinem Geist das Höchst' und Tiefste greifen,
> Ihr Wohl und Weh auf meinen Busen häufen,
> Und so mein eigen Selbst zu ihrem Selbst erweitern . . .

And what is allotted to all mankind, I would enjoy within my own sole self, reach with my mind the heights and depths of things, heap all their weal and woe on my own breast, and so extend myself to all their Self...

This was not an entirely original ambition. Hamlet feels something similar when he says:

O God, I could be bounded in a nutshell and count myself a King of infinite space, were it not that I have bad dreams

and it has been the aim of a certain kind of mystic since time immemorial. The particular emphasis given in the nineteenth century was on the rebelliousness involved in an ambition tantamount to a claim to divinity. As Goethe says, 'Nemo contra deum nisi deus ipse', 'No man against God, unless himself a god'. Faust engages diabolical help at the moment of expressing his purpose, and the preoccupation of the Romantics with the occult, the forbidden, the revolutionary forces, is all of a piece with the idea that the hero who rivals God has something of a devil in him.

Here lies a basic idea of Ibsen's plays. Many of his heroes and heroines seek metaphorically or in imagination to extend their dominion over the entire earth, and though the usefulness of this analogy varies a good deal – it is most remarkable in *Peer Gynt*, scarcely present at all in *A Doll's House* – it is often perceivable as a matrix or a fount of ideas. Each time, however, that Ibsen returns to the topic, the heroes realise that their all-embracing ambition involves setting themselves up in competition with the Almighty. Like Hamlet, they have 'bad dreams', which in one shape or another bring them to ruin. Seen in this pattern, these plays are a reiteration, almost a ritual, of Ibsen's never-satisfied impulse to enact the sequence of Lucifer-like revolt and defeat in yet another drama.

The first play, *Catiline*, appearing in 1850 at a time when revolutions had only recently swept over almost all Europe, is named after the conspirator who attempted to overthrow the established order of Rome. But Ibsen's purpose, though he had already written poems of passionate homage to the Magyar uprising, was barely political. Like his later plays, *Catiline* is related to topical issues, but also, more deeply and symbolically, to his own desires. He wrote in his youth, to his sister Hedvig, that he wanted to 'attain to the utmost possible clarity of vision and fulness of power,' and though he does not use Faust's or Hamlet's language, he gives Catiline similar words. Catiline too has 'visions of power, of greatness, of a life of deeds.' He is outraged by the baseness of the life he sees around him, and determined to restore it to its former nobility and splendour, though if he fails he will destroy it root and branch. He also begins to speak in terms which foreshadow developments in later plays. His soul is 'noble, worthy of a ruler'. A 'sovereign's throne' is before him; he has a 'princely soul', and dreams of 'greatness and regal power'. He is not, then, a revolutionary on behalf of the people, as the fact that the play was written so soon after 1848 might suggest. But then again, he is not simply attempting to be a king. He speaks of his 'high and daring goal' as 'unattainable', as though something more spiritual were at stake, and at one point becomes cryptically allusive: 'My purpose here,' he says, 'is higher than you think – perhaps than any thinks.' It would have been natural for Ibsen in his youth, with Romantic ideas pressing strongly on him, to have meant by this that Catiline's ambition was more than mere earthly rule. Catiline does in fact feel himself endowed by the gods with power to restore Rome to its ancient splendour, as Ibsen, living in a backward, stiflingly straitlaced Norway still dominated by Denmark, looked for inspiration to the Viking past. Esoterically, Ibsen could have read more into this: the possibility of being a 'King' himself was never far from his mind. As early as 1850, he had planned a novel about a man who was to be given a kingdom: his imagination fed on the subject.

In *Lady Inger of Østraat*, performed in 1855, there is a significant development. This is the story of a great heroine of Norwegian history who becomes here the leader of her people against the Danish overlordship – another theme suited to Ibsen's personal aspirations. Lady Inger is seen plotting to outwit the Danes and place her own son on the throne, yet in her desire to see her son crowned she reveals what such a victory would mean to her. Early on, she is described as 'a queenly woman', and the cause of her inward conflict is that she both feels a mother's love for her son, and is determined, through him, to rule. When she sees the pretender to the throne killed, at her command, she entertains the thought of a vicarious reign: 'Whom will they elect in the dead man's place? The King's mother – lovely name.' Only repentance for her deed brings her back to the thought that it is her son who must rule, not herself, and already 'unquiet dreams' begin to beat down her desire for kingship. Remorse at length bites so deep as to affect her mind, and, as it does so, she feels the urge not merely to rule Norway but to set herself up against God. She believes, in her madness, that her son is already proclaimed King, though in fact he is dead. 'The honour was hard to come by,' she says, 'for it was the Almighty himself I had to contend with,' and again, 'Who conquers, God or I?' Her ambition is presented as insane, it is true. But the scene of action has come nearer home: it is not Rome now, but Norway. Almost forty years later, in *The Master Builder*, the challenge to God, as well as the possible insanity of the challenger, was to be still a fundamental issue.

In *The Vikings at Helgeland*, performed in 1858, the heroine is again a woman who wants kingship for herself through a man. 'We will go forward with invincible might,' Hjørdis says to her lover Sigurd, 'to fight and strive and never rest until you are seated on the King's throne!' The language is heady, but the situation is close to that of other plays, including much later ones. Catiline is urged on by the dark vestal virgin aptly named Furia, Sigurd by the Valkyrie warrior-woman Hjørdis, Rosmer (in 1886) by the 'bird of prey' Rebecca West, master-builder Solness (in 1892) by Hilde Wangel. Like Rosmer also, the humane Sigurd is urged to celebrate a union with the wild, conscienceless Hjørdis, and when this is seen to be impossible, Hjørdis kills first him, then herself, rather as Rebecca perhaps tempts Rosmer to join her in death. In the earlier play, as in the later, this has wider meaning: Hjørdis wishes to be not only wife to the King of the Vikings, but also to wrest the power from the old gods now yielding before the advance of Christianity, and use it for her own ends. What she foresees is a kind of royal, divine marriage beyond death: 'Out of this life, Sigurd, I will set you on the throne of Heaven and sit beside you there!'

Ibsen was not writing straightforwardly historical plays at this early stage in his career, so much as a dramatised account of a self-aggrandising, self-expanding passion, so powerful as to repeat itself in play after play, in a concentration that few other dramatists have ever shown. Where others turn to a variety of themes, Ibsen continually reverts to the same one, often with the same basic characters in slightly different guises, and even when his dramatic skill is less evident than his obsession. There is a conventionality about some of these early works which can perhaps be explained by his efforts to provide what the public would be prepared to pay for. His plots are gnarled with complexities, and motivations often implausible in the extreme; he contrives painfully artificial misunderstandings, two-dimensional characters, his language can be turgid and rhetorical. Yet the persistent necessity to dramatise the conflict between self-assertiveness and self-abnegation drives him inexorably through all these comparative failures to the point where his private dream becomes publicly acclaimed.

The play which first brought Ibsen real fame – omitting *The Feast at Solhaug,* which had been well received as early as 1856 – was *The Pretenders*, performed in 1864. Like several of its predecessors, this was again ostensibly about Norwegian history. The plot concerns the struggle between two rival claimants to the throne of Norway in the thirteenth century: Haakon, the established king, and Skule, the earl who feels his rightful claims have been disregarded. It is the situation of *Macbeth*, even more of the Austrian Grillparzer's *King Ottokar* of 1824, which Ibsen may also have known. Yet again he put into it not only his own situation, using the protagonists to cloak his own relationship with Bjørnstjerne Bjørnson, the king of the Norwegian stage at that time, but also his mythical interest. For the first time, a direct male contendant for a throne is presented in the foreground: the progression through various masking devices has been completed, and now Ibsen confronts the issue in broad daylight.

'Every night in my dreams I am King of Norway' – this gives the keynote to Skule's character. But he is separated from the fulfilment of his dreams by impassable hindrances – 'on the other side are the kingly title and purple robes, the throne – power – everything!...but I never can cross the gulf'. The gall to his wound is that Haakon wears the crown with so easy a grace: he has the confidence and calm bearing of a man who never doubts his mission. Skule, however, is constantly haunted by doubts, and this because he wants something greater than Haakon could imagine. Haakon, like the Emperor Rudolf in Grillparzer's play, is settled in mind, he is king, and it does not occur to him to want more. Yet the one occasion on which he gains Skule's respect is when he goes further, when he proposes to unite all Norway, not merely the provinces he now rules, under one overlord. This 'great kingly thought' fires Skule's imagination. He is so convinced that this is his mission and his alone that he is deeply hurt by the idea having originally sprung from Haakon's mind. 'All shall be one, and all shall be conscious of it and know that they are one,' he repeats, recalling Haakon's words. From the moment Haakon spoke them Skule knew him to be the rightful king. Only such a desire for unity, he believes, endows a man with the right to kingship. Skule, whose first reaction was to pronounce the idea mad and impracticable, sees now that Haakon is in the right, and he himself only a pretender.

This theme is connected with Norwegian nationalism, a burning issue at the time the play was written. As always with Ibsen, its roots are more personal. The significant thing is that Skule concedes Haakon's claim because it is an attempt at achieving unity. He becomes aware that Haakon is attempting to achieve in the real world what he himself has only imagined, though his imaginings were on a far grander scale. For him, kingship means more than the overlordship of a part or even the whole of Norway. He is first impelled forward by the scheming Bishop Nicholas, who places the matter in an entirely different light. Nicholas mocks at Skule's impotence before Haakon's supremely confident sway. Cannot Skule see, he asks, that Haakon is assisted by a far greater power than that of his rabble of followers? 'His help comes from above – from the powers that fight against you and have been your enemies ever since you were born!' Skule must realise on which side he stands, and what his claim to power implies. 'Remember,' Nicholas continues, 'that the first great deed that ever was done, was done by one who dared to revolt against a mighty empire!...The angel who stood in revolt against the Light!' Here, in mythological and Romantic form, is the crux of the situation, now more Faustian. Skule is forced to see what his desire means, in its fullest symbolical force. The question of the throne of Norway recedes into the background in the face of this more far-reaching implication. If Skule can be measured against Lucifer, then his claim too must pass beyond any merely earthly dominion and reach out to the entire universe: he must need to be, in Goethe's words, 'a god himself'.

Nicholas is not making a passing utterance without relationship to the rest of the play. Skule takes over Haakon's idea and makes it his own. 'My father,' says Skule's son Peter, 'has a great kingly thought to bring into being; it is no matter who or how many are sacrificed to that end.' Skule sets himself up as king in his own right, disdaining any position inferior to Haakon's, though realising dimly that he has taken an impossible path: 'My kingdom? It is a dark one – like that of the angel who set himself up against God.' Nicholas has put the matter to him in these terms, and he has accepted it. His whole attitude is a *non serviam*. Yet for all that, he does not fully realise the position until, in a melodramatic moment, the shade of the dead bishop appears to him in the guise of a monk and offers him complete victory over Haakon's armies. At first Skule is all eagerness, and his ardour does not diminish when the monk offers 'to take you up on a high mountain and show you all the glory of the world'. His terror begins when he realises that this is in fact the bishop he once knew, sent by the Devil to grant him assistance. But even terror is banished at the thought of the armies of Hell which will march at his command. (Borkman will later use a similar though inexplicit image in which he summons up vast armies from below. Goethe's Faust also has diabolical troops at his command.) 'Yes, give me the crown!' is Skule's answer. But as with many legendary pacts with the Devil, an oath is first required. This too he is prepared to yield, until he learns what it is – that his son shall be completely at the Devil's command. At this, he falters: 'Ah, now I understand you – it is the damnation of his soul that you seek!' He drives the Devil's emissary from him, and goes in Christian humility, somewhat like Schiller's rebel, Karl Moor, to seek pardon from God, and death at the hands of Haakon's followers. As in all Ibsen's plays, death is the end of the ambitious rebel.

In its bare essentials, the play is a re-enactment, in different costume, of the Faust legend, with the difference that in this case the 'Faust' is unable to accept the bond. There is nothing, however, to suggest that Skule's ambition is meant to seem repugnant. On the contrary, there is an echo of the extremely well-known words of the Lord in Goethe's *Faust*: 'es irrt der Mensch so lang' er strebt'; 'man errs so long as he strives'. Skule, we are led to feel, must strive in this way and must consequently err, must even risk his soul's damnation. That is the sense of the concluding lines of the play, where Haakon, returning to the scene amid the rejoicings of his followers, after his men have killed the unresisting Skule, discovers the corpse. He replies to the congratulations of his marshal that Skule has been misjudged – 'there was a mystery about him'. And to the uncomprehending question this evokes he replies: 'Skule was God's step-child on earth; that was the mystery.' So also Lady Inger says of herself, 'Hush, let me tell you something. They hate me – away up beyond the stars – because I brought you [my son] into the world. I was meant to be God's standard-bearer through my country. But I went my own way.' The suggestion is that the desire for kingship is paradoxical – that, while on the one hand it sets a man up for defeat by the universe, at the same time succumbing to it is the only way for him to proceed. The revolt is an essential act if a man is to be brought nearer to God. With Haakon, the case is different. He is what Goethe and Schiller would have called a 'schöne Seele' – one who feels no need to reflect on his situation, but is born to be king. Once doubts commence, however, the whole cycle must begin, descending to the nadir before its upward path can bring it back to zenith. That path was Ibsen's, he may have felt, as he saw it in contrast to his rival's, as Schiller felt it was his, in contrast to Goethe's.

Brand, coming in the sequence immediately after *The Pretenders* (though with a gap of two and a half years), appears almost as an act of contrition after Skule's hubris. Brand too, the lonely, ambitious parson, has had his visions of glory:

> Dreams of beauty, dreams of might,
> Came like wild swans full in flight,
> Lifted me on stretching pinions,
> Bore me high through wide dominions,

> ...Incense streamed upon the air,
> Silken flags, and anthems loud,
> Alleluias from the crowd,
> Round my life's work, all were there.

He also comes in the first place to set himself up against God, or at least the God of established religion, 'a bald, grey, skull-cap-pated God'. His faith is in a young, powerful God, like Hercules, yet all-loving. At first, he can scarcely tell if he himself is a Christian, proclaiming 'there's beauty in a true Bacchante'. Moreover, he wants Unity and is dismayed at the distractions which divide other men's personalities. 'Whate'er you are, be whole-souled in it,' is his advice to the artist Einar whom he meets on the mountain-side. His God will restore such unity to all men:

> But from these fragments of the soul,
> These spirit-torsos that remain,
> These heads and hands, shall spring a whole,
> That God shall know His own again.

Brand is as much involved with the Will to Power as any other of Ibsen's heroes: he is curiously like Nietzsche in this, despite un-likeness. Dominion, unity, youth and vigour are at first as much his watchwords as they are Lady Inger's or Skule's. But in him the Will takes a different course. He comes first as a preacher, hoping to fashion all men afresh, 'to make them like God'. His first defeat comes when he finds men burdened down with feelings of guilt, unable to break through into a gay, free world of ruthless action, and at this he turns from converting others to the salvation of his own self. If he cannot make gods of men, he will at least make himself a god, in his inner being. Inspired by his wife, who sees a vision of the world which Brand is to create, he regains his ardour. A new Will begins to swell within him, as his wife, Agnes, says:

> Within
> Smoulder powers, I feel them glow:
> I can feel floods overflow,
> I can see a dawn begin!
> For the heart extends its bounds,
> Grows a mighty world and great, –
> And again the voice resounds:
> *This* the world thou shalt create! –

Here the parallel with Goethe becomes closer than in some earlier instances: the heart which becomes a world sounds decidedly Faust-like. But this is a Will not to power, but to renunciation. Brand believes that he can only 'be himself' through the total annihilation of the Will, that is, essentially, by the path of the contemplative. But the final result will be the same. Brand will become God, or at one with Him, not by the active path of the Dionysian reveller, but by the passive path of the mystic.

> Heart, my own heart, is the sphere,
> Ripe for God, created new!

From this birth of God in his own heart the imaginative mastery of the world will begin to grow.

This sounds like hubris in another form; certainly it leads to the same end. From the moment of Agnes' vision, Brand hurls himself into the work of annihilating selfhood with a fury only paralleled by his earlier Dionysian egoism. One selfish passion after another is ruthlessly stripped away; he denies himself the sunlight which formerly was his source of life, he casts off all wants, and sacrifices – as Skule was unwilling to do – even the life of his child to his ambition to become selfless. At length he comes to see that even his wife still means something to him, that he is still attached to, and thereby dependent on, another creature, still has personal desires. These too he casts away from him, going off alone into the mountains, to the crazy girl Gerd, whose

> mind distraught, whose giddying flight
> Makes foul seem fair and wrong seem right.

With her he goes to the mountain-church where, as he thinks, God can be worshipped most purely of all, in total isolation. He cuts himself off entirely from all organised religion and all contact with his fellow-men. But when he arrives there disaster overtakes him. His utter disregard of self, practised in the hope of yet a greater return of perfect selfhood, brings about its own destruction, and an avalanche sweeps down upon Brand and all his works. He has forgotten the fundamental idea which concludes the play: as the supernatural voice proclaims out of the avalanche, 'He is *Deus caritatis.*' Brand has not had the confidence to throw himself on the waiting though ambiguously destructive arms of Love.

In the same way Skule's rebellious armies were swept away by the avalanche of the forces of Haakon ('to defy me is to defy Heaven'), who came 'pouring down over Ekeberg in thousands'. Ibsen's last play was to end in the same way, for the artist Rubek's final effort at becoming himself a Creator is dashed to pieces by just such another avalanche. Disaster attends all these attempts at wresting power from the universe. Brand fails in his passive, self-destructive path as much as does Skule in his way of self-affirmation.

Between *The Pretenders*, *Brand*, and the ensuing play, *Peer Gynt*, there is an oscillation between these two poles of activity and passivity. Peer Gynt returns again to the active role of Skule (Eric Bentley, indeed, has called Peer a 'counter-Faust' and parallels between the two plays have been drawn ever since Ibsen's first appeared). He is the embodiment of the desire for kingship, its fullest expression in all Ibsen's earlier plays. 'I'll be a King, an Emperor,' are among the first words we hear from his lips. His dreams of 'Emperor Peer Gynt and his thousand retainers' are, paradoxically, almost identical with those of Brand. But where Brand meets with savage bitterness, Peer receives humorous treatment at Ibsen's hands. Audiences feel sympathy for Peer in his impudence and egoistic folly, and the early scenes are among the most successful Ibsen wrote. Yet Peer can be ruthless in self-assertion, like many other Ibsen heroes. The motto 'To thyself – be enough' is characteristic of all those described hitherto, and of some later ones. Catiline declares, once he has made the pact with Furia (corresponding to Skule's attempted pact with Nicholas), 'Now for the first time I am myself.' It is said of him that only when full of wrath, and brooding on revenge, was he truly himself. Falk, the hero of *Love's Comedy*, whose name, the Falcon, expresses the nature of his striving, proclaims:

> See, Personality's one aim and end
> Is to be independent, free and true,

or again:

> ...freedom's all-in-all
> Is absolutely to fulfil our Call.

Half Skule's tragedy lies in the fact that he cannot 'be himself' to the full, with all the ruthlessness which that implies, and must envy Haakon's self-assurance. Brand also plaintively asks:

> Cannot room on earth's whole round
> Just to be one's self be found?
> Man's one right, 'tis all I ask!
> To be one's self!

Peer is not alone in his philosophy, and though Ibsen shows him in the end to be not the ruler of the All he fancies himself to be, but a Nothing, an onion whose layers can be peeled away to reveal no core, the play is not a moral lesson on the folly of selfishness. It is rather a comic, amoral demonstration of what happens to a man who tries to follow out an egoistic philosophy. The last lesson Peer learns is the ambiguous one taught him by the Button-Moulder. 'To be one's self is to slay oneself.'

Yet this does not mean that Brand was right after all, for Ibsen shows clearly enough what happens when the path of self-annihilation is taken. Brand and Peer Gynt, like Wilhelm Meister and Faust, are counterparts. They are also interpreted as Ibsen's response to the Christian Kierkegaard and the ego-fulfilling philosophies based on Hegel. Ibsen sides not with the one or with the other but with both and neither. To quote Goethe again: 'We are in a situation which, although it may seem to drag us down with its oppressive weight, nevertheless affords us the opportunity, indeed, makes it our duty, to fulfil the intentions of the Godhead by, on the one hand, being obliged to emphasise our selfhood, while on the other hand we do not neglect to observe the rhythmical pulse of self-denial.' Neither the one nor the other alone, is what Ibsen seems to admire, though he seems to have been interested in a synthesis of both at once, an intensification of both to their uttermost limits, whereby each comes round full circle and meets its opposite.

That this was in Ibsen's mind – though at other times synthesis seemed tragically impossible – is shown by the massive, unwieldy play, *Emperor and Galilean*, conceived and partly written shortly before *Brand* and *Peer Gynt*, completed later. Ibsen found, in the historical accounts of the Emperor Julian the Apostate, the very type and example of the man who would best portray a more complete version of his own strivings. He shows Julian first as a young man brought up in Christianity, but revolted by the practice of the religion which he sees about him. Julian too has hopes one day of becoming Emperor, but they are better founded than Peer Gynt's or Brand's, for he is soon named Caesar, and thereby becomes heir to the throne. This places him in an advantageous position for the execution of his plan, and at the same time affords Ibsen the possibility of going further with his own project. Julian's disgust with the religion of his contemporaries leads him to Athens, where he learns from Maximus the Mystic to want more than the Emperorship. He is introduced, amid occult rites and ceremonies, to the neo-Platonic conception of the union of all opposites in harmony. A voice tells him that it is his destiny 'to establish the empire', the 'third' empire – not that founded on the tree of knowledge which led to Adam's fall, nor that founded on the tree of the cross, but 'that empire which shall be founded on the tree of knowledge and the tree of the cross together, because it hates and loves them both, and because it has its living sources under Adam's grove and under Golgotha'. Julian eagerly clutches at the hope of such a kingdom, in which it would be possible to combine the freedom and happiness of the Greeks with the self-denial of the Christian way of life. (While Goethe's Faust does not precisely attempt this, his union with Helen of Troy is meant to symbolise a similar synthesis of classical Greek and Northern, Romantic ideals.) Yet, like Skule, Julian realises that the task demands a ruthlessness which he is at first not prepared to show. He must become the associate of evil men, of Cain and Judas Iscariot. For what he demands on the one hand – the pagan's full life of the emotions – while it may liberate generous love and ecstatic gaiety, liberates also hate and greed and envy. It is this which makes any union of Christianity and paganism impossible, as Rosmer is later to discover in his turn. Either the life of the senses is rejected in favour of a life beyond the grave, as Brand rejects it, or it is accepted, with its double gift of love and hatred. Ibsen does not present the view that, if the senses and the emotions, and the unconscious too, are given full play, the result will be good. He emphasises that the result will quite probably be evil, at the least frustrating.

Realising this on his own account, Julian at first hesitates. But the prize is too great for him to resist, and before long he is seen as crowned Emperor, oppressing the Christians and attempting to restore the forgotten rites of Dionysos. It is a miserable failure from the start – the rites are either lascivious or languid, never a bold expression of delight in the bounty of Nature, as he intended them to be. Nevertheless he goes on with his plan. The rights of the senses must be re-established before they can be combined with the life of self-denial in a higher union. He plans to beget within himself the 'Messiah of the two empires, the spirit and the world', to be himself 'Logos in Pan, Pan in Logos'. 'I will possess the world' is still his defiant cry as defeat draws near.

Ibsen had only once before dealt with this problem of a synthesis of good and evil at all closely, in *The Vikings at Helgeland*, and then it had not been fully clarified in his mind. There, the question had been that of union between the ruthless Hjørdis and the humane, law-respecting Sigurd. As Hjørdis came to realise the impossible nature of her striving she fell into a frame of mind akin to Julian's. She was defiant to the end, but she was also distraught, almost mad, and haunted by visions of glaring eyes. In this state, she watched the flames burn down her husband's house with indifference, mindful only of her ambition to place Sigurd 'on the throne of heaven' and to sit beside him there. So also in *Emperor and Galilean*, Julian is driven by military defeat into frustrated hope. He too sees flames surrounding him – the fire-symbol is a significant one in several later plays – with indifference to his fate. He too is pronounced mad by those around him, and he too sees the path to dominion still open before him, though to all appearances his cause is totally lost. Watching the fire consume the fleet which is his only hope of escape and safety, he sees the miracle come about.

In that glowing, swirling pyre the crucified Galilean is burning to ashes; and the earthly Emperor is burning with the Galilean. But from the ashes shall arise – like that wondrous bird – the God of earth and the Emperor of the spirit in one, in one, in one!

An early version of Hilde Wangel's 'castles in the air, with firm foundations', in *The Master Builder*, can be heard here. But Julian is deceived, for the destruction of the fleet only makes his own

defeat more certain. As he falls, wounded to death, he acknow-
ledges this – 'Thou hast conquered, Galilean' – though he also
appeals to the old god, in paradoxical allusion to Christ's words on
the cross: 'Helios, Helios, why didst thou betray me?' As with
Hjørdis, his dream is fulfilled only in a mood of madness; as in
almost all Ibsen's plays, the Christian or anti-pagan, anti-individua-
list forces triumph in the end. But yet again the effort has not been
for nothing. Skule was called by Haakon 'God's step-child on
earth'. *Emperor and Galilean* ends on the same note. Two Christians left behind to watch over Julian's body (like Ella and Mrs
Borkman at the end of *John Gabriel Borkman*) are overcome with
the conviction that 'here lies a noble, shattered instrument of God'.
One of them at last bends over it to cover the face, and as she does
so concludes the play with words, very close indeed to the lines
from *Faust* about the saving grace of error (see p. 11 above):

Erring soul of man – if thou wast indeed forced to err, it shall surely be accounted to thee for good on the great day when the Mighty One shall descend
in clouds to judge the living dead and the dead who are yet alive.... !

It is the situation of Faust once again. Julian, like Faust, perhaps
must err, perhaps must make the pact with the forces of evil, since
otherwise life would destroy itself in a paroxysm of ascetic other-
worldliness. Thus in accepting evil Julian damns himself; that is
inevitable. But just as Lucifer is both the Devil and the Bringer of
Light, so Julian restores life to a world perishing beneath its own
self-flagellations. The third Empire is never established, and can
only appear to be established in the delusions of a madman. But
if men are not constantly engaged in the effort to achieve it, they
fall either into wanton lewdness or pious self-destruction.

Ibsen, then, is not committed to Julian. He stands back and
watches the fall of his creation. Nevertheless, by portraying that
fall, he indicates its necessity and emphasises the need he feels in
himself to go on dramatising a striving in the same direction.
Neither Brand on the one hand, nor Peer Gynt on the other, nor
yet Julian, who attempts to combine both their attitudes, could
ultimately satisfy Ibsen. He himself, however, is enabled to go on
by a faith which seems always to have afforded him a sure foundation. 'God is Love' are the concluding lines of *Brand*. Peer Gynt

comes home at last to Solveig, who, in the final scene, personifies the Mother of God, and in whose faith and hope and love he has, in her own words, always been maintained. (The parallel here is unmistakable: it is Goethe's Faust ascending after death to 'the Eternal Feminine'.) Even Julian receives a promise of salvation on the Day of Judgement, by virtue of the everlasting power of love. The 'diabolical' revolt is contained within an unshakable universal framework.

That a certain common pattern underlies many of the first thirteen plays is incontestable. But with the exception of *Peer Gynt* and to a lesser extent of *Brand*, the plays written up to 1873 are not the ones commonly performed, and most of them are unknown to the majority of audiences. They have their dramatic qualities to thank for this: the contrivances and awkwardnesses of the greater part of them outweigh the passion and the personal concern which went to their making and though several have been revived none has caught on. *Peer Gynt* is a different matter. The high spirits of the opening scenes, the Norwegian fantasy which is still kept in its place and does not descend to folksy whimsicalities, the pace of at least the first half, and the exposure of egotism and of the contemporary philosophy which advocated it are still highly entertaining, though the invention does not keep up consistently till the end, and the pace slackens tiringly in places. *Brand* is less often performed, but remains, like *Peer*, an intensely written play on one of Ibsen's main concerns.

There was a time when the agument that *Brand* and *Peer Gynt* were the two works on which Ibsen's reputation truly depended was advanced (by Ronald Peacock and Raymond Williams) and seemed likely to carry considerable weight. That ground may still need to be gone over again, though the argument must always encounter the difficulty that any solidly based judgment must rest on the verbal poetry, which translations often reproduce as though it were something near to jingle. The quality of Ibsen's poetic language, difficult enough for any reader not Norwegian to appreciate, is nowhere more crucial than in these two plays. Meanwhile, the emphasis in more recent criticism has tended to go in a different direction. While Raymond Williams believed – what may still prove to be well-founded – that Ibsen's real genius was hampered by the attempt in his final years to fit the realistic theatre of his time, the trend in the last twenty years has been towards seeing the last plays as the crowning achievement, even to seeing the prose in which Ibsen deliberately cast them as a form of concealed poetry, and the 'social criticism' as a mere means to the creation of drama of the highest excellence. George Steiner wrote in 1961 of 'this magnificent body of drama' (p. 297), singling out the late plays as having 'the kind of inward motion that we find also in the late plays of Shakespeare' (p. 295). James McFarlane wrote in 1970 of the 'towering stature' of the later dramas. It is this trend towards hyperbole that most needs critical examination at the present. By most of those who write about Ibsen it is now accepted as no more than his due.

The twelve, beginning with *Pillars of Society* in 1877, and ending with *When We Dead Awaken* in 1899, are readily grouped together not only on chronological grounds, but because they follow after Ibsen's final decision never to use verse again, implied in a letter to Edmund Gosse of 15 January 1874. In all of them, echoes of the earlier preoccupations can be heard: there are still characters who seek to embrace the whole world within their single grasp, and still attempts at a fusion of opposites, in a Hegelian sense, such as had been attempted by Julian the Apostate; there are even distant hints of a diabolical pact. Other themes and symbols run through from beginning to end in Ibsen's whole work: the mysterious fire, the death of children, the glaring eyes expressing the fear of retribution – it is clear that essentially the same man is urgently involved in essentially the same problems, though the settings have changed completely. Ibsen is writing now about the scandal of unseaworthy shipping, the status of married women, euthanasia, and many other contemporary issues, or so it seems, and it was very largely on this score that he was attacked by dramatists like Yeats and Synge, who saw in him only a proposer of problems. Neither Yeats nor Synge seems to have been aware of Ibsen's personal involvement, or of the pattern in the plays, taken as a whole, which suggests they are something of an autobiography of his inward self, rather than objective presentations of topics of the moment.

Yet the fact of personal involvement, taken by itself, does not turn Ibsen into a great dramatist, nor does the fact that his skill as a dramatic craftsman increased with the years. That improvement in skill has been well documented, and stands beyond question, but need no more conduce to good drama than the skill of a first-rate joiner need lead to fine furniture. The quality of the work still remains to be defined, and here some hesitation has been expressed, even by some who accept Ibsen's reputation without serious qualms. P. F. D. Tennant, for example, in a much-used work on Ibsen's dramatic technique, observed almost in passing a matter of vital importance in any attempt at appreciating Ibsen's work as a whole. 'The great majority of his characters,' Tennant wrote, 'are mere cyphers, whose behaviour is conditioned by the structure of the play...' (p. 32). Since it was not his concern to write a critical study, Tennant takes this point no further. But it was a point similar to one which Yeats had made, when he observed that 'even the most momentous figures are subordinate to some tendency... some process of thought whose very logic has turned it into mechanism – always to "something other than human life".' Knut Hamsun, Ibsen's fellow-countryman and younger rival, had spoken in much the same way when he held that Ibsen used an extremely simple kind of character-psychology; there was an 'inherent obviousness and insensitivity' about Ibsen's feelings, which, like his perceptions, were 'too much in whole numbers, definite and typical, and not in fractions'.

What James McFarlane says about Brand is relevant here, though McFarlane does not extend this criticism to all the plays, and he is in any case dealing with the character of Brand rather than the play as a whole:

[Brand] stands not so much for a way of life as a code of conduct – a code, indeed, of easy three-word brevity: 'All or Nothing.' The difficulties and anxieties of this mode of life lie not in the usual anguish of deciding what to do for the best, not in resolving a series of difficult alternatives, but simply in doing as one's code requires. Life is lived by a simple, portable yardstick which is offered up to all life's problems and a decision read off. The pain lies all in the doing, not in the deciding [...] There is no dialogue within the soul, only endless reaffirmation of the sovereignty of the code. [...] Those moments when Brand's mind seems open to alternative instructions are for him moments of weakness. Right and wrong are curiously matters of quantitative, not qualitative concern: all or nothing. McFarlane, *The Oxford Ibsen* (III. 17)

Although this is about one man within the play, it could be applied to a great many more of Ibsen's characters, and helps to account for the impression of almost mechanical rigidity in them.

With this we arrive at a crux. The passion of Ibsen himself was often that of the All-or-Nothing man: as he said on one occasion, 'Brand is myself in my best moments,' and although he was able to distance himself from this *alter ego* – the mere fact that he put him in a play sufficed for that – the question remains whether he distanced himself sufficiently in the writing of his plays to avoid the manipulation of characters which would serve his overriding purpose rather than the interests of the play.

Further criticisms concern Ibsen's use of the form and some of the devices of nineteenth-century French drama. That he imitated the French may well have increased his popularity, since certain formulae for drama evidently appealed to audiences. Bernard Shaw confessed that in writing *The Devil's Disciple* he had deliberately used the stock elements of Victorian melodrama: 'Every old patron of the Adelphi pit would, were he not beglamoured [...], recognize the reading of the will, the oppressed orphan finding a protector, the arrest, the heroic sacrifice, the court martial, the scaffold, the reprieve at the last moment, as he recognizes beefsteak pudding on the bill of fare at his restaurant.' Similarly, Ibsen in his later plays used the delayed letter, the dastardly schemer, the blackmailing villain, the heroine confronted by him with a fate worse than death, the message that arrives just in time to save the hero from disaster, or the well-intentional advice whose meaning is mistaken, with tragic consequences. Methods like these may contribute to a passing success, but are liable to oversimplify complex issues and by that very fact damage the plays both as drama and as reformist theatre. The issues are, whether in using such means Ibsen gained impact for his ideas, or merely coarsened them to the point where it mattered little whether they had impact or not, or achieved some special success from the combination.

Equally important in thinking of what Ibsen means for the theatre in our own times is his use of language. There were always doubts expressed about this, from the moment that he became internationally known: it was often felt that some natural force which Ibsen must have had in the Norwegian had been lost in translation, and for this William Archer's version was often blamed. Muriel Bradbrook has brought out something of what has been lost, in showing the difference between the last words of Act Three of *Hedda Gabler* in their original and in Archer's form. Where the Norwegian has 'Nu brænder jeg dit barn, Thea! – Du med krushåret! Dit og Ejlert Løvborg's barn. Nu brænder, – nu brænder jeg barnet,' Archer put 'Now I am burning your child, Thea! Burning it, curly locks! Your child and Eilert Løvborg's! I am burning – I am burning your child.' Of this, Professor Bradbrook observes the loss of the heavy stresses, of the telling vowels and rasping consonants which are the very life of the passage (pp. 24–25).

But to find that life is impossible in terms of present-day English. The power and beauty of Norwegian is peculiar to itself and can never be rendered properly in a foreign tongue. On the other hand, the question of how well Ibsen himself uses his own language is a matter of dispute. John Northam, who writes with a close knowledge of the original, tells us that translations of Ibsen obscure distinctions in manners of speech and the full character-istics of the moments of high rhetorical utterance. He calls for an expert who will illuminate the difficult words in the Norwegian a little more brightly for the great, inexpert majority. By contrast Tennant, who seems to rely on translations, remarks that Ibsen's treatment of prose dialogue is strikingly lacking in variation. 'Nearly all his characters,' Tennant writes, 'speak the same lan-guage.' Michael Meyer, yet again, who sides with Northam on this issue, has made translations in which the more colourful turns of phrase turn out, on comparison with the original, to be strictly unwarranted, except as providing a more popular version.

The criticisms of Ibsen's language were at one time thought to be decisive. It was not that he had turned to writing prose, but such prosy prose, as it seemed to English-speaking readers. Against this view it began to be urged that despite appearances Ibsen had not, by his own account, given up writing poetry after 1873. As he declared ten years later, in a letter, 'I myself during the last seven or eight years have scarcely written a single line, but have exclusively devoted myself to the incomparably harder task of

writing poetry in straightforward, realistic, everyday language,'
and some have been convinced by this, though 'writing poetry'
was not exactly what Ibsen said. (see p. 214 below). F. L. Lucas, in
treating of *Pillars of Society*, wrote that 'Ibsen has not yet learnt his
peculiar secret of transfiguring his prose with a poetry hardly sur-
passed by any verse; of transforming the world of everyday with
an unearthly light, as magic as an Irish sky' (p. 126). Lucas did not
go on to substantiate that extravagant claim. But at least two recent
writers on Ibsen, Francis Fergusson and John Northam, have since
gone on to set out in detail a more closely defined account of the
so-called poetry in Ibsen's prose, to which we will need to return.
Meanwhile, what James McFarlane says of the general situation is
instructive: 'the central issue in the twentieth-century debate about
Ibsen' has become 'the notion of *poésie de théâtre* and its relevance
to his drama' (*Anthology* p. 66). This applies more to the last
twelve plays than to any others, and seems to imply that the
poetry is to be sought not only in language, but in symbol, décor,
the whole impact of the plays in performance.

Whatever the weight of these criticisms and the replies to them
may be, no doubt remains about the popular reputation Ibsen's
work enjoys. The list of performances in England, printed in the
volume of *The Oxford Ibsen* published in 1966, shows no sign of
any slackening of public interest up to that year, and the record of
television productions is equally emphatic. Ibsen's influence on
the whole of European and American drama has been so great that
even doubters are obliged to concede that the criticisms they make
may prove to be not merely criticisms of Ibsen but of drama as a
whole. Thus Eric Bentley (voicing one part of his own dialogue):
'If you think Ibsen lacks the skills of Henry James [as a novelist]
you should realize that he has others which James lacks, the skills
of the theatre rather than of the book. If of course you simply
prefer the novel to the drama, there is no more to be said: you will
naturally prefer James's gradual, word-by-word definition of his
subject to Ibsen's definition by upheaval' (p. 314).

There is a degree of truth there – not because there is no other
kind of drama than Ibsen's, but because his kind has become so
large a proportion of the whole that the discussion of his real
place in the history of drama is of extraordinary importance.

There is room for some disagreement, but not for such diametrically opposed views as are put forward in this case by the different camps. The question whether Ibsen can be accounted a great dramatist who, for all that, had next to no power of characterisation, manipulated his characters as he pleased and allowed his plots to dictate to them, did not differentiate essentially between their forms of speech, or create any genuine poetry out of his prose, who built his plays on the model of ordinary popular successes and thumping melodramas, and repeatedly used essentially the same themes, is not answered by saying that in his very passion he aroused a livelier debate, stimulated more audiences to take action, than any other dramatist.

Only a view of each play as a separate whole, linked with all the other separate wholes, can come near to establishing the balanced picture that is needed for a just estimate. This means taking each play of the twelve in turn, experiencing it so far as possible as one would do in the theatre, in one's own ideal performance. The task is made more difficult, since a text is never a performance, can never have the emotional effect of a play in the theatre, and will always be open to more than one interpretation. But so will every stage production; all that a writer, as distinct from a producer, can do is to give a coherent account not only of one but of several plays, within a particular frame of reference. At least the text, unlike the production, remains in view indefinitely, and allows contemplation as well as discussion. With so much solid basis we are obliged to be content.

LIBRARY
OF
MOUNT ST. MARY'S
COLLEGE
EMMITSBURG, MARYLAND

2

Pillars of Society

The play which appeared four years after *Emperor and Galilean* was an unusual one for Ibsen to have written. There is no resemblance at all between the huge philosophical, all-embracing drama which Ibsen at least for a time, perhaps always, regarded as his masterpiece, and the comparatively simple account of a Norwegian ship-repairer who allowed himself to send a vessel to sea in the virtual certainty that it would sink. The story of *Pillars of Society* is in itself enough to mark the great change in policy that Ibsen had decided on. The construction, far from repeating the prolixity of the earlier work, is closely knit, the dramatic pressure constantly applied and, though the taut unity of plays like *Ghosts* and *Hedda Gabler* still looks remote, a new mastery already begins to show itself.

Act One brings in many incidents and reports in a short space of time. Ibsen establishes that Consul Bernick is a ship-repairer by introducing Aune, his foreman, who is something of a socialist – this immediately sets the ladies' sewing-party, already visible on stage, in a special light. Their supposedly charitable efforts become open to criticism, and so does Rørlund the schoolteacher's wordy, narrow Norwegianism. The number of ladies is large, and the cast-list is by far the longest of any of the later plays, but this is essential in order to give an impression of the 'society' to which the title refers. Hollow pretensions are quickly shown up in a simple way, through Hilmar Tønnesen who boldly talks of seeking adventure but is afraid of the empty cross-bow pointed at him by the boy Olaf Bernick, and by Mrs Rummel who deliberately leads the conversation towards revealing a scandal, only to declare that she herself never uttered a single word of it. These are rough and ready devices, but bold and definite in effect.

Once scandal is mentioned, the preliminaries are over and exposition begins. Ibsen chooses for this the long established device of the newcomer, here a Mrs Lynge, who is ignorant of local gossip and has to be told about one of the vital events preceding the time of the play. (Johan Tønnesen, stepbrother of Bernick's wife, was discovered in the house of a married woman by the woman's husband, and emigrated almost at once to America; Dina Dorf, the daughter of the same woman, is sitting with the ladies at this very moment. It also has to be related that Johan is held guilty of stealing a cashbox before his flight. This is a complex story, but essential for understanding later developments.) Mrs Lynge also needs to be told, as a stranger, how Mrs Bernick's stepsister, Lona Hessel, followed her stepbrother abroad after she had slapped Consul Bernick's face, though the audience is left in suspense about the reason for this attack.

The relationships are complicated, with references to an 'old Mrs Bernick', and the necessity to distinguish between Hilmar Tønnesen, Mrs Bernick's cousin, and the absent Johan Tønnesen, her stepbrother, as well as between her sister, Martha, and the absent stepsister. A sense of the family as distinct from the visitors is better gained from actors on stage than from the printed page: Ibsen has not yet achieved his later economy.

There are two more developments to come. Bernick himself now enters, and discusses the railway which he and some others intend to build. And finally, in a way typical of Ibsen's developments, a stranger appears from the boat just arrived at the harbour. She is Lona Hessel, whose comment on the pile of sewing is 'all this moral linen smells bad', and who brings down the curtain with another typically metaphorical line – 'I want to let in some fresh air, my dear pastor.'

It was a feat to have included so much in about twenty pages of dialogue. By the end of Act One all nineteen characters except Johan Tønnesen have appeared, and nearly all of them have spoken. Though the significance of events is still obscure, the impression is given of a coiled spring, which the arrival of Lona Hessel will release, and the impression is strengthened by Ibsen's dramatic irony. It is just when Rørlund is talking about 'a house like this' (where family life is seen at its best, and peace and harmony prevail), that Mrs Bernick observes how loud the voices are getting in her husband's office next door. And as Bernick himself is saying that the family is the nucleus of society, where nothing disruptive casts a shadow, he receives the scandalous order from the American owners to send the *Indian Girl* to sea without regard to her real seaworthiness. By such means Ibsen stokes the fires.

So much was achieved, it is true, at the expense of characterisation: it is clear that Hilmar is self-deceived, Mrs Rummel a tattler, Dina Dorf a straightforward innocent girl, and Lona Hessel an unconventional woman, but inevitably all this is only briefly sketched in, and little insight is gained into anybody's real nature. Even so, the targets have all been announced: Norwegian insularity and its contempt for 'foreign immorality', the contrast between the interests of workers and employers, the ruthlessness of the American shipowners who are prepared to risk their ship sinking rather than forego possible profit, the shame and poverty forced on Dina's mother by the suspicion of adultery, matched by the contempt felt for a woman who sings for money and gives public lectures, as Lona is said to do. There is plenty to be brought to a head in the remaining three acts, in fact too much.

Act Two is conducted for the most part in a contrasting mood, almost as a slow movement, though the pace quickens towards the end. Where in Act One the stage had been thronged, the curtain now goes up on Mrs Bernick and her husband, alone, and nearly all the Act consists of encounters between only two or three people, almost as though in a classical tragedy. There is drama in this change. The reason why the Bernicks are now on their own is that none of the women present earlier will come to the sewing-bee today: the presence of Johan Tønnesen in the house, brother of Mrs Bernick though he is, is too much for them. One sees now why Ibsen included in the cast such very minor and seemingly superfluous characters as the daughters of Mrs Rummel and Mrs Holt, whose only function is to swell the numbers in Act One and thereby increase, by their absence, the sense of ostracism in Act Two.

In the privacy of a conversation between man and wife, Ibsen is also able to deploy his irony and prepare for more. Bernick is praised by his wife for his magnanimity in insisting that the supposed theft of money by Johan, before his escape to America, was only a rumour: a slight abruptness introduced into the acting of his reply can quickly suggest that Bernick's reason for dismissing the whole business so readily may do him less credit. His irritation with his wife a moment later, bringing her to tears, adds to the impression that he is suppressing something. By constant touches of this kind Ibsen keeps subconscious expectation alive: a revelation must come.

The expectation has barely been allowed to flicker up when Ibsen introduces the second scandal, which is to be wound in with the first. Aune, the foreman, who has already appeared briefly, now returns to say that the job of repairing the American vessel, the *Indian Girl*, is proving too much for him. There is a brief argument between Aune and Bernick about socialism and the attitude of working-men to labour-saving machinery, which puts both sides of the case fairly. Ibsen is not concerned with making a propagandist case for either socialism or capitalism, though one of his accusations will be against the readiness with which men are prepared to risk the lives of others for their own profit. The point of this piece of dialogue is rather to demonstrate that for the sake of his reputation Bernick is determined to have the *Indian Girl* sail the day after tomorrow, despite Aune's protests that she cannot be made seaworthy in so short a time, if at all.

Bernick's motivation here is not wholly convincing. His pretext is that the brawling and loose-living American crew of the *Indian Girl* have been causing resentment in the town, and that he is being slyly accused of concentrating his resources on another ship, the *Palm Tree*, belonging to a local citizen, instead of ensuring that the Americans leave as soon as possible. Though not altogether implausible (surely he stands to lose more of his reputation if a ship he has just repaired sinks), this does not explain Bernick's strong insistence that both ships, not merely one, must be ready to sail in two days' time. It is necessary for the complicated plot that they should leave more or less together, as we see in Act Four, but Ibsen forces the pace a little here. It is of no great consequence that he does, merely a minor example of motivation being skimped in the interests of the general construction.

The dialogue between Bernick and Aune shows no differentiation in speech between the two men of the kind one would expect between employer and employee. Though the pros and cons of the workers' and employers' positions are deftly brought in, they are abstract, and one has no sense of Aune as a working-man, so far as his speech is concerned. He speaks in the same somewhat impersonal way as Bernick does, without idiosyncrasies, and can even perpetrate such a line as 'My poor home is also a small community, Mr Bernick', or 'Even a common man has some things in this world he must preserve.' Schiller and the German 'Sturm und Drang' dramatists (as well as Büchner, of whom Ibsen is unlikely to have heard) had long before re-introduced a naturalism of common speech such as Shakespeare also occasionally used, and even Victorian melodrama went in for 'Cockney' speech and 'Mummerset'. Ibsen as yet remains formal in this respect.

A brief interlude of comedy, with Hilmar Tønnesen, a crudely sketched character who is continually saying 'Ugh!', and asking how the flag of idealism is to be kept flying, precedes the entrance of Lona and Johan, who have scandalised the town by their mere presence. These are the healthy, natural people whom Ibsen contrasts with the hypocritical Norwegian stay-at-homes, and they associate themselves with Dina, who is also troubled by the stifling rectitude of the place (though both she and they call it 'morality', which is confusing).

The mainstay of the Act arrives with the conversation between Bernick and Johan, which takes us back to the first scandal. It emerges at once that the real reason for Bernick's apparent magnanimity, which so won his wife's approval, was that he, not Johan, was the man who had the affair with Dina Dorf's mother, though Johan took the blame on himself. The mask is removed from Bernick's face, so far as the audience is concerned, though Johan seems still untroubled by all that has happened. Here again, however, the motivation asks for some credence. Johan was nineteen at the time of his exile, and unversed in the ways of the world. Even so, the offer or agreement he apparently made, to allow himself to be suspected of adultery with Mrs Dorf, and then to emigrate to America, seems to have been made in an uncommonly noble spirit:

JOHAN: Never you worry, my dear Karsten. We agreed that was how it should be. You had to be rescued, and you were my friend. Yes, I was really proud of that friendship. Here I was, a miserable stay-at-home, plodding away, and then you came back, all proud and posh, from your grand tour abroad, you'd been in London and Paris. And you chose me for your particular friend, although I was four years younger than you – that was because you were walking out with Betty, and I can see that now. But how proud I was of that; and who wouldn't have been? Who wouldn't have gladly sacrificed himself for you, especially when it meant no more than a month of town-gossip and then off out into the wide world? (Act 2) (V. 63)*

Again, the story Johan tells here is not without all plausibility, but it does argue a wide-eyed innocence and naivety in Johan, such as is often required in order that Ibsen's plots may work – it is the opposite of the double-dyed villainy required on other occasions for the same purpose. The retailing for the audience's benefit of facts which Bernick already knows is also uncomfortably prolonged.

Bernick does not yet supply villainy of quite the later quality, though he does prepare the way, in what he now goes on to say to Lona Hessel. She had supposed, before she left for America, that he was in love with her, until he married Betty, his present wife, and he confirms now that he did in fact love Lona. But he protests that he only threw her over because Betty was to inherit money, and he needed money badly to set his mother's business on its feet. The surprising thing here is the apparent absence of any awareness in Bernick that Lona might be hurt by this treatment, and by the announcement that he naturally had to prefer money to her. (John Gabriel Borkman will speak in similar terms.) As for Bernick's protest that he did not act from selfish motives, that he renounced Lona for the sake of avoiding the suffering for the entire community which would have followed a collapse of his firm, one hardly knows whether to call it hypocrisy or a naivety greater than Johan's; it is so blithely unquestioning. The even more complete disregard of other people's interests which Bernick is to show later is well prepared for, here, in his relation with Lona.

Lona, on the other hand, shows a strange insistence that Bernick

* Volume and page references are to the passages in *The Oxford Ibsen* with which my version may be compared. (See Preface.)

should reveal his guilt publicly. Though we do not know it at the moment – it does not emerge till Act Four – she has come back from America expressly to make him reveal to his wife and his fellow-citizens the truth, that he was the man in Mrs Dorf's room on the fateful evening, and that he has falsely laid the blame on Johan. She knows no more than that, at this moment, and why the revelation is so important to her is something of a puzzle. Johan is doing well in America, and would not have come back except at Lona's instigation: he has in fact lost nothing, so far as living in America is concerned, by the bad name still attaching to him in his native town, and clearly does not even realise he needs to worry about it. There is nothing to gain for him from any public confession by Bernick. Mrs Bernick can scarcely be helped by learning that, before marrying her, Bernick went to Mrs Dorf to break off his liaison with her (the only reason given in the play for his presence in her room). Even had Bernick's relation been adulterous, Mrs Bernick need not be forced to realise it. As for the public, Lona apparently expects them to be scandalised, and that is about all: certainly she does not believe Bernick will prosper in his relations with the town through any confession he may make. It is really hard to see why she should take it on herself to dictate to Bernick's conscience, which need be troubling him only a very little, if he believes Johan to have accepted guilt as willingly as Johan says he has. Lona's determination that the truth be told at all costs, for the good of everyone's soul, has a touch of the fanatical: Ibsen presented a similar character more critically in Gregers Werle, in *The Wild Duck*. In *Pillars of Society* the Puritanical zeal, the Alceste-like demand for the truth at all costs, does not seem to strike Ibsen as dubious. Nor does Lona take seriously the risk that by persuading Bernick to tell all she may ruin him, personally as well as financially.

To understand Lona properly we should perhaps see her not so much as a real person, and a busybody (she does not know, for instance, that Bernick deliberately spread the lie that Johan also stole money before leaving; she only knows that he was the man in Mrs Dorf's room, and that he has let Johan take the blame, which Johan does not mind), but rather as a dramatic form of Bernick's conscience. Like Goethe's Iphigenia, she also represents the agony of soul which some feel at the merest breath of untruth.

At this point the third scandal begins to weave its way into the plot. We have so far only the barest intimation that Bernick is involved in a matter concerning the building of a railway. Nor do we hear much more yet, in Act Two. But as the schoolmaster Rørlund detonates the bomb laid in Act One, revealing to Dina that Johan is the man (as Rørlund thinks) who was the cause of her mother's shame and misfortune, a business associate of Bernick's rushes in to announce that 'the whole railway is hanging by a thread'. We have no idea as yet of what this may mean. Yet Ibsen's craftsmanship, in keeping the audience agog even as he partly relieves its tension, is undeniable. It is only in the human aspects of the play, the characterisation and motivation, that he falls short of the same extraordinary competence.

In Act Three, far from letting the tension drop, he keeps us waiting to hear about the railway, while he gets on with the second trail of gunpowder which leads to the sailing of the *Indian Girl*. Both of Bernick's schemes form the twin strands of this Act, though the ship-repair begins and ends it.

In taking up the theme of the profiteering of unscrupulous ship-owners Ibsen was echoing the scandal which had earlier for many years been made public by Samuel Plimsoll, in his campaign to prevent ships being sent to sea, heavily insured, with the virtual certainty that they would sink. Plimsoll's book *Our Seamen* had been published in 1873, and the British Merchant Shipping Act which dealt with many of the malpractices was passed in 1876, just one year before Ibsen's play appeared, although Ibsen's concern with the topic began as early as 1869. So far as reform was concerned, the play was, however, flogging a rather dead horse.

Plimsoll's condemnation was not exactly Ibsen's. It was not for personal, emotional reasons that the ship-owners Plimsoll attacked acted as they did, but purely for financial ones, to collect the insurance. Bernick is less hard-headed. His chief motive hitherto in insisting on rapid repairs has been in order to avoid the not very damaging accusation that he is failing to encourage the American roisterers to leave town as quickly as possible. In Act Three, he seems not to have been aware that such rapidity might endanger the crew, to judge by his shocked comment to himself made when

he is alone (and can thus not be merely masking his own carelessness). The real implications have to be made plain to him by his
clerk, Krap, who supposes that the foreman, Aune, is deliberately
making a shoddy job of the repair in the expectation that the ship
will sink, and so discredit the new machinery to which he is
opposed.

Such combinations of naivety and ruthlessness – for Bernick
is not daunted by his new realisation – are not uncommon in
Ibsen. What he now provides is a pressure on Bernick which will
seem to compel him to go ahead with the plan to send the *Indian
Girl* to sea, for reasons which he had not expected when he first
thought of it.

There are two pressures, acting in contrary ways. On the one
hand, Johan now learns for the first time that Bernick has not
merely allowed the suspicion of adultery to fall on Johan (which
Johan knew all about), but has also allowed rumours to be spread
that Johan stole money before escaping. This leads to a demand by
Johan that Bernick should clear his reputation of the second false
charge. Bernick, however, cannot agree to do this because, he
says, the plan he has almost carried through, of buying up large
areas of land in order to build a railway, will be frustrated by any
revelation that he is not a perfectly upright citizen. Thus Ibsen
cunningly winds together two further strands in his complex plot.
Bernick cannot defend Johan, who must therefore, if he wishes to
marry Dina (as he now announces he does), make the return
voyage to America. At the same time, Johan is a potential menace
to Bernick's reputation. He can at any time make revelations
which Bernick, at any rate, thinks would be highly damaging:
Bernick is convinced that the whole purpose of Lona's and Johan's
journey has been to blackmail him.

Now the screw is applied with rigour. The foreman Aune comes
in to make it quite clear to Bernick that the risk to the *Indian Girl*
is great, especially in rough weather. Almost at once it is announced that a gale is expected, and with this virtual confirmation
that the *Indian Girl* must sink, Bernick begins obscurely to speculate on the morality of the action he evidently means to take. He
discusses with Rørlund whether a man who has some project in
mind that will benefit thousands of people – by which he hints at

his own railway project – is entitled not merely to risk the lives of workmen, but to go ahead with the project even in the knowledge that one particular workman is certain to be killed. Though the question is not settled between them, Bernick evidently sees it as akin to the question whether a general may engage in battle, knowing that some of his troops will die. The remoteness of this from his own relation with Johan is irrelevant to him: he has practically persuaded himself that he is entitled to let Johan perish. The persuasion becomes certainty by the end of the Act, when Johan, frustrated in his expectation of marrying Dina, loses his temper and announces that he will sail on the *Indian Girl*, but return to 'smash as many of you as I can'. With this threat hanging over him, Bernick feels fully justified in his dramatic curtain-line:

KRAP   Excuse me coming back, Sir, but there's a tremendous storm blow-
        ing up. (*He waits a moment; there is no answer*) Is the *Indian Girl* to sail
        all the same?
            (*After a short pause*)
BERNICK (*answering from inside his room*)
        The *Indian Girl* sails all the same.
            (*Curtain*)   (Act 3) (V. 100)

It is a situation of melodrama, not merely in the sense that it needs today to be considerably underplayed to avoid the intended but embarrassing shiver of apprehension as the scene closes, but in the sense that Ibsen has turned the whole affair into a personal vendetta. The unscrupulousness against which Plimsoll had been protesting had none of this heady quality, and required no more than a careful concealment from the insurers of the true condition of the ships. It was not really dramatic material. Ibsen makes it dramatic by ingenious contrivance which paradoxically requires extremely straightforward reactions. Aune is prepared to repair the ship badly, fully aware that it may sink, for fear of losing his job – a motive is provided for him, and no complexity is allowed for. (Might he not, if he were anxious about the crew, have a word with the captain of the *Indian Girl*, or confide in other workmen; might he not use his position to blackmail or shame Bernick, if he wanted to take the very reasonable course of preventing mass murder?) Johan, who has shown no signs of being a violent man, suddenly plays into Bernick's hands with the declaration of his intention to smash him, and again the words are enough. The captain and crew of the *Indian Girl*, we have to assume, are perfectly willing, though drunk, to put to sea in a tremendous storm, presumably on Bernick's orders. Even the pilot, who is not drunk, is expected to do what Bernick prescribes. In each case, a dramatic situation is achieved by extreme simplification, as though on the supposition that a proffered motive is sufficient in itself.

Dramatists, it is true, may foreshorten events, compress them so tightly into the short space of time available that on closer inspection they seem improbable. It is the effect on stage, and the purpose for which it is used, that counts. Tolstoy, in his attack on *King Lear*, makes havoc of the gulling of Gloucester by Edmund, and one can justify Shakespeare here only in terms of the play as a whole, most of which Tolstoy factually misrepresents. In *Pillars of Society*, however, the motivation is consistently of the same kind; characters behave throughout as though only one thought could occupy them at a time, and the total impression does nothing to redeem this, despite admiration for Ibsen's ingenuity.

The final Act is heavily, almost grotesquely, ironic. The great public demonstration, the torchlight procession in honour of Bernick, is meant to bring out the hollow sham of such occasions, several of which, made in his own honour, Ibsen had himself experienced. Bernick's craven questions to his partners about the likely results of the storm underline heavily the villainy in which he is engaged. The falsity of his situation bears in on him, to the point when he begins to yield to the pressure which Lona has been applying ever since she arrived, to come out with the truth.

The precise form of his conversion is the final weakness of the play. Up to the last minute, Bernick is prepared to let his plot proceed. Only when he realises that Johan is no longer a menace to him, and has sailed with Dina on the *Palm Tree*, while his own son Olaf has secretly boarded the *Indian Girl*, does he falter. The thought of the death of the only living person who could continue in his spirit the work he has begun brings Bernick to see that he must make a clean breast of it. Why the one should lead to the other is not logically clear, though motivations are not always logical. At all events, having heard that Olaf has been retrieved, Bernick goes out to meet the torchlight procession and reveal all.

The revelation is a disappointment. Bernick begins, rather abstractly, surprisingly so for a man in his emotional frame of mind, by declaring that 'a lust for power, a craving for influence and for position has been the driving force behind most of my actions'. This curiously formalised statement, however, does not convey anything of which he is ashamed. On the contrary, he charges himself not with lust for power, but with following 'somewhat devious ways, simply because I recognised and feared the way our society is inclined to impute base motives to whatever a man does'. This is an astonishing self-exoneration, after what we have just seen of Bernick. For him to lay the blame at society's door can hardly be what Lona Hessel intended. He goes on to confess that he has been buying large quantities of land entirely for his own profit, which is strictly untrue, since he has offered a cut-in to three of his friends – as indeed they half-heartedly protest. To make amends, he now proposes, without having consulted the friends, to float a public company in which shares may be bought by anyone. How this salves his conscience is not explained: if there was any guilt at all in this deal, it was presumably in the buying of land on the cheap, before sellers knew a railway was planned. Critics in the town may be mollified by the chance of a share in the profits. Nothing seems to be gained, morally, by increasing the original four shareholders to a large number, for the sellers remain cheated of their higher prices.

Finally, Bernick confesses that fifteen years ago he was 'the guilty party'. This, though it might be obscure to the crowd, is clearly understood by his wife to mean that he was the man in Mrs Dorf's room, but does nothing to indicate that he lied about the theft attributed to Johan. And at this point, he breaks off, saying that he still has much to repent of, which concerns his own conscience alone. He says nothing of his expectation that the *Indian Girl* would sink with all hands, or of his murderous feelings towards Johan, and we must assume that since his plot was frustrated, he feels no obligation to make his mere intentions public knowledge. Johan still remains under a false accusation, and Bernick is far from having made a clean breast.

The ending is something of a damp squib, since the only thing that could have justified the interference of Lona would have been a full confession with a full realisation of the consquences. A zeal for the whole truth that can be fobbed off with such half-measures as Bernick offers is dramatically dull. Lona, for her part, is fully satisfied – she does not know, yet, about the intended death of Johan – but precisely on that account the play seems more devious than ever. Where Molière, in *Alceste,* allowed the tragi-comic consequences of the demand for truth to be clearly seen, Ibsen makes the demand and then only pretends to have satisfied it. Apart from the continuing deception of Lona, there is the reaction of the citizenry. Up to the last moment, it has appeared that for Bernick to admit even a peccadillo would be disastrous for him. Now that he has offered a token confession, coupled with what might almost be accounted a bribe, in the offer to share the railway profits, it is not certain what the public will do. Had Bernick told the whole story, it is difficult to suppose he could ever have shown his face in the town again. As things are, the final impression is of a good deed done. Lona decides to stay on in Bernick's household, and even the storm gives way to a clear sky, so that Johan and Dina have a good prospect of reaching land safely, in the *Palm Tree* (there had been serious, though unpublished, doubts even about that). At the final curtain, Lona's sententious words ring on with their spurious suggestion of a moral drawn from the events – 'the spirit of truth and the spirit of freedom – these are the pillars of society'. But there is an unintended irony in the whole situation; she is simply deceived once again, and Ibsen has connived at the deception. Nothing has been said about what the pillars of society are, beyond what any sceptic already knows.

The advance on the earlier plays, technically and humanly speaking, has been slight. Before leaving *Pillars of Society*, however, there is something to be gained from comparing it with a play at first glance very dissimilar, not in respect of technique but of underlying themes. Certain themes, as we saw, had an obsessive hold on Ibsen, and though the variations he makes on them may conceal similarities, they are often there, just below the surface, and may determine the course of his plays more than the situations with which the plays seem to be concerned. *The Pretenders*, for instance, is quite plainly concerned with the rivalry between Skule and Haakon, and only a little biographical knowledge is needed to see a parallel between this and the rivalry between Ibsen and Bjørnson. It is less obvious that Bernick stands in a similar relation to Johan Tønnesen, though clear enough that they are also as dark to light and guilt to innocence. Bernick and Johan do not go to war, as Skule and Haakon do, but in the modern conditions Ibsen has chosen he comes close to the point of letting Bernick encompass Johan's death. And then there is the curious similarity that Johan is not merely Bernick's morally guiltless superior, but that he marries – or at least elopes with – Dina Dorf, the girl whom Bernick has brought up in his household since early childhood, though she is not in fact his daughter. In *The Pretenders*, Haakon marries Skule's daughter: one might almost think some personal concern of Ibsen, apart from, though no doubt including, his illegitimate son born in 1846, was involved here.

Bernick is close to Skule in another sense. In a modern setting, there could be no question of allowing Bernick to seek a throne. What he does do – opening up a railway for the benefit of the whole community – is as near as Ibsen could bring such a figure, at this time, to the 'great kingly thought' of the Pretender. Later, John Gabriel Borkman was to express that thought in a more obviously symbolical form, by means of his steamship-lines that encircle the globe. The symbol in that case is closer to the cosmic mastery which Skule's 'thought' represents. Bernick remains, by comparison, an adumbration. Yet the way in which his plan to defeat Johan is thwarted again bears a resemblance to the earlier play. In both plays, the hero is unable to achieve his end because of the peril in which his son stands. The peril is entirely different – Skule's Peter incurs the anger of his father's supporters by sacrilegiously dragging out the shrine which will properly confirm Skule's coronation; Olaf Bernick tries to run away on the ship in which his father intended that Johan should drown. But in each case the father is hoist with his own petard: it is because Skule requires final confirmation of his kingship that Peter places his own life at risk, and because Bernick insists that the *Indian Girl* put to sea that Olaf almost drowns in Johan's stead. Ibsen seems to have in mind a similar retribution in each case, and it is this that governs the development of the plot, so far as Ibsen's personal inwardness is concerned. The two plays are closer to one another than might be supposed.

The old preoccupations, then, continue. What has not yet been set right is the sacrifice of observed humanity to dramatic convenience: the play is still, technically speaking, too dependent on improbabilities and lucky coincidences, showing not very much progress in that respect on much earlier works. The plays of the next few years were to show a more marked difference.

3
A Doll's House

It was not until six years after *Emperor and Galilean* that Ibsen achieved a real simplicity of form and an immediate popular appeal, though the appeal was at first more of an outrage. The nineteen characters of *Pillars of Society* have, in *A Doll's House*, been reduced to seven, and of these only three are needed to carry the plot, with two others whose rôle is rather that of confidant. The variety of misdeeds perpetrated or attempted by Bernick have been reduced to Nora's one, and the dénouement which required so many wordy confessions in the final Act of the earlier play has been simplified to one striking gesture. The discipline Ibsen had imposed on himself shows throughout.

There remain certain basic similarities, though not precisely the same kind of similarities as those which link *Pillars of Society* with *The Pretenders*, rather a traceable pattern showing once again Ibsen's personal involvement. He is closer, in this respect, to Goethe, who spoke of all his work as 'fragments of a great confession', than to Shakespeare, say, whose plays differ so widely from one another. Though Leontes and Othello and Posthumus betray a continual concern with marital jealousy, and Brutus and Hamlet may be compared in their response to misrule, the two themes are wide apart, and have nothing in common with *Lear* or *Henry IV*. Ibsen's plays, however widely different, are closely bound up with a single prepossession.

Like Bernick, Nora has long ago done something wrong, and now has to face the consequences. In each case the wrong, in Bernick's case the initial wrong, was of a minor kind. The play is set in motion by the arrival of a character who insists that the wrong be confessed, though here differences begin to emerge. Where Krogstad uses his knowledge for selfish and hostile purposes, to blackmail Nora, Lona Hessel's demands on Bernick were made, as she believed, entirely for his own good. This is in keeping with a constant theme of Ibsen's drama, the ambiguous effects of ideal demands.

Nora herself, a light-hearted innocent young woman, is also at the furthest extreme from the deliberately power-seeking, deceiving Bernick. But this is a feature of another pattern which runs not through a single play but from play to play: Ibsen progresses after 1873 by an almost regular sequence, whereby each new work tends to reverse the situation of the previous one. We shall come back to this: for the moment the mirroring of Lona and Bernick by Krogstad and Nora is enough to keep the connecting thread in view. In *A Doll's House*, however, there is one feature which joins the play, however tenuously, with *The Pretenders*. Not only is Krogstad evil-minded; there has also been an agreement, a pact, between him and Nora, whose indirect implications he now enforces. Since Nora has no ambition remotely comparable with Faust's, the similarity can be over-stressed. Yet this bond will recur in later plays, in *John Gabriel Borkman* (where the Faustian parallel is more apt), and in *The Master Builder*, in a different guise again. The hint of it in *A Doll's House* is worth noting, at this stage. It is a hint strengthened by the fact that, as before, the final result is the loss of a child, or, in Nora's case, children, although this formed no part of any contract.

The essential point about *A Doll's House* is that, taken as a whole, it triumphs over many of the misgivings it can occasion on the way. There remains some cause for embarrassment; there are obscurities about the situation, some of which need more explanation than they get, and even Nora's final leave-taking is coloured by a motivation that at first sight looks too theatrical – or perhaps operatic would be a better word. Yet apart from that leave-taking the play generates a powerful impetus, which must largely account for its success, as a *pièce à thèse*.

A novel which opened with a scene between a man and wife so caricatured as the first scene in *A Doll's House* might quickly tire. A producer might well be tempted to substitute for Helmer Torvald's 'little squirrel' and 'little songbird' some simpler phrase – 'my love', or 'my sweet', repeated sufficiently often, would be enough to convey to modern ears the fact of Helmer's uxoriousness. The substitution is impossible in many cases, since the phrases form parts of sentences which require them.

Now, now! My little singing skylark mustn't start drooping her wings, eh?
What's my little squirrel doing, sulking like that?
What do we call little birds that are always squandering money?
(*wagging his finger*) Now my little sweet-tooth hasn't been a naughty girl in town today, has she...Are we sure little sweet-tooth hasn't been running in to the confectioner's, eh?   (Act I) (V. 203–5)

Helmer drips with sentiment, to a degree that makes Ibsen seem unsure of convincing his audience. He makes Helmer grotesque, and reduces the tragic quality of the ending correspondingly. A less stridently, more unconsciously dominating male could have attracted more sympathy without destroying the sense that Nora leaves her husband because she must. The 'all or nothing' quality in Ibsen's writing shows through here. But it is not a quality inherent in dramatic writing, as opposed to the writing of novels. It is rather a quality of the melodrama in which Ibsen was still involved.

The exposition is handled expertly: the temptation Nora feels to boast to Mrs Linde of her unusual mode of raising money is a matter of character-drawing, and leads the audience naturally to the later revelation, made through the blackmailer Krogstad, of precisely how unusual her action was. Here the exposition creaks slightly. In order to get it over quickly, Ibsen makes Krogstad assume that Nora has not remembered the details of the loan he made her some years ago: 'At that time you were so worried about your husband's illness, and so anxious to get the money for your journey, that I don't think you paid very much attention to all the incidentals. So it isn't out of the way to remind you of them.' She presumably remembers them very well, seeing how much the whole affair preys on her. But the more important point, critically, is the nature of the agreement Nora made, the reduction of her wrongdoing to so small a deed. Needing money to get her sick husband a holiday abroad, she borrowed from Krogstad, who required her father's signature as a security. Since her father died two or three days after Krogstad made his request, she forged the signature, a fact which Krogstad had already suspected and which she at this point frankly admits. (Unlike Laura Kieler, on whose true life-story Nora's was based, Nora has not forged a cheque, but signed her father's name on a security after his death, having been unwilling to trouble him earlier because of his illness. Ibsen has decidedly diminished the crime in Nora's case.)

Krogstad now uses this confession in order to blackmail Nora into persuading her husband to allow him to remain in his job at the bank, from which Krogstad has just been dismissed. With this an element of melodrama enters: Nora is almost innocent, as most audiences will feel; her forgery is something of a technicality, to non-lawyers, and as she says, she did it for love, to help her ailing husband. We are not far from the situation of the silently suffering heroine, accused of a crime she has never committed, trapped into choosing between disaster for her loved ones as well as herself (disaster for Helmer Torvald is what Krogstad has in mind) and submission to the villain's demands. The manipulation of legal niceties against uninformed young women is another device characteristic of villains in melodrama.

But although he uses traditional means, Ibsen does so for wider purposes. After Krogstad has left, Helmer Torvald tells his wife that Krogstad himself has been guilty of forgery (which apparently does not render him, in his turn, vulnerable), and that as a result his whole family has become infected:

A fog of lies that spreads disease and infection to every part of a home-life. Every breath the children take in that kind of house is full of germs of the nastiest kind.   (Act I) (V. 233)

When he adds that practically all juvenile delinquents come from homes where the mother is dishonest, Helmer plants a barb in Nora's conscience which will lead in the end to her leaving him. As the curtain goes down on Act One, she is 'pale with terror', trying to disbelieve that she, a forger after all like Krogstad, could be an evil influence on her own children. It is one of the factors in her decision to leave her husband, this half-belief in her cor-ruptive power. She does, it is true, throw off the thought in her final words – 'It's not true! It could never, never be true!' But the force of her denial shows the grip that the idea has over her.

Nora needs to be extremely suggestible to fear so much. In this respect the near-melodramatic situation exacts its penalty. Yet the play does not succumb to the melodrama, which is constantly in the background and becomes more prominent from time to time, but is constantly outweighed by Ibsen's serious intention. We may compare here the play by Augier, *Le Mariage d'Olympe* (1855), inferior to *A Doll's House* in every respect. In Augier's play, the son of an aristocratic house has innocently married an adventuress, whose designs on his family fortune he has begun to realise. The adventuress is unmasked by virtue of a series of somewhat improbable coincidences, and while that part of the plot progresses it becomes clear that her husband would much prefer to be married to a woman of his own station in life, who has dutifully suppressed every inclination she has felt towards him. In the final scene, the adventuress tries to blackmail her husband's uncle, an aristocrat of the old school, into allowing her to make off with another man, while retaining both the family title and a large annual income. Rather than submit to this, the old marquis shoots her dead, and is preparing the pistol for a second shot, presumably at himself, as the curtain goes down. Here is sheer melodrama: the good are rewarded, since the husband and the woman he would really prefer can now be happily united, the evil are punished, and the suicide of the marquis can really be looked upon as rather noble, within the melodramatic fantasy, especially as it allows a happy ending at least for the young people. Augier uses melodrama and intrigue to bolster up the audience's sense of the propriety of marriage, while adventuresses are seen to get what they deserve. Ibsen uses the same means for the serious purpose of questioning the nature of marriage, and is hampered in this only by the simple-minded quality of the husband and wife he portrays in their final scene.

A Doll's House gains also by comparison with another earlier play, Friedrich Hebbel's *Herodes and Mariamne* (1850), which may well have influenced Ibsen, since Hebbel was well known in Scandinavian countries. In Hebbel's play, set in Judaea about the time of Christ's birth, Herod is so enamoured of his wife that he leaves instructions with his servants to see that she is put to death, if he should chance to die in battle. Mariamne, hearing of this, is outraged. When news does arrive that her husband has died – false news, as it turns out – she orders a banquet to insult the memory of the man who trusted her so little and showed his love in so possessive a way. Herod returns unexpectedly, and, finding her engaged in revelry, has her put to death. The three Wise Men thereupon enter in search of the new-born Christ, and to herald symbolically the advent of an age (still some two thousand years off) when women will be treated as the equals of men. The indirectness of Hebbel's approach to the issue of women's rights, coupled with an ineptness in his verse, and an over-symbolical conclusion, allow it much less force than Ibsen achieves. *A Doll's House* is still potent enough to have been filmed in the 1970s in the cause of the Women's Liberation movement.

When Act Two opens, Nora is still in extreme anxiety at Krogstad's threat: she can scarcely bear to think of the Christmas preparations – the scene is ironically set at that season – and screams aloud when she supposes 'them' to be at the door. Christmas is the chosen time for another reason, that it affords a pretext for the party at which Nora will dance her wild tarantella, the symbolical expression of her as yet unuttered desire for freedom. For the time being, though, this lies in abeyance. Dr Rank is referred to again – he has already appeared briefly – but his inclusion in the play is more often to provide a *rallentando* than for any stronger structural reasons. With his inherited disease and his pessimism he foreshadows Oswald in *Ghosts*, and as an admirer of his friend's wife, though an undesigning one, he foreshadows Brack, in *Hedda Gabler*. He has no such important part to play as either of these two, and may owe his existence to some still only partly formed impression in Ibsen's imagination, that he had to create such a man. Yet he has at one point an essential rôle, all the same.

The part of the Act which promotes the action is thus put off till nearer the middle, by which time the audience's appetite has been whetted enough. Nora decides to do as Krogstad asked, and plead with her husband for Krogstad's reinstatement at the bank. Here Ibsen uses the occasion to spread still further the causes of Nora's self-doubting. It emerges incidentally that her father's professional conduct was not above suspicion and, though she makes no overt comment on this, her words 'Yes...yes, that's right', and her prompt flattery of Helmer for his help in clearing her father's name, provide a chance for this second blow to her confidence to be brought out in the acting. Like father like daughter, like mother

like child, must be her unspoken thought, and the physical infection inherited by Rank, of which she has just been speaking,
must also strengthen the sense she has of a family corruption.
Ibsen was to make this the central theme of *Ghosts*; here, he merely
allows Rank's example to increase the sense of Nora's helplessness.
No character or theme is wasted, or unrelated to the total effect
intended.

Helmer's refusal to do as his wife asks, and Nora's insistence,
precipitate the fatal action: Helmer sends the written notice of
dismissal to Krogstad at once, and relents only to the point of
reflecting that Nora's plea is caused by her fear that Krogstad
will libel him in the newspapers (on some unspecified count, and
despite his known history as a forger). From now on, the pace
quickens. But Helmer's immediate comment, and Nora's reply,
remain mysterious: it is not until the final scene that the audience
may see the significance:

HELMER Come what may, when the moment arrives, believe me, I shall have
 enough strength and enough courage. You'll see I'm man enough to take
 everything on myself.
NORA (*terrified*) What do you mean?
HELMER Everything, I say...
NORA (*controlling herself*) That is something you shall never do in all eternity.
(Act 2) (V. 244)

This exchange is toned down by Helmer's remark that of course
they will share as man and wife, but Nora clearly means something
Helmer does not suspect, as she shows by her renewed terror after
he has left her on her own. The mystery is allowed for the moment,
however, to have its dramatic effect, and the dialogue passes on to
Dr Rank and his inherited disease.

Rank is something of a grotesque. His grisly promise to send a
card with a black cross over his name, when he is finally certain
that 'the final horrible disintegration has begun' – another fore-
shadowing of Oswald – does, however, underline Nora's insouciance, confronted with what could be a similar corruption of
herself in the moral sphere. It also allows Rank to make the odd
remark, really not justified by his own condition, that 'Somewhere,
somehow, every single family must be suffering some such cruel
retribution.' This is puzzling, since it is clearly untrue, and is only

to be explained by Rank's all-enveloping pessimism. Yet its purport for Nora is clear enough, and she stops her ears to it. At the same time, Ibsen uses this conversation with Rank to build up a side of Nora's character which will be needed if her final decision to leave Helmer is to be convincing. The woman who answers Helmer in kind, when he calls her his little squirrel, could have no strength to go out and live on her own. The woman who affects not to understand that Rank's disease is due to his father's sexual profligacy (which Nora has already mentioned to Mrs Linde as the cause), but to suppose it comes from his father's over-eating, is capable of a self-distancing from her situation, such as Nora is going to need. She is playing up to Rank's expectation that women know nothing about such things, and no doubt plays up to Helmer's adulating vocabulary in the same way – or to some extent at least. Her flirtation with Rank, ending with the light blow on the ear which she gives him with the silk stocking she has let him inspect, is another indication of the more spirited woman beneath the convention-respecting surface. The whole scene with Rank, which still continues a little while, is full of subtleties, insights into a genuine femininity in Nora, which contrasts strongly with the masculine caricature of Helmer. Not the least part of this is Nora's confession to Rank, when she has chided him for speaking openly of his love for her, that she can't tell whether she did or did not know of it already (she has also, of course, some hopes of Rank providing her with the money she needs): Ibsen uses none of the cut-and-dried motivation here, for which he has been criticised elsewhere.

The remainder of the Act, it is true, reverts to something very close to melodrama. Krogstad returns to make his final demand on Nora, and is refused. The form of her refusal is, however, ambiguous. When Krogstad announces that before long it will be he, and not her husband, who will in reality be running the bank, her replies lead him to believe that she hopes to frustrate Krogstad by suicide: 'You'll never live to see the day!...Now I have the courage...I'll show you! I'll show you!...You can't frighten me' (Act 2) (V. 254). An uncompleted sentence seals his interpretation: when he points out that even if she drowns herself he will still have Helmer in his power, she replies 'Afterwards? When

I'm no longer...' – and the audience at first hearing is likely to supply only the word 'alive'. What is not clear as yet is the implication of the word 'Afterwards?' Nora does not mean by this that she will be beyond Krogstad's power, once she is dead. She is thinking of a quite different sacrifice, knowledge of which Ibsen withholds for the sake of dramatic suspense.

Accordingly, Krogstad now leaves the fatal letter in the hall letter-box, revealing to Helmer Nora's crime, in the best traditions of nineteenth-century established theatre. The door into the hall can be opened, revealing the letter, or closed, allowing for a possible substitution or other tampering, according to need, and there the letter remains for many hours, well on into the next Act, a physical threat alternately 'on' stage and just off it, deliciously menacing.

And again Nora uses her ambiguous language, revealing to Mrs Linde what has happened, and speaking of the possibility that something might happen to her 'which meant I couldn't be here'; she adds even more mysteriously that something miraculous is going to happen, but something terrible as well. Nora could probably not say herself quite what her words mean, though they become clear later.

The final scene of the Act is unexpected, in that Nora's tarantella, danced in rehearsal for her performance at the party, but really to distract Helmer's thoughts from the letter-box, has a depth of meaning not found in melodrama. The tarantella is often said to be a dance simulating the furious whirling movement of those who have been bitten by the deadly tarantula spider: it is at one and the same time a frenzied activity and a symptom of death. Ibsen makes nothing of this point, explicitly, leaving it to the performer to suggest Nora's mingled feelings: she is, as she agrees, dancing as though her life depended on it, but also dancing in the knowledge that Helmer will open the letter after the party, and that she thus has at most thirty-one hours to live. The curtain then goes down on a powerfully symbolic and dramatically exciting moment, still leaving the audience with little other expectation than that Nora will soon take her own life in despair at her situation.

Act Three opens a little disappointingly, in so far as it has seemed apparent that Ibsen is using melodrama without being naively

committed to it. Krogstad has till now been a villain of the deepest
dye; even his name suggests, in Norwegian, 'hook', or 'crook'. His
blackmailing of Nora has been given a certain justification – he
needs this particular job, at Helmer's bank, rather than at any
other and rather than any sum of money, because he expects to
become Helmer's right-hand man, and within a year to be running
the bank himself, though this seems something of a fantasy (again
in view of his forgery), and has been undermined by his decision
to put his blackmail into writing. The fatal letter is theatrically
effective, but puts a counter-weapon into Helmer's hands which
could annul Krogstad's present advantage.

As Act Three opens, a change sweeps over Krogstad. From being
so ruthless a character, with no mercy for Nora in her imaginings
of suicide, Krogstad is suddenly converted by Mrs Linde's offer to
marry him. The influence of a Good Woman is too convenient
here: as Eric Bentley allows one partner in his dialogue to say,
'Krogstad is a mere pawn of the plot. When convenient to Ibsen,
he is a blackmailer. When inconvenient, he is converted' (p. 366).
This need not be ascribed to the brevity of drama. Even Ibsen's
principal characters are capable of equally sudden volte-faces.
What he required was that Krogstad's threat should be lifted – or
rather, that it should remain in force till the moment that Helmer
read the letter and made his first intolerant reaction to it – and then
that both Helmer and Nora should take their decisions freely,
without external pressure. This Ibsen might have achieved in other
ways: Helmer might have pointed out to Krogstad that, thanks to
his letter, the situation was perpetual check, with no prospect of
checkmate. But the characters do not have this relationship to
one another; their reactions reflect that mechanical quality which
Yeats perceived.

When Nora returns with Helmer from her triumphant dance,
Krogstad has disappeared, and Mrs Linde does not have time to
do more than briefly urge Nora to confess, which she refuses to
do. There follows a moment of married bliss for Helmer as he
contemplates his wife's beauty, only to be shocked by the realisation that she is unwilling to satisfy him tonight. His indignation,
and evident conviction that, as his wife, she has no right ever to
refuse him, is a further insight into their relationship. Ibsen is not

writing melodrama here, but a critique of a marriage (not, it is true, of marriage in general).

The entry of Rank is one final confirmation to Nora of the untenable position she is in. Rank makes clear that he is now certain to die very soon of the disease he has inherited. He has had a final fling this evening, at the party, just as Nora has. Shortly after, when Helmer has opened the letter, the moral which Nora draws from Rank's life is pushed home by her husband's attack: 'I should have known something like this would happen. I should have foreseen it. All your father's irresponsible ways – Be quiet! All your father's irresponsible ways you have inherited. No religion, no morals, no sense of duty...' (and then, after a few moments) '...You will not be allowed to bring up the children, I daren't trust you with them.' (Act 4) (V. 276). This effects what Ibsen planned in an early draft, made in 1878, the year before that of the final version – 'Depressed and confused by her faith in authority, she loses faith in her moral right and ability to bring up children.'

At that earlier stage in the writing, however, Ibsen seems not to have had in mind the ending which he finally made. 'The catastrophe approaches, ineluctably, inevitably. Despair, resistance, defeat.' Those are the last words of the outline of the plot, in what Ibsen described then as a 'tragedy of modern times'. The change to 'play in three acts', with its positive ending, may well have been a late idea. The scenario which seems to have been drawn up at the same earlier date does not explicitly say why Nora leaves Helmer, and Ibsen may still have not been clear in his mind on that score.

Certainly, there has been no sign so far, in the final version, of Nora's coming rebellion, despite the occasional flaring up of the distinct self in her. There is nothing that would have made the earlier tragic ending unlikely – it would even have been in accordance with Ibsen's habit of writing plays in contrasting pairs, if he had followed up the portrayal of the revelation of truth bringing happiness, in *Pillars of Society*, with a play showing the exact opposite. (The mirror-image is visible in the essentially good Nora and essentially evil Bernick, with their prompters, the evil Krogstad and the good Lona Hessel; where Bernick keeps his child, Nora loses all hers, and it would have completed the pattern if Nora had gone to her death, as a contrast to Bernick's happy reunion with his wife.)

To see the full effect of Ibsen's new inspiration, if that is in fact what it was, the profusion of treatments of the sinning wife in the literature of his day may be recalled. The dramatised version of Dumas' *La dame aux camélias* appeared in 1852, and its success was only exceeded by the operatic version, *La Traviata*, in the following year. Here, the courtesan who marries a good man dies of consumption: the breach of the purity of marriage is not condemned, but the marriage is not allowed to succeed. The less popular *Mary Magdalene* of Friedrich Hebbel (more widely known, however, in Germany and Scandinavia), of 1844, was more closely analogous to *A Doll's House* in that it involved a notion of self-sacrifice very close to that which inspires Nora for much of the play. Hebbel's Klara, having an illegitimate child, drowns herself rather than bring disgrace on her family, hoping to make her death seem an accident. Her last words, 'O God, I come only because, otherwise, my father would kill himself', are close to the thoughts Nora has, of taking her own life rather than that Helmer should selflessly take the responsibility for having himself forged the signature.

In 1879, when *A Doll's House* was first performed, there were three theatres in London offering a dramatised version of Mrs Henry Wood's novel, *East Lynne* – the first (American) performance had been in 1862, and the play became so successful that nine different dramatisations, and even more adaptations, had appeared by 1899. *East Lynne*, which concerns a young woman of noble birth who marries beneath her, who suspects her husband of infidelity and then lives in sin with a villainous lover, was one of the greatest popular successes in England and America in the late nineteenth century. Its crude melodrama makes the touches of the same genre which Ibsen borrowed look slight by comparison: nothing could equal, for sheer improbability, the scene in which Lady Isabel, having returned to her husband's home in disguise as a French governess, is forced to witness the death from illness of her own son, unable to reveal to him her parentage. She dies soon after, of grief, but has already addressed the audience in terms which they must have loved hearing. One version reads here:

(Chamber. Lady Isabel discovered seated at a fireplace, wrapped in a large shawl, very pale and very ill)

Alas! What is to be the end of my sufferings? How much longer am I to bear this torture of mind, this never-dying anguish of soul? From what a dream have I awakened! Oh, lady, wife, mother! whatever trials may be the lot of your married life, though they may magnify themselves to your crushed spirit as beyond the nature, the endurance of woman to bear, yet resolve to bear them. Fall down on your knees and pray for patience; pray for strength to resist that demon who would flee them. Bear them unto death, rather than forget your good name and your good conscience. Oh! I have sacrificed husband, home, children, friends, and all that make life of value to woman – and for what? To be forever an outcast from society, to never again know a moment's peace. Oh! that I could die, and end my suffering and my misery. *(Sinks her head on table.)*

Despite the great differences in language and technique, it was towards some such conclusion as these earlier plays had had, that Ibsen's seems to be tending until past the middle of Act Three. Nora, like Mrs Alving in his next play, was due to pay for her past misdeed, however slight. The reversal of expectations was the bombshell which set the whole of European theatre by the ears, and made Ibsen the centre of great controversy. As Shaw said in *The Quintessence of Ibsenism* in 1891, 'Up to a certain point in the last act, *A Doll's House* is a play that might be turned into a very ordinary French drama by the excision of a few lines, and the substitution of a sentimental happy ending for the famous last scene....But at just that point in the last act, the heroine very unexpectedly...stops her emotional acting and says: "We must sit down and discuss all this that has been happening between us." And it was by this new technical feature: this addition of a new movement, as musicians would say, to the dramatic form, that *A Doll's House* conquered Europe and founded a new school of dramatic art...' (p. 192).

Some fifty years later Brecht wrote, in the notes to his *Three-penny Opera*, that he had written it as a 'report' on the kind of play his bourgeois public liked to see. He might well have taken his cue from Shaw, whose remarks on *The Devil's Disciple* have already been quoted (p. 22). Brecht's intention was to allow the public to take a long look at its favourite form of entertainment, distorting it only enough to arouse a sceptical frame of mind.

Ibsen, in *A Doll's House*, did much more than merely distort: he followed familiar patterns – how deliberately we need not inquire – to the point of almost assimilating himself to them, but the ending was a wrench to the whole fabric.

The surprise, the shock, and the fact that women's rights were already highly topical, assured Ibsen's success as a playwright of ideas. He himself declared that he had not intended to write a tendentious play, that not all women needed to behave like Nora, and that he was not even very sure what women's rights actually were. His disclaimer was a demand to have his plays experienced as plays. Yet the form and mood of *A Doll's House* are so closely akin to those of the most popular works of his time as to illuminate the relationship between theatre and public which must always exist.

The theatre, unlike the novel, must bring in its public at specified times and places to see particular productions, and the successful dramatist has to gauge public taste to a degree uncommon among artists. A successful drama, with few exceptions, is one that has caught on in its own day, and bears the stamp of its own day's audiences. By the nineteenth century, those audiences had ceased to be drawn from small court circles or fashionable society, and had increasingly been made up of middle-class and working-class members. So much was this the case that a man of aristocratic leanings like de Tocqueville began to despair of drama, seeing it as the literary form most natural to a democratic and revolutionary age, and deploring its violence and over-simplification. 'The spectator of a dramatic piece,' de Tocqueville wrote in his chief work, *Democracy in America*, (published in 1835–40), thinking chiefly of America, 'is, to a certain extent, taken by surprise by the impression it conveys. He has no time to refer to his memory, or to consult those more able to judge than himself. It does not occur to him to resist the new literary tendencies which begin to be felt by him; he yields to them before he knows what they are.' This analysis holds good rather more for the period after de Tocqueville wrote than for that preceding it. So does his later remark, 'As for the probability of the plot, it is incompatible with perpetual novelty, surprise, and rapidity of invention. It is therefore neglected, and the public excuses the neglect. You may be sure that if you succeed in bringing your audience into the presence of something that affects them, they will not care by what road you brought them there; and they will never reproach you for having excited their emotions in spite of dramatic rules.' This cynical review of popular taste was echoed (before his own career as a dramatist had gone very far) even by Strindberg, who spoke of the theatre as a *Biblia Pauperum*, a Bible so to speak in strip-cartoons, and by Nietzsche, who saw it as a place for demagogues. In terms of the greater part of nineteenth-century drama, at least, de Tocqueville had some justification.

So far as Ibsen was concerned, even *Pillars of Society* had been intended as much more than melodrama: ostensibly, his topic had been the need for or consequences of truthful relationships, and the same thought underlies *A Doll's House*. It is time to ask, now, what had been sacrificed in the process of winning a public. The immediate effect of the play was to arouse controversy, and in so far as this was about the right of wives to abandon their husbands and children, it must surely have been valuable. But the play, as Ibsen pointed out, is not about any such general right, it is about Nora's right to leave Helmer, and here the melodrama plays a certain part, the characterisation a greater part, in determining the quality of the answer. The fact that Krogstad's blackmail is not presented convincingly in every detail is of small importance compared with the crudity introduced by the caricaturing of Helmer. Such egotistic silliness places the whole relationship on a level much lower than that between Racine's Titus and Berenice – two lovers who never marry, but who see the necessity to withdraw from what is almost a marriage. Anna Karenina's husband (Tolstoy's novel, so similar in several ways to *A Doll's House*, was published only a few years before Ibsen's play, in 1875–6) becomes unbearable to her, but he has his feelings, and one is moved by his plight when Anna leaves him. Helmer has no feelings, apart from pain at being abandoned, and naive pleasure in Nora's beauty. At no moment has he shown any awareness of others, so that even the discussion of such a position as his is restricted. His faults are too exaggerated to be fruitful.

Nora, on the other hand, is drawn in the round. Her potential independence has already shown through, in her mixture of submissive complaisance and of play-acting the part for which Helmer has cast her. The limitation of her capacity to cast light on the intricacy of married relations arises from the motivation of her leavetaking. Her belief that she is hereditarily almost unfit to bring up her children, though its growth is precisely outlined, is cut-and-dried; no shadow of her earlier joyful relation with her children (so like the scene near the beginning of *Anna Karenina*) is allowed to intervene, and the very precision of the playwriting jars here. We have seen the good, dependable Nanny with whom Nora will be leaving her children, but Nora's coldness is surprisingly abrupt: 'Goodbye, Torvald. I don't want to see the children. I know they are in better hands than mine. As I am now, I can never be anything to them.' Ibsen's circumspection, if one thinks of how mother-love was commonly presented on stage in his time, is understandable. Yet the provision of a good Nanny feels like a partial justification of Nora's departure: it impedes full recognition of how bleak and unrealistic her decision really is. She makes a 'dramatic' exit, but that is just what renders it suspect. Her model in real life entered a mental home.

The other feeling that prompts Nora has been obscured till now. The revelation of it explodes at the same time as her reversal of all traditional expectations, and is structurally the climax of the play. From soon after Krogstad's first threats, Nora has spoken mysteriously about the miracle she expects, but the impression has steadily grown that she will, like Hebbel's Klara, choose death rather than the dishonour of a close relative. When she now reveals why Helmer has forfeited her love, a much more complex motive is shown:

NORA I've been patiently waiting for eight years now. Because, heavens, I knew very well that miracles don't happen every day. Then came this crushing blow, and I became absolutely convinced the miracle *would* happen. Krogstad's letter was lying out there – but it never so much as crossed my mind that you would ever submit to that man's terms. I was so absolutely convinced you would say to him: tell the whole wide world. And when that was done...

HELMER Yes, then what? After I had delivered my own wife to dishonour and shame...!

NORA When that was done, I was so absolutely sure you would come forward and take everything on yourself, and say: I am the guilty one.

HELMER Nora!

NORA You mean I'd never accept such a sacrifice. No, naturally. But what would my assurances have counted for against yours? – *That* was the miracle I went in hope and dread of. It was to prevent it that I was ready to end my life. (Act 3) (V. 284)

In the travesty of Ibsen's play by Henry Arthur Jones and Henry Herman, *Breaking a Butterfly*, according to Harley Granville-Barker's account, Nora's expectations were satisfied. In this version, it appears, in Granville-Barker's words, that Helmer 'behaves like the paste-board hero of Nora's doll's house dream; he *does* strike his chest and say "I am the guilty one"' (p. 167).

To imagine such a scene actually taking place is to bring home the melodramatic quality of Nora's expectation. Her dissatisfaction with what Helmer does offer as love is caused by an ideal of love equally romantic and unreal. Self-sacrifice is the first and only thought that still governs Nora's mind, but it is intensified here to the point that she means to sacrifice herself to prevent him sacrificing himself.

This is a different decision entirely from the suicide from despair which seemed to threaten. Desperation compels; by contrast, to make up one's mind that one must kill oneself in order to prevent someone else from taking blame requires either a powerful will, stoicism, and a rational appraisal, or an impetuous, mistaken chivalry. Nora shows no sign of having seen the kind of man Helmer is; her expectations of him sound fantastic. They are made with no thought of the consequences. A noble Helmer who publicly claimed responsibility for the forgery himself would incur for them both a greater penalty, seeing that even an innocuous forgery, when made by a bank official, is more serious than one by a housewife. What is worse, such a protective action in the name of love is all of a piece with the attitude to which Nora is objecting in Helmer's treatment of her hitherto. She blames him now for not thinking of undertaking precisely the kind of knightly rescue of a damsel in distress which would assert his male superiority all over again. As for suicide, she could not expect the chivalrous Helmer of her imagination to refrain from clearing her name after death, any more than he would refrain if she were alive. The kind of man she thought he was would merely be hurt still more by her suicide: he would not be saved by it from the need for a false confession.

At this moment, when she is breaking through to a self-realisation that could be genuine, Nora proves to be as unrealistic as her husband. If the miracle she speaks of in the final lines were ever to happen, and Helmer were to change into the man she looked for, a sentimental ideal would still govern them both. She is in an impossible situation, since the man she looks for is the very man she cannot bear to see becoming a reality.

This circumscribing of the breakthrough, confining the heroine to an essentially unchanging standard, is characteristic of later plays also. Hedda Gabler's ideal is similarly undermined by its close resemblance to the ideals of the very world she despises. Yet the effect of *A Doll's House* is not wholly limited by Nora's insistence on the need for an absurd sacrifice. The great impact which the play had is partly to be explained by the realisation that Helmer's ridiculously overdone self-seeking has over-reached itself. When, opening the first letter from Krogstad, he thinks only of his own position, and opening the second feels only relief for himself, the justness of Nora's decision to leave him is a good deal strengthened. The egotism is so blatant and Nora's femininity in the opening scenes so exaggerated that, a hundred years later, it is almost surprising that there should have been any scandal. The vilification Ibsen had to face for even offering the matter for debate is a mark of the level of popular taste and judgment with which he had to contend. Yet – again from a later vantage-point – the concessions he made to that taste are also clearly visible, not only in the earlier scenes, but at the vital moment of Nora's decision. Her departure announced a great awakening, in European drama as well as in women's egalitarianism. But it was strongly conditioned, if not crippled, by the fact of its conformity to crude though popular standards.

4

Ghosts

'The condition of the world,' Hegel said in a passage no more paradoxical than the rest of his *Philosophy of World History*, 'is not yet known; the aim is to bring it about'. If Ibsen had read that definition of the task of the 'world-historical man', which he possibly had, since he had studied Hegel while still a student at the university, he might well have applied it to himself, after *A Doll's House*. Such world-historical men, Hegel went on to say, were always aware of the inadequacy of the present moment, as they found it: they were unable to find in it any satisfaction for the consciousness of something better or greater that they had within them, and they stood at least in their early years in continual opposition to their circumstances. Yet this very negativity merely prolonged their opposition: without an affirmative attitude, which could not come while they still opposed, they remained helpless. Those who became great leaders, however – whether military, political, or religious – had discovered what it was that they truly wanted or 'willed' to happen in the world, and from that point on the very self-criticism to which they had subjected themselves made them irresistible. Other men did not know what they themselves really wanted. The world-historical men, by contrast, not only knew, but knew that it was what the rest wanted. Thus they brought about the 'condition (*Zustand*) of the world' which till then had been unknown, though latent and essentially always present:

To oppose these world-historical individuals is a hopeless enterprise. They are irresistibly impelled to perform their life's work. That is then what is right, and the rest, even though they may not have thought that this was what they wanted, adhere to it and endure it; it is a power within them that rules over them, even though it may appear to them external and alien and contrary to their consciousness of their supposed will. For the mind (*Geist*) that has progressed further is the inner soul of all individuals, albeit the unconscious inner soul, which the great men bring to their consciousness. It is, after all, what they themselves truly want, and therefore it exercises a force to which they surrender even when their conscious will contradicts; for this reason they follow these leaders of souls, for they feel the irresistible power of their own inner spirit, stepping forward to meet them.

Ibsen had moved in much this way, almost from his earliest plays onwards: the consciousness of speaking on behalf of and in criticism of the Norwegian nation was always with him. With time, however, and especially after his stay in Italy, his aim became wider: he was speaking to, and perhaps for Europe. Yet it was not until the last act of *A Doll's House* that 'the affirmative', in Hegel's sense, truly took over from the negative. As an unsigned notice in *The Manchester Guardian* of 8 June 1889 said – it has since been identified as being by Bernard Shaw – the audience at the first London performance was curiously in sympathy, and although this remained instinctive, the reviewer felt that he knew what was going on:

It would of course be absurd to pretend that Nora's assertion of her intention to leave her husband and home in obedience to an impulse of duty to herself before which all the institutions and prejudices of society must yield was felt to have the irresistible power of an awakening social force behind it. Audiences are not yet trained in the dynamics of the 'will to live', and when Miss Achurch said 'I *must*, I *must*', the audience, not having studied Schopenhauer, did not quite see it. It is all the more significant that they submitted to Ibsen on the point without a murmur.

Schopenhauer or Hegel, the point is the same. Ibsen seemed to Shaw, at that moment in history, to have hit on the ending which would fire imagination, not merely about women's rights, but about the whole concept of the liberated self. He might very well not have done so: if his original notion of a 'tragedy' had been adhered to, *A Doll's House* might have gone down to history as one more play about a married woman's disgrace and suicide – more tightly knit, and less sentimental than the average run, but not otherwise remarkable. The change to an affirmative ending for Nora was a change to the affirmative in Ibsen himself.

Yet he was still misunderstood, inevitably and almost appropriately, since his position was dialectical. The play, as he insisted, was not about women's rights, it was about Nora's lines 'I have another duty equally sacred [as the duty to her husband and children]...My duty to myself.' This duty was not exhausted in the mere affirming of it – speculative members of the audience might well have asked what hope Nora could have of surviving alone after leaving the family, without money or prospects of a job, and with only a romantic innocence to protect her. It was a duty that moved in a dialectic of opposite forces; as Peer Gynt had been told much earlier: 'To be oneself is to slay oneself.' The play which followed *A Doll's House*, at what was from now on to be an almost regular two-year interval, was like a slap in the face to those who had naively welcomed Nora's emancipation. 'Let those who think themselves emancipated realise what the word means' could have been Ibsen's private thought in writing *Ghosts*. It might require not only the abandoning of children, but the merciful killing of one.

Mrs Alving, James McFarlane argues, goes even further in her search for liberty than Nora does. (*The Oxford Ibsen* V., pp. 2 seqq.) Nora merely knows that an attempt at breaking out of the family's grasp has to be made: she does not know how it will turn out. Mrs Alving has failed once in the past to take her chance of achieving freedom from her husband, but since then she has steadily grown towards emancipation. She has read the new books, has condemned, perhaps only half-heartedly, her own preference for duty over self-fulfilment, and now not only condones free love but is even willing to contemplate an incestuous marriage for her son, if that is what his greatest fulfilment needs. In Mrs Alving the concept of free self-fulfilment goes further than it had done since *Brand* and *Peer Gynt*, and it does so in terms of the society of Ibsen's own day.

Underlying all Ibsen's ideas on emancipation there was, however, a deep pessimism about the chances of the ideal ever being realisable. A note written on a torn wrapper postmarked 1881 puts the position as he himself saw it at that moment (and in a letter to the Danish critic Brandes ten years earlier he had said something very similar):

The fault lies in the fact that the whole of mankind is a failure. If a man demands to live and develop as a man should, then that is megalomania. The whole of mankind, and especially Christians, suffer from megalomania.

'To live and develop as a man should' – that is, presumably, in terms we can deduce from the plays, to develop every facet of human nature in Faustian expansiveness. It is to be like Rebecca West, unconscious of any restriction of conscience in her contriving of Beate Rosmer's suicide, or like Dr Stockmann, the 'enemy of the people', defying the compact majority, all alone. That is what the world calls megalomania, and on this view Christians suffer from it, as Brand did, in an inverted form, denying the self in order to have it crowned with glory. But Ibsen goes further: the whole of mankind suffers from the same mania, and on that account the whole of mankind is a failure.

There is something related to megalomania in the sweepingness of that very assertion. It is at the least open to question whether a freedom so complete for each individual that no individual could possess it is really the goal towards which a man should strive and develop. A responsible self-realisation within a society is another matter. Ibsen's concept here implies a total freedom from concern with all other individuals. The only enjoyer of such freedom would have to live in a world where limitations were so completely absent that freedom would not be noticed: it would be the freedom of solipsism.

In *Ghosts*, for the first time in the plays after 1873, Ibsen writes as though the situation he is describing has not only a wider social validity, but a universal one. Neither of the two preceding plays had been about more than the characters themselves and their societies, neither had such generalising lines of central importance as Oswald's, after the fire at the Orphanage: 'Everything will burn down', 'we are all ghosts', or such general application as is implied in the title itself, with its suggestion of the omnipotent hand of the past. (A parallel is Rank's remark that all families must suffer like his, but *A Doll's House* is not mainly concerned with this.) There are moments when *Ghosts* seems to be about the tragic consequences of *joie de vivre*, and though it is true that the play does not represent Ibsen's personal philosophy as a whole, merely a negative pole of it, the intention is clearly to state that negative, for the present, with great emphasis.

In the construction, Ibsen follows two paths. The story which is to lead to the catastrophe is not one that lends itself to much dramatic development. Oswald returns home to Norway from Paris, aware that he may at any moment experience the softening of his brain which will end his sane life. The revelation of this must be kept back until the catastrophic climax, and the causes must be expounded, but for the purpose of dramatic action a different story is needed, and this is provided in the intrigue whereby Engstrand involves Pastor Manders in disaster.

The first Act begins with both strands at once, Engstrand's conversation with his 'daughter' Regine being a concise piece of exposition. From the talk between these two emerges the fact that the young son of the house, Oswald Alving, has just returned from Paris, that the Orphanage in memory of his father is to be opened by his mother tomorrow, that Pastor Manders is to conduct the opening ceremony, and a good deal else, which the audience will remember as it slots into position in the mosaic of events later revealed: Regine's mother was in service with Captain Alving, and may have had an illegitimate child – but by an English sailor, so far as it is yet known; Regine herself is perhaps on the lookout for a wealthy match like Oswald; the Seamen's Home which Engstrand is planning will be in fact a brothel. All this is necessary for the complications to follow, and is told in a minimum of time. In twelve short speeches, less than a hundred words, Ibsen establishes that it is raining – and this is not merely to tell the audience about the weather, it is to prepare the audience for the final curtain; that Engstrand is, or seems to be, Regine's father; that a 'young master', Oswald, is asleep upstairs; that Engstrand is at least a shade hypocritical, perhaps a drunkard. He also plants in the same passage the first indication of the rôle Engstrand is to play. The carpenter's limping steps into the room are caused by the heavy boot on his club foot, to which Regine draws special attention. (The economy is neat – she upbraids him for the noise, which may wake Oswald, whose name is thereby introduced, at the same time that Ibsen ensures the audience is aware of the foot.) The brief exchange about this also involves a distant suggestion: a literal translation here would read:

REGINE (*in a low voice*) What is it you want? Stay where you are. It's dripping off you.
ENGSTRAND That's the Good Lord's rain that is, my child.

REGINE That's the devil's rain, is that.

(Act I) (V. 349)

At this stage the audience will make nothing consciously of the suggestion that Engstrand's machinations have a touch of the diabolical. There is, however, a shadowy reminiscence of Bishop Nicholas and his machinations against Earl Skule in *The Pretenders*, in the way Engstrand involves Manders in his toils, and the seemingly casual blasphemy could conceivably be a deliberate touch.

Engstrand's plot is not thrust into the foreground, and it has even been regarded (by F. L. Lucas) merely as a matter of suspicion, rather than a virtual certainty. Ibsen gave no direct answer, when questioned about it. The coherence of the references to it can leave no doubt, however, that he meant his audiences to sense that a plot was evolving. There has already been one fire in Engstrand's workshop, the previous day, and the carpenter is said by Mrs Alving to be careless. Regine suspects him early on of having designs on Manders 'once again', and now he invites the pastor to conduct a service in the workshop on the eve of the opening, which can scarcely be for devout reasons. By this means, having established that the shavings in his workshop are a fire-risk, he ensures that there are candles there as well, and this enables him to lay the charge of having started the fire directly at Manders' door – the candles are essential, since Engstrand will claim in Act Three that he saw Manders snuff them with his fingers and throw them among the shavings. Immediately after the fire, Engstrand says to Regine 'now we've got him nicely, my girl,' and proceeds to blackmail Manders into promising support for his 'Seamen's Home'. The pattern of events and the motivation fit together so closely as to point clearly at what is intended.

There is no presentation of all this in the form of events on stage, and the audience hears of the incidents at such long intervals that it can scarcely do more than accept them. (The dramatic *action* is restricted to the fire at the Orphanage and its climactic effect.) On only a little scrutiny, it is true, the incidents are less convincing. Engstrand presumably worked it out in his mind beforehand, that if he could implicate Manders in the starting of the fire he would be able to secure his support for the Seamen's 'hostel' by offering to take the blame himself, as he does offer to do in Act Three. That is why he let it be known that there had already been a fire at his workshop: another fire started accidentally by him would be equally credible. At the same time, he had to arrange things so that Manders, and only Manders, would believe that the fire was started by his carelessness in snuffing the candles. Once Manders had capitulated, nobody else need ever know what really happened.

Like the blackmailing in *A Doll's House* – and indeed in *Hedda Gabler* – the plan, though defective, is immediately successful. 'I don't suppose the papers are going to let *you* off very lightly, Pastor,' Engstrand says, and at once Manders falls into the trap: 'No, that's just what I'm thinking. That's just about the worst part of the whole affair. All these spiteful accusations and insinuations ...! Oh it's terrible to think about!'

Manders does not say what spiteful accusations and insinuations might be made. What possible gain, one wonders, could anyone see for him in his letting the Orphanage burn down without having insured it? He may be attacked in the newspapers if it becomes known that his carelessness started the fire, and Engstrand will see to it that that information becomes available, if Manders does not submit. But what has Engstrand to gain for his Seamen's Home from having such a confession of his own guilt published? And even if Engstrand's guilt does not stand in his way, has Manders, the respectable, unblemished parson, anything to fear from a well-known drunkard like Engstrand? It is not as if the story of snuffing the candles were remotely credible in itself. Manders does not ask Engstrand why, if he saw a still smouldering candle being thrown into the shavings, he did not take it out again, as, if he had a moment's presence of mind, he would ask, and as others would ask, if the story were made public by Engstrand. Manders has to be highly suggestible, if Engstrand's plot is to work. (As John Northam concedes (p. 112), 'Manders need not be as inadequate as he is to give a reasonable representation of society's inadequacies.') But in addition to that, Engstrand has to be completely sure not only of Manders' unthinking acquiescence, but that his own story of negligence will be generally believed without incurring discredit for himself, and that Manders will not, by an inadvertence which would come naturally to him, let the cat out of the bag himself, before long. To cap all, Engstrand has to be presented as believing that Manders will go on subsidising or protecting the Seamen's Home after it becomes known what the place really is, if it is not widely known already, for it does not take much guessing. A man of Manders' rigid principles would be at least as likely to turn against the immoral establishment, whatever the cost to himself. In naturalistic or realistic terms, the plot is naive, though it would do well enough in an Elizabethan comedy of gulling. Its effectiveness in the theatre is due not only to the remoteness of the events from the stage, but to the fact that there is no real social background either: the confrontation is restricted to the two men concerned, and we are not given any means of guessing what the newspapers are like, how the other clergy would react (would they in fact blame Manders for trusting in Providence rather than insuring?), or what influence a man like Manders could really exert. The play and its problems exist, in this respect, in a social vacuum.

Yet Engstrand's plot leads, all the same, to one of Ibsen's most suggestive symbols. He has been criticised for breaking off Act Two, just at the moment when Mrs Alving is about to make a crucial revelation, by staging a fire at the Orphanage, and so prolonging the action unnecessarily for a further Act. But the fire was a potent element in his imagination; far from being merely a convenient device, it is a means of expressing more than words could say. It is no coincidence that Hedda Gabler, at a comparable moment, burns the manuscript, the so-called 'child' of Løvborg's brain, on which he had set his hopes: her relation to Løvborg resembles in some ways the relation of Engstrand to Manders, or rather of Engstrand to Mrs Alving, through Manders, for the two strands of *Ghosts* coalesce at the moment of the fire. Nor is it a coincidence that Solness, the master builder, feels so guilty about the death of *his* children by fire, which he attributes to his need for diabolical 'helpers and servers'. The fire is ambiguous, for Solness – without it, he says, he would never have succeeded – but so it was for the Emperor Julian, when his fleet was consumed: the phoenix that he expected to arise from the flames was 'the God of earth and the emperor of the spirit in one...' A strand of symbolism involving sometimes a diabolical pact, sometimes evil machinations, sometimes a resurrection, sometimes a destruction, connects all these fires.

To see the significance of the fire in *Ghosts* it is better to work through to it from the beginning again, following the other thread, the account of Mrs Alving's relation with her husband and the upbringing of Oswald, to the moment of his return.

The conversation between Mrs Alving and Pastor Manders, which follows almost immediately on the one between Engstrand and Regine, deals first with the question of insuring the Orphanage. It is rather late in the day to be doing this, it is true, but for neatness and to keep a unity of time Ibsen is driven to the expedient of having the matter of insurance discussed after the building has been completed. There is, however, a certain ambiguity too, as there will be also in the account of Mrs Alving's early married life. According to Manders, there are many influential people in the town who would regard the insuring of such a building as showing lack of faith in the will of Providence to protect it. In Act Three, on the other hand, the fact of the building not being insured is used to increase the awkwardness of Manders's situation after the Orphanage has been destroyed. Both to insure and not to insure are shown as equally reprehensible. There are in the plays several more such ambiguities about the nature of public opinion, as was already the case in *Pillars of Society*.

Similarly, but with more damaging consequences for the play, it emerges from a later conversation in Act One that Mrs Alving's life was made miserable from the very beginning of her marriage by her husband's 'excesses'. He was, she says, 'debauched [or profligate, or abandoned] all his life', and she was driven by his profligacy to run away from him after only a year, though she soon returned. Late in the play, however, she accuses herself of having made the house unbearable for Captain Alving, in the early days of their marriage. She sees herself at that later point, in Act Three, as having been too concerned with doing her duty when she came back to continue life with him: the impression is created that this preoccupation with duty destroyed the *joie de vivre* in her husband as well as in herself, whereas it appears that, at least so far as Alving was concerned, it was already perverted.

The two versions are presented so far apart in the play that the second tends to colour one's interpretation, which is also easily led astray by the fact that the early years are not enacted, only narrated. Actions are more vividly remembered than narrations in words: it is easier to suppose, with words, that one has forgotten some qualifying remark. Yet the text is clear enough on these points, when one goes back to it.

There may be some misgivings, on the other hand, during Mrs Alving's speeches, in Act One, particularly when she goes on to say that, having returned to Alving, she 'took complete control' and maintained for him a spotless reputation, while he continued exactly as before. Is it possible, one wonders, for such deception to be practised for eight or nine years, when a husband lies all day long on the sofa, reading a government gazette, and holds secret drinking orgies with his wife in the evenings, which end with his having to be dragged into bed? Did servants and visitors never notice? If nobody saw him, how did he get so great a reputation that a memorial is to be unveiled in his honour? Did his nose never change colour or his breath smell? And did Mrs Alving bring his women to him, or allow him to run the risk of finding them outside? Ibsen's concern with presenting a whited sepulchre leads him, as in earlier plays, into some unlikely situations.

(The medical situation is even more unlikely, it seems, but few spectators will know whether it is unusual for syphilis to be transmitted only to one child, and not to the other child or the mother, whether a man can suffer from the disease for years without its being obvious from his appearance – but did Mrs Alving never let her husband have any medical attention all that time? – whether a sudden outbreak can follow after a complete absence of any signs in childhood, and whether it is normal for only the central nervous system to be attacked. These are improbabilities, according to experts, but they affect the play only a little. The view put forward by Derek Russell Davis (in McFarlane's *Anthology*, pp. 369–383), that Oswald suffers not from syphilis but schizophrenia, is weakened by the psychiatrist's addendum, written six years after his original article, in which he says that the term schizophrenia now tends to be avoided, since it 'only has meaning within the context of an outmoded theory.')

But it is not the unlikelihood that matters, so much as the impression Ibsen gives of never having brought alive in his mind the events of the Alvings' past, (however detailed the story becomes) and thus having allowed it to remain so vague that Mrs Alving could speak about it in such contradictory terms, now as though it were her own fault that Alving was debauched, now as though it were his own, or society's.

The other vital moment in Act One, before the curtain-scene, is Oswald's reminiscence of his happy days with the Bohemians of the Norwegian community in Paris. This, though sentimentally idealising, establishes something of importance for the whole play, that there is a possibility of enjoying life without the trammels of morality as Manders understands it, and without the fatal consequences which Alving had to endure. It is true that, in Act Two, Oswald imagines he has contracted syphilis by 'overtaxing his strength' while living with the Norwegians in Paris. But it is hard to know how to interpret this passage – he may be saving his mother the pain of thinking her husband has transmitted the disease, or he may be as naive as he sounds, or Ibsen may have meant to imply that even the Bohemians were infected, too. It prepares the ground for two later moments in the play, to which we shall return.

The last lines of Act One, however, aim more at theatrical than at dramatic success. Arnold Bennett indeed found the curtain of every act 'dreadfully "stagey"', and it is difficult to imagine such endings to the chapters of novels with any claim to be remembered. The over-acting implied in the stage directions need not be followed closely today; it is merely an indication, presumably, of conventions current at the theatres Ibsen knew:

(*From the dining-room comes the sound of a chair being overturned. At the same time Regine's voice is heard.*)

REGINE'S VOICE (*in a sharp whisper*) Oswald! Are you mad? Let go!

MRS ALVING (*stiffening with horror*) Ah – ! (*She stares wildly at the half-open door. Oswald is heard inside, coughing and humming. A bottle is opened.*)

PASTOR MANDERS (*agitated*) But what is all this? What *is* it, Mrs Alving?

MRS ALVING (*hoarsely*) Ghosts. The couple in the conservatory – Come back to haunt us.

PASTOR MANDERS What do you say? Regine? Is *she* – ?

MRS ALVING Yes. Come. Not a word – ! (*She grasps Pastor Manders by the arm and walks unsteadily toward the dining-room.*)

(Act 1) (V. 378)

In any production, however, Mrs Alving's horror must be conveyed in some way, and it is the horror itself, rather than the melodramatic expression of it, that invites the charge of staginess. The moment in the inner room is only a mild flirtation, shocking enough to Manders, no doubt, but without any real similarity to Alving's seduction of Regine's mother. To all appearances Oswald is behaving not abnormally, for a young, unmarried man (though we learn more of his real motives in Act Three). Alving, by contrast, already married, and to his wife's knowledge a debauchee, was beginning to seduce a young servant. There is no 'ghost' here. Oswald is innocent of any serious charge, and Mrs Alving's reaction seems to occur not because of any fear that Oswald is about to show himself as profligate as his father. If she had a horror of incest, the pretext for her use of the title of the play in her curtain-scene would be stronger. But it soon appears she has not, and Ibsen's concern for a 'good curtain' becomes the more apparent.

At the beginning of Act Two, despite her shock of a few hours earlier, Mrs Alving is willing to contemplate even an incestuous union between Regine and Oswald, and blames only her own cowardice for her inability to propose it to them, if that will make Oswald happy. Considering that Oswald has so far done nothing more than put his arm around Regine, this is indecent haste. Mrs Alving has not been driven into a corner; her conjectured proposal is grounded on no better reason than her belief that plenty of married couples all over the country are as closely related, and that seems to be enough for her. She has no idea whether Regine or Oswald would wish it, or whether the strong social pressures which are presumably represented by Manders would make life intolerably difficult for them, she merely moves from frightened conventionality, to an equally frightened unwillingness to oppose incest. As with Manders, at the moment when Engstrand springs his trap, the audience is left unaware of the serious arguments which might be put forward on either side. It is 'all or nothing' again.

By contrast, a play by a man usually accounted an inferior of

Ibsen's shows how such a debate might have been held in a social context that gives it meaning. In Harley Granville-Barker's *Waste* there is a discussion at Cabinet level of the consequences of the death of a young woman during an abortion, made necessary by her affair with a Member of Parliament who is now a candidate for an appointment in the Cabinet. There is the attitude of the dead woman's husband to be considered, the problem of how the scandal will affect the Party, the moral condemnation of the one outright Christian present, the indignation of the M.P. at the woman having presumed to do away with the child of his begetting, the advisability of hushing the whole thing up, the likelihood of rumours circulating. The debate, having this complexity, is tensely interesting, and owes its strength partly to the fact that the author envisages a real political party of his own day, and writes with politicians in mind who were known to him personally. Ibsen, on the other hand, throws up the question whether incest may be admissible without allowing his characters to consider it in terms of his own day or any other. What at one moment is unthinkable is almost at once the natural and obvious course, one more of the endless possibilities of self-realisation, even though ultimately as disastrous as the rest. This is not a question of 'consistency' of character – of course people contradict themselves and are ambiguous on vital issues. The distinctive feature here, which is distinctive of many other of Ibsen's characters, is the 'dialectical' plunge from one extreme to the other which allows innocence and guilt to seem equally valid, since neither is associated with any basis of fact.

In Ibsen's defence, it might be said here that he is concerned with ideal speculation, not mundane detail. It is true that as he progresses his plays tend to become more remote from everyday reality (despite the strong social implications of *An Enemy of the People*). But this issue of Oswald's marriage demands some awareness of the real consequences. *Ghosts*, despite its generalising tendency, is not simply a play about the dead hand of the past strangling the present; in its specific content it is about the advisability of an incestuous marriage at a particular time and place, and it is just on this question that Ibsen gives no insight into the nature of Mrs Alving's decision.

The middle of Act Two is taken up with a development of Engstrand's plot, when Oswald returns, and there follows the moving scene, in which he tells his mother the hideous facts of his illness. At least, his fear and her loving sympathy make this a moving scene at first acquaintance, so long as Ibsen seems to be writing simply and directly about a mother's love, and the torment of undeserved pain. The awfulness of inherited disease is brought home here. But Ibsen is attempting more than this: 'we are all ghosts', all suffering from the same inherited disease, and it is the means of escaping not merely syphilis, but the effects of the Christian belief in original sin, that really occupies his mind. As Brand says, there are men

> into whose souls a stain
> Eats its way, that toil nor time
> Ever shall erase again...
> They who cannot burn away
> The foul carcase of their thought...
> And from them, perchance, outruns
> Link on link of sin...
> Because they were their fathers' sons!

Sickness is the bad dream that holds back several of Ibsen's characters from the fullest realisation of themselves. In one of his earliest plays, *The Warrior's Barrow*, Christianity is called 'the Southern plague' which destroys the hardy Norseman's will. Rebecca West will later declare herself to be 'infected' with Christian ideals. Earl Skule cries out in envy of King Haakon, 'I am sick! I am sick!', but it is sickness of the will that he means. Falk, in *Love's Comedy*, determining to live a life 'made strong by truth', makes up his mind that it shall not be 'in sickness', which is synonymous for him with restraint, self-denial, and all that Ibsen himself tended, in his dichotomies, to sum up as Christianity.

There is only the briefest direct association of Christianity with sickness in *Ghosts*, when Oswald speaks of people in Norway seeing work as a punishment for their sins, and contrasts them with people abroad, where 'nobody really believes in ideas of that sort any more'. Allowing for the exaggeration, this can only refer to such writers as Nietzsche, whose works began to appear in 1872, and to his predecessors. It is unlikely that Ibsen, who devoured newspapers but read few books, had read Nietzsche at that early date. Before long, Nietzsche was to become notorious for having, allegedly, advocated the killing of the weak by the strong, but there seems little likelihood that Ibsen was directly influenced by him at any stage in his life. Besides, the motive underlying Oswald's conversation with his mother does not represent him as weak. The similarity with Nietzsche is rather in Oswald's view of Regine as a strong, healthy woman who would have no qualms about putting him to death if he were to ask her. The 'life-affirming' philosophy of Nietzsche is distantly echoed in Regine, though no more than that.

The first hint that Oswald and Mrs Alving's conversation is not a normal scene between a sick son and a doting mother is given when Oswald takes up her words 'how could I refuse you any-thing now?', and eagerly asks if they are really true. His eagerness is unexplained because at this point Regine enters, and, as soon as she has gone, he begins to ask his mother whether she does not think her 'splendid'. Mrs Alving takes this to be a sign of Oswald's having fallen in love, and anxiously begins to speak of Regine's having many faults. But the conversation, though the audience cannot know it at this moment, is at cross-purposes. Oswald goes on, it is true, to say that Regine is his 'one salvation', but this also is ambiguous, like his comment on her splendidness. What he goes on to say about Regine is never an avowal of love, though Mrs Alving takes it that way. He calls Regine 'goodlooking', 'sound as a bell', 'vital', 'well-built', and eventually speaks of marrying her, or at least going away with her. But what he sees in her is 'joy in life', or 'joy of life',★ what Nietzsche might have called 'life-affirmation', the unscrupulous self-regard which will

★ The Norwegian *livsglede* is translated by John Northam as 'the gift of happiness', on the grounds that 'joy in life' is inflated in English, where the Norwegian is not, since *glede* is the common word for 'happiness'. There is a difficulty here, since *lykke* is closer to 'happiness', while *glede* certainly means 'joy' and 'delight' as well as merely 'pleasure'. A similar difficulty arises over translating into English the German *Lebensfreude*. I prefer 'joy in life', or 'joy of life' inflated as both sound, since some quality of exulting in life, in a sense akin to Nietzsche's, seems implied, rather than the milder 'gift of happiness', and since what Oswald expects of Regine is consonant with what Nietzsche would have ex-pected of an exultant 'life-affirmer'.

not be daunted by any feeling of a need for compassion, if Oswald's disease should reach the point at which a quick death is preferable to prolonged agonies. This is still not explicit, to the end of the Act, or even for much of Act Three. So far as Mrs Alving understands, Oswald is telling her that he is in love with Regine and wants her for his wife. Nor does Regine herself know the rôle for which Oswald has cast her.

What Mrs Alving does make of the occasion is ambiguous, and more meaningful than at first appears. At Oswald's declaration that in other countries nobody believes in a vale of tears any longer, and that he is afraid to go on living in Norway on account of the ugly degeneration he might undergo there, she rises and says, pensively, 'Now I see it all. . . And now I can speak.' She evidently means to tell Oswald that he is half-brother to Regine, and to let him choose whether to marry her or not: in fact she says 'you shall know everything. And then you can choose.' We may suppose that, like Lona Hessel, she is inspired here by the thought that truth will make them free. Yet only a few lines later she tells Oswald that he will neither go away with Regine nor stay at home with her – 'because now I can speak plainly': the implication is, now, that he could not possibly choose to marry his half-sister. Mrs Alving has, then, no precise expectation about the effect of her revelation: she is merely presenting Oswald and Regine with the truth that will leave them with their own free, or relatively free, decision. Before she can do so, the fire breaks out at the Orphanage, and the revelation is postponed to the last Act. But the significance of the fire is now redoubled.

The moment bears comparison with the scene in Part Two, Act Four, of *Emperor and Galilean*, when the Emperor Julian decides to stake everything on success, and gives orders to burn the fleet with which he could still make a retreat. (Earl Skule, in a similar situation, is urged to break down the bridges, and as defeat nears an ominous red glow shines half across the sky, like a flaming sword.) The decision is made at a moment of great exaltation: Julian sees himself as a new Messiah, and requires his soldiers, including the Christians among them, to offer incense to him as to a god. When the Christians revolt at this, Julian gives orders for them to be killed, but in the very moment that he speaks the words, a bright glare spreads across the sky, and flames leap up from the ships.

The sequence is not unlike that which leads to the ending of Act Two, in *Ghosts*. There also Mrs Alving has just allowed herself to inveigh a little against the 'Christian' conception of suffering, and is on the point of making the breakthrough to complete truthfulness, at least so far as Oswald's relation to Regine is concerned, when the fire breaks out. Though the expression is adapted to the modern setting of the later play, Ibsen seems to be pursuing a course, as though the rejection of Christianity and the assertion of personal liberty inevitably involved a retribution, expressed through the fire-symbol.

Julian finds almost at once that he has been betrayed. He has burned his boats at the instigation of a deserter from the enemy camp, who persuaded him that they were useless. As soon as the flames have caught, he learns that the deserter, whom someone calls a 'crafty devil', has seemed to 'vanish into thin air', 'like a shadow'. Though a rational explanation is possible, there is a certain suggestion here that a diabolical figure, with whom we may compare Engstrand, has been the principal agent in bringing the fire about.

The similarities, however much veiled by the change of location and epoch, are less likely to be fortuitous than to come from a powerful experience of Ibsen's own. Yet there is some truth in the criticism that the fire merely ends the Act conveniently and postpones the revelation for a while. It is natural for Julian the Apostate, a historical figure with mystical beliefs, to interpret the flames from his ship both as a fearful portent and as the funeral pyre of Emperor and Christ, from which the Third Empire, synthesising both, will arise. The fire in *Ghosts* can be taken as a retribution only by Manders: what Mrs Alving herself has done, or intends to do, does not strike one as requiring punishment for her. She means merely to speak the truth, and then to leave Oswald and Regine to choose for themselves. The fire, which has strictly nothing to do with her own actions, can only be regarded as significant from the superstitiously pious view of a Pastor Manders, which Ibsen satirises throughout the play. The fire is thus, for all its coherence with the pattern of some of the other

LIBRARY OF
MOUNT ST. MARY'S
COLLEGE
EMMITSBURG MARYLAND

plays, as unconnected with the sequence of events as it seems to the play-goer who knows nothing of Ibsen's work as a whole. The ending is 'stagey', as much as the ending of Act One is, in that it provides a sensational curtain-drop incommensurate with the action.

Act Three begins with a step down from the sublime, when Mrs Alving, despite the burning down of the Orphanage, becomes anxious about Oswald's having gone out without his hat. A note of comedy continues when Engstrand reveals his hand to Manders, and Manders accepts the whole improbable yarn. But from this point onwards, the final climax of the play is prepared, and the meaning of what has gone before is uncovered. First, the possibility of Oswald's appealing to Regine to kill him when the disease breaks out again is dismissed; as soon as she hears of his illness, Regine decides to leave and blackmail Manders into marrying her, or giving her money, instead. Regine is consistent here. All through the play she has never thought for an instant of anything but her own advantage. She flirted with Manders from the first, before she realised that Oswald might be serious in his attentions. She detests Engstrand, but only because he is not respectable enough for her purposes, and because none of the seamen he knows is a good enough match for her. When Mrs Alving now reveals that Regine is Captain Alving's daughter, Regine's only comment is a sneer at her natural mother, and a request for permission to leave straight away. Her rejection of Oswald is extreme – 'No, you don't catch me staying out here in the country, working myself to death looking after invalids.' And while her reluctance to stay is understandable, her reasons are not only brutally direct, but explanatory in a way that casts light on her rôle in the play:

A poor girl's got to make the most of things while she's young. Or else you find yourself left in the lurch before you know where you are. I've got this joy of life in me too, Mrs Alving.   (Act 3) (V. 414)

Here we are given a clue to what it was that attracted Oswald to Regine. None of his praise of her was for any qualities of mind or heart; he was simply impressed with her robust strength and what he too called her 'joy of life'. Now, it appears that this joy is also the expression of a capacity to be completely ruthless, to care nothing for the life of another. Regine, as Oswald sees her and Ibsen portrays her, has something in common with Rebecca West, in *Rosmersholm*, who actually does bring about the death of another woman without, at the time, feeling the slightest compunction. It is a notion of fearless action that would have been listened to with respect by some, in a decade when Nietzsche was shortly to write of the 'blond beasts', and Ibsen produces it so often that we should not dismiss the idea of a connection between *livsglede* and ruthlessness as though it were not meant to be worth serious attention.

The monstrosity is that Oswald, being disappointed in Regine, turns to his mother and expects her to behave in precisely the same way. There is a ruthlessness in him, matching Regine's, and this is what makes the ending of *Ghosts* less seriously moving than it might be. He is so brisk:

OSWALD Regine would have done it. Regine was so marvellously light-hearted. And she'd soon have got bored with looking after an invalid like me.
MRS ALVING Then praise and thanks to God Regine isn't here!
OSWALD Well then, now it's up to you to give me this helping hand, Mother.
MRS ALVING (*with a shriek*) Me!
OSWALD Who is better fitted than you?
MRS ALVING Me! Your mother!
OSWALD All the more reason.
MRS ALVING Me! Who gave you life!
OSWALD I never asked you for life. And what sort of a life is this you've given me? I don't want it! Take it back! (Act 3) (V. 420)

It is not, in fact, Mrs Alving who has given him this sort of a life, yet so powerful is the suggestiveness that many critics are led to think it is. To quote one of many, John Northam writes: 'Mrs Alving observed the dictates of that dead morality so that her son might grow up morally healthy; the result is disease and the impossibility of health of any kind' (p. 103), and 'Mrs Alving has at last [at the moment when Oswald demands that she kill him] been made to know the consequences of her past compromises' (p. 104). But this is unfair to her, and ignores a gap in the chain of events. Mrs Alving, as Northam himself says, 'always fights to control and shape events, never allowing herself to be overwhelmed. She is indeed a strong woman' (p. 107). There are many ways in which she has not compromised, and it is impossible to blame her at all severely for what has happened from the time she married till Oswald's return. She chose to marry for money, which could have been a fault, although even marriages of convenience can turn out to be loving. Having married, she found Alving's debauches intolerable and ran away to Manders, who rejected her. Only then, after trying for an unconventional solution, did she return to Alving, having no other obvious choice, and bore him a child. Her efforts since then have been admirable in many ways: she has brought up Alving's daughter by another woman in her own household (not revealing to her her true parentage, it is true); she has sent Oswald away, rather than have him contaminated by Alving, and succeeded, until the disease made itself known, since Oswald was evidently free-minded and independent till then. To accuse her of lacking motherly love would be over-severe: she has not ceased to care for him, and clearly made a painful decision in full awareness of the facts. She did not nag at Alving, as a conventionally minded woman might have done, but nursed him, letting him have his way as far as she could, though there can have been no possibility of enjoying with him the debauches he indulged in. And though the façade she built for him was false, it stood a reasonable chance of preserving her money for the good purpose she had in mind. None of this was culpable; she was making the best of a bad job, by her own lights. To saddle her with all the consequences, as though she had brought them on her own head, would be unjust. The Orphanage burned down not because she lied about Alving – that was a successful compromise so far as it went – but because of Engstrand's fantastic machinations, a fortuitous sequel to her careful plans. Oswald is suffering now not because she failed to follow her emotional promptings – she tried in vain to follow them in the first year of her marriage – nor because she did her duty in looking after her husband, but because Alving contracted syphilis at some uncertain time, presumably before Oswald's birth, perhaps even before his marriage. The lack of connection between her conduct and the two catastrophes is a serious fault in the construction of the play. At most an indirect connection can be made, by ignoring Mrs Alving's remark that her husband was living a loose life before she married him, and laying responsibility on her for his having gone to prostitutes and for their having infected him. It is in that sense, no doubt, that critics see her as incurring her own penalty. But Ibsen has presented the past so ambiguously, in this respect, allowing it also to appear that Alving was alone responsible for his being infected, that we can only speculate.

For Oswald, on the other hand, the situation is as clear as daylight. His motivation is starkly simplified, and, like Regine's, Engstrand's, and Manders's, purely egocentric. At the beginning of the play, a few hours before the final scene, he appeared (rather like Nora in *A Doll's House*) to be a naive, cheerful young man with scarcely a care in the world, though his heavy drinking was a clue to his inner state. His general run of conversation was idealising – his account of the Norwegian in Paris is either a little starry-eyed or innocent (does he really believe he 'overstrained' himself in Paris?) – and devoid of any perceptive insights. He took everything on trust and saw the world in plain black and white. When it comes to the revelation that he is convinced he is going to die, the picture of him changes almost completely. He now lets no consideration obstruct him. His impetus comes from an initial naive trust: a doctor has told him that the next time he experiences an attack it will be the end of his sane life, and what doctors say is true. On the basis of this trust he has come straight back to Norway, non-stop, to persuade either Regine or his mother to give him an overdose of morphine at the first sign of incipient madness, and the flirtation with the maid at the end of Act One was evidently not what it seemed, but all part of his plan, a means of acquiring Regine's help. That having failed, he turns to his mother with no thought that she might find the rôle he has in mind for her impossibly painful or criminally dangerous and wrong. When she runs to fetch a doctor, he slams the door in her face and locks it, compelling her to face the choice he has determined for her.

These are the cruelties of a naivety resulting in a desperation so gross that it sees no interest but its own. The only way to sympathise with Oswald here is to share his view that the next attack is certain to be so devastating that he can override anyone else's scruples. Yet Mrs Alving's first instinct, to run for a doctor, was not wrong, it was an instinct to preserve, to seek a cure, to hope for the future. The peremptoriness of his tone, and disregard for *her* torment of mind, are far from being an adult response – a plea would have been more moving than this hectoring. Ibsen has arranged a dilemma for Mrs Alving only by giving Oswald the egotism of a small child.

Yet Ibsen is no fairer to Mrs Alving. Once she has given in to Oswald, and promised to give him the morphine if ever it should become necessary, Ibsen turns her into a soothing, almost twittering caricature of motherly love, with a capacity for sentimentalising the situation as great as Manders's:

> MRS ALVING (*bent over him*) What terrible ideas they were to get into your head, Oswald. But all just imagination. You couldn't stand all these upsets. But now you'll be able to have a rest. At home, with your mother beside you, my darling. Anything you want you shall have, just like when you were a little boy. There now. The attack's over. You see how quickly it went. Oh, I knew it would…See what a lovely day we're going to have, Oswald? Brilliant sunshine. Now you'll be able to see your home properly.
>
> (Act 3) (V. 421)

She is such an Aunt Sally, one is loth to criticise her; the strong woman who dealt so boldly with her circumstances before the play began is now reduced to a butt for Ibsen's sarcasm, and the level of interest has sunk to a confrontation between a spoilt son and his doting mother. The criticism has to be directed rather at Ibsen himself, for devising such a scene, which allows a vindictive pleasure in seeing Mrs Alving put on the spot.

The final curtain can only bring a sense of contrivance, after this. There is, of course, a dilemma, the whole dilemma of euthanasia, and Ibsen's *succès de scandale* was caused by his having dared to suggest that the traditional condemnation of euthanasia might be questioned. After *A Doll's House, Ghosts* was a second blow at convention, if only in its presentation of a shocking ending. Ibsen had that capacity for questioning received ideas which suited the rapidly changing society of his day at the same time that he flouted it. But it was a capacity for persistent childlike questioning, for saying 'why?' to everything, not for reasoned exposition. People were stirred to talk about euthanasia as they were to talk about women's share in marriage, simply through Ibsen's boldness. There was no matter in the play for deep consideration in human terms, when the characters remained so petty in their thoughts and responses to one another.

Again, in so far as the play is a *pièce à thèse*, it carries too little weight, too little social reality to do more than create a stir. Mrs Alving observes that we are all ghosts: 'It's not just what we inherit from our mothers and fathers that walks again in us. It's all kinds of old defunct theories, all sorts of old defunct beliefs, and things like that. They are not *alive* in us; they are simply lodged there, and we cannot get rid of them.' The question to be asked of *Ghosts* is what these defunct beliefs and theories are. It does not show us that the condemnation of incest is defunct, or even that it is unreasonable: it merely suggests it may, conceivably, be an unnecessary taboo. Nor does it show us that performing an unpleasant duty – in this case nursing a husband whom one dislikes or detests – is either a defunct or an undesirable notion, or that in general the traditional values of a society are unnecessary in themselves. To say this about *Ghosts* is not to defend all traditions of all societies, it is merely to say that the play is too unrelated even to the Norwegian society of its day to do more than place a question mark against marriage, duty, and other socially binding conceptions. Of course these conceptions inhibit the absolute freedom of the individual. The serious issues begin with an attempt at defining the rights of the one against the other. But when Pastor Manders is the only representation of society that is afforded, the question-mark can be little more than a printer's sign; it has no clear function in any political or social debate.

The scene at the end is not simply about Mrs Alving's dilemma, and Ibsen was not writing a problem-play, as he always insisted. As Oswald's disease attacks for the second time, he calls out for the sun, and though this is the first sign of his insanity, it also seems to have a meaning, however difficult it may be to say what the meaning is. In a sense, the sun is what Mrs Alving has always tried to give him: the freedom to be himself, to live joyfully. In a sense, it is what Ibsen had sought himself, and what Julian the Apostate expected when he resolved to go 'up into the daylight'. Oswald's words are also reminiscent of Julian's at the moment of his death, when he cries, 'Oh sun, sun, why didst thou deceive me?' Oswald and his mother have been deceived by the sun, or deceived in their search for it, one can hardly say which. Yet at the moment when Oswald speaks his words, the stage directions require that the glacier and mountain peaks, seen through the conservatory window, should gleam in the morning light. Oswald does not see them, as they are behind his back, so that it seems as though he were deliberately turning away from the very thing he wants. There is, it is true, no deliberateness about it. The sun certainly seems symbolic here, but Oswald's response is not willed, and the meaning of the symbol remains doubtful. Northam suggests that at last the truth shines forth: 'for all the pain and disaster, the existence, the beauty and majesty, and the irrepressibility of truth have been affirmed' (p. 106). Perhaps that is so, if it is merely the presence of the sun that affirms it – but the events of the play have done nothing to show the beauty or majesty of truth, or even that it is irrepressible. (Engstrand, for one, has got clean away with his lies.)

Perhaps also there is a comparison to be made with the ending of *Brand*, where at the moment of catastrophe a voice is heard proclaiming 'He is the God of Love'. The simultaneity of disaster and salvation may have been in Ibsen's mind, as a pure paradox, just as 'joy of life' can find expression either as the pure, unsullied Arcadia of the Norwegians in Paris or as the cruel, self-regarding will of Regine. The contrast of 'polar' opposites is a familiar feature of all Ibsen's plays, and his attachment to a dialectical philosophy may account for the crude divisions between innocence and vice, knowingness and innocence, which are so characteristic of them. At all events, the sunrise at the end of *Ghosts* leaves the way open for a further turn of the eternally recurring wheel. The climax is a double moment of triumph and defeat.

Yet despite the strong reservations that have to be made, this play remains a work of art, by contrast with the purely social and medical purposes of a work like Brieux' *Les Avariés*. Brieux is infinitely better informed about the symptoms of venereal disease than Ibsen, and the purpose of his play is immediately obvious: he shows in the clearest terms how an infected husband who ignores medical advice can involve both his wife and their child in his own disease. *Les Avariés* (*Damaged Goods*), first produced in 1905, met with the same kind of opposition as *Ghosts*, and needed to be strenuously championed by Shaw and others to gain a showing at all. But though it may have had more effect on medical opinion and sexual hygiene, its dramatic movement is negligible in comparison with Ibsen's; it lacks the thrill of Ibsen's carefully devised theatrical moments, and the brisk exchanges of his dialogue. The point is not simply that Ibsen attempts a more far-reaching implication than anything Brieux envisages – so far as that is concerned, Ibsen attempts more than he can manage – but that the play is a genuine piece of creative self-expression. He really cares about the deadening hand of the past – he cared about it all his life – and he is attempting to state a tragic frustration of his own. But the play is confused, and the self it expresses is too little aware of the realities of other selves to be able to create a great dramatic work; it is in places naive, or excessively black-and-white in its characterisation, and succeeds partly because its naivety is masked by the conditions of theatrical performance. But it has pace, climaxes, dramatic thrust and counter-thrust, surprise, revelations, reversals and repeated excitements, and these, coupled with the genuine personal concern, are the features that still gain its audiences when the pedestrian good purpose of Brieux has long ceased to appeal at the box-office. The talent of Ibsen as a dramatist is curiously distinct from his ability to be enlightening about human nature or the large topics with which he attempted to deal.

5
An Enemy of the People

The hostile reception of *Ghosts* was not necessarily a sign of its having hit the mark. For many years, it is true, none of the bigger Scandinavian theatres would touch it. In Germany the police refused to allow public performances. In England, when at last it was performed in 1891, the Press reacted with violent abuse. Ibsen had good cause to feel that his diagnosis was correct, and so had his supporters. Yet the fact was that he had simply had the audacity to imply that a dutiful married woman might drive her husband to drink, that a husband who went to prostitutes might transmit disease to his son (though Ibsen was far from giving accurate information about this), and – more controversially – that the incurably diseased might have to be put to death. The almost fanatical efforts at suppressing the play, or condemning it for even dealing with syphilis, showed that the smothering of truth, which Ibsen had exposed, was all too prevalent. Yet this success was not achieved by the subtle analysis of society, but by simply telling people they were rotten within, and that tells us nothing about the play as a play. Preachers had been telling people as much for centuries, without being abused for it. The reaction of theatre-goers may have come partly from the fact that they had come to expect only entertainment from the theatre, partly from the all-embracing yet not specifically grounded accusations which Ibsen levelled at them, in which case it was a hysterical reaction. So far as dramatic criticism is concerned, Ibsen had again created a play with a good deal of crude characterisation and motivation, although with effective theatrical moments, and again, through the flat contradiction to established values which he represented, sent the pigeons flying. He had succeeded in 'bringing about the condition of the world' once again, by virtue of being so closely involved with its own crudities of response.

Something of his feelings at the time can be gauged from the tenor of his next play, *An Enemy of the People*, which appeared after only one year, in 1882, and bears many marks of an impatient reaction. Though begun before *Ghosts*, it was now splendidly appropriate to the new situation: the *Zeitgeist* was going Ibsen's way again. But by comparison with the plays which were to follow, this was a 'Sturm und Drang' work. No other of the later plays has so much pace, so much violence of speech and action, or so much outright conflict.

It is easy, by over-simplification, to see in the plot a straight-forward allegory of the reception of *Ghosts*. It is also clear, though neither of these interpretations exhausts the new play, that *An Enemy of the People* reverses the situation of *Ghosts*. There, the attempt at concealing truth seemed to lead to unmitigated disaster. Now, the attempt at revealing truth leads to disaster, of a kind, but to a triumphant reaffirmation. Like Nora in the previous play but one, the persistent seeker after truth is left at the end alone, but secure in his self-esteem.

For speed of development, the play has no rival in Ibsen's work. In Act One, Dr Stockmann, the medical officer at a Norwegian spa, receives confirmation that the water supplied to visitors at the pump-room is badly infected. In Act Two he enlists the help of the Liberal editor Hovstad, and the proprietor of his newspaper, Aslaksen. In the next Act the full implications of the medical findings for the prosperity of the town are realised by the Mayor, as well as by the 'compact majority', and Stockmann begins to see his prospects of effecting an improvement disappear. The fourth Act, far from supplying the *ritardando* which it often does in a five-act play, shows Stockmann addressing a public meeting, which turns into a riot against him. Finally, not only the Mayor and the businessmen, but the Liberals, including both Hovstad and Aslak-sen, and most of the town, in short the 'compact majority', turn against Stockmann. He loses his money and all but one of his supporters, apart from his wife and children, but finishes up determined to continue the fight.

From the brief résumé, it sounds like a play in defence of a real liberty, a denunciation of so-called Liberals who are in fact only concerned with their personal profits. It is not, and in some places it sounds like the reverse of such a play. The ambivalence found in the other plays is found here too.

For two Acts, only the radical reformer in Stockmann is in evidence, though presented with a jollity that might have been meant to demonstrate a point about the supposedly pessimistic author of *Ghosts*. The atmosphere is unusually hearty as Stockmann's wife hands round plates of roast beef, and Stockmann keeps open house in a genial way, also seldom found in an Ibsen play. This hospitality also serves the purpose of neatly bringing Hovstad and Aslaksen into Stockmann's house as guests, and, since the Mayor, who is of the conservative faction, is Stockmann's elder brother, there is nothing complicated about bringing him in either. A little suspense enters in Act One, as Stockmann drops a hint that the analyst's report on the spa-water is expected and, by the end of the Act, the news of the poisoned source has broken, just before the curtain comes down. In Act Two Ibsen introduces briefly Stockmann's father-in-law, Morten Kiil, who is to play a large part in the catastrophe at the end, then goes on to a demonstration of how the opposition to Stockmann develops.

At first sight, the opposition seems at least a little unlikely. Even though the replacing of the pipes is expected to last two years, a man working solely on business principles would see that if there is a risk of a serious outbreak of typhoid fever – only a few cases having been reported so far – the reputation of the spa might disappear for a generation. It would be worth losing money for two years to avoid the worse consequence. (It is true, however, that Ibsen was basing his play on an actual event of a similar kind, businessmen being as irrational as anyone else.) The Mayor's rooted objection to believing Stockmann's report is, therefore, difficult though not impossible to credit so long as only business seems to be at stake.

Ibsen wins the sceptic over when he lets Stockmann accuse the Mayor of having originally insisted, against opposition, that the spa-water be tapped at a place where it was likely to be infiltrated with foul water from a nearby tannery. That vanity can override business interests is clear enough, and, when this vanity swells by the end of the Act, to the point where the Mayor is ordering Stockmann to keep his information secret, all pretence of adequate measures to be undertaken without too much public clamour is demonstrably hypocritical. The Mayor, for reasons of his own, intends to do nothing at all about the report, and Stockmann has good reason to be preparing to make a stand.

By Act Three, however, Stockmann is doing more than making a stand. When he comes into Hovstad's office with instructions to the editor to print his report for publication in the paper, he announces that he has four or five similar articles in mind, not about the same thing, but 'all connected with the question of the water-supply and the sewers'. It soon appears that he has more than four or five, and that they have nothing directly to do with the sewers. He is, in fact, in a barely controllable rage, as Ibsen is careful to indicate when Stockmann speaks of 'slamming down' his report in front of the public, only to change the phrase, after he has heard somebody echo it, to 'submit it to the scrutiny of every intelligent citizen'. But such assumed humility lasts for only an instant. Stockmann sees himself as the descendant of an old Pomeranian pirate bombarding the people from off-shore with one explosive article after another and, as he soon goes on to say, 'it's no longer just the water-supply and the sewers now. No, the whole community needs cleaning up, disinfecting.'

In the following speech, Stockmann goes further: 'All these dodderers have got to be got rid of! Wherever they are! My eyes have been opened to a lot of things today.' A moment later he is talking of revolution and, though he does not yet develop the point, by the time he leaves Hovstad's office he has said enough to show that he is looking forward to all-out war.

The reasons for this are obscure, though partly due to Stockmann's aggressive personality. Ibsen has been at pains to show, in Act One, that Stockmann has only recently come to the town after a long stay in the North and that he is full of enthusiasm for what he now sees. Though he does say that he looks forward to young people 'stirring things up a bit' in the years to come, there is no indication of what he thinks needs to be stirred up, and what he says to his brother – which may be played as a quick covering-up of the slip about the young people – is that he now feels immensely happy, 'surrounded by all this vigorous, growing life':

What a glorious age this is to live in! It's as if a whole new world were springing up all around

and

...there's life here...and promise...and innumerable things to work and strive for.   (Act 1) (VI. 28)

If Stockmann were a shrewd plotter, the covering-up might be made more convincing. But he is not. On the contrary, he is a man of completely straightforward emotions and ideas. All the more unfortunately for the play, his outburst in Act Three is enough to alienate from him the sympathy that a more realistic liberal might attract, and this is damaging to the balance of the contending forces. Stockmann's overjoyed response to the town in Act One looks euphoric. His total disillusionment in Act Three might be dyspeptic.

He has learned nothing more about the town in the meanwhile. All that has happened is that his brother, largely from injured vanity, has refused to take his report seriously and has threatened him with dismissal. Hovstad and Aslaksen are still on his side. No one else as yet knows anything about the adverse report on the pump-room water, except the analyst. Stockmann has suffered – as yet – only a personal snub and a threat from an elder brother. Yet he launches into an attack that takes in the whole of the town, and goes on to include not only the whole of Norwegian society but the whole civilised world: by Act Five, Stockmann is longing for a piece of primeval forest or a South Sea Island to be alone in. Where, one might wonder, did he gain the experience on which to base his several other papers, or his attacks on the world at large? He has been living in remote parts: his attacks could well be derived from fantasies. The rapid swing from one extreme to the other is, on the other hand, rather like Mrs Alving's, in a different situation, and equally baseless.

An essential point here concerns the timing. When Stockmann leaves Hovstad's office after his first visit in Act Three, he has only his brother's egotism to resent, and if he were capable of tact he could keep Hovstad and Aslaksen on his side. As things are, his outburst has already begun to incline Aslaksen to turn back to sympathy with the authorities, who have never been far from his thoughts.

It is true that Ibsen now includes a scene in which Hovstad's hypocritical attitude is shown up by Stockmann's daughter, Petra. But this does not show Stockmann to have any better grounds for his outburst. Hovstad temporises because he has to sell his newspaper: Petra cannot see this, and denounces him rather smugly. But Hovstad is clearly shown to be a man of conscience:

HOVSTAD You shouldn't say that too boldly, Miss Petra. Least of all now.
PETRA Why isn't it just as good now?
HOVSTAD Because your father can't do without my help.
PETRA (*looking down at him*) So you're one of those too, are you? Puh!
HOVSTAD No, no, I'm not. It came over me so unexpectedly. You mustn't believe that.
PETRA I know what to believe. Goodbye!

(Act 3) (VI. 74)

The degree to which Hovstad is affected for the worse by the necessity to compromise, and the degree to which he still remains able to maintain a freely critical stance, are both shown in that nicely balanced passage.

The point remains that Stockmann's exaggerated outburst has already alienated Aslaksen, and has at least annoyed Hovstad. The issue thus begins to arise, for the play as a play, whether the level of argument is going to be interesting enough to keep the spectator's attention to the end. A dramatic confrontation is in the offing, but any clash is dramatic to some degree, so far as that goes. Will this one be worth more than the kind of notice that one might give to a crank orator at Hyde Park Corner?

The first doubt occurs when Hovstad, as soon as he realises that the Mayor is opposing him, begins to crumble. Aslaksen, Hovstad's proprietor, has not yet decided against publishing Stockmann's report – he may be wavering, but he has not yet come down either way. Hovstad, however, begins to toady to the Mayor as soon as he is asked whether he is expecting to print the report, and this is too servile a capitulation to supply a continuing interest: the opposition to Stockmann is being too obviously put in the wrong. Nothing has happened yet to change Hovstad's situation, and his volte-face is craven. The Mayor then insists to Hovstad and Aslaksen that Stockmann has been impetuous, which they are too ready to believe, although Stockmann's behaviour in the office may have conduced to their believing it.

The two are still wavering when Stockmann returns, full of bonhomie ('Back again!' are his first words), to see how the printing of his report is getting on, and shortly begins to talk in paranoid terms. He is surely meant by Ibsen to be seen as a naïve egotist, when he speaks of a mass movement, with only a half-hearted and momentary attempt at disclaiming any interest in leading it:

My fellow citizens, you know – good heavens, these good people, they're really so fond of me...Yes, and that's just why I'm afraid...What I mean is... a thing like this comes along, and they – especially the underprivileged classes – take it as a rousing call to take the affairs of the town into their own hands in future.   (Act 3) (VI. 80)

The egotism is put in its place, to some extent, when Stockmann, sensing that he has said too much, pretends – it can be played or understood as a pretence – to have meant he wanted no public parade or banquet as his reward. It would take an un-self-centred man to see Hovstad's reaction so quickly, and to deflect the remark into something more harmless. But the correction of the balance is only temporary, and naivety again reasserts itself before long.

Stockmann now announces grander visions: 'Oh, I see the whole liberal middle-class (*borgerstand*) flocking to join a victorious army.' In high spirits, he puts on the Mayor's official hat and pretends to be 'head of the whole town', replying to the Mayor's indignant objection:

Pooh! when a people rises from its slumber like a lion, do you think anybody's going to be scared by official hats? Because we are having a revolution in town tomorrow, let me tell you.   (Act 3) (VI.83)

An actor may go on presenting this as a bit of a lark, if a ponderous one, even when, still wearing the hat, Stockmann dismisses his brother from office and assumes it himself. His self-conscious but strong egotism may be expending itself by such tomfoolery, just as Ibsen expends his own bitter feelings about the reception of *Ghosts* by projecting them into this semi-ridiculous figure. There is a certain raillery about it all, aimed partly at Ibsen's own reactions to the mud slung at him. But the play is now on a knife-edge. Hovstad and Aslaksen have just heard Stockmann speak, in terms they never suspected him of using, of a full-scale people's revolution, the likelihood of which is extremely remote. Though he has not mentioned any specific grievance apart from the sewage, he seems in earnest. The boisterous game with the hat must be a self-deflating joke, and the reference to a 'revolution *tomorrow*' sounds like a deliberate toning down, rather than a serious political prophecy. Yet there is a touch of egomania about it: one suspects something like Skule's 'kingly thought' in *The Pretenders* to be in the background. Why, otherwise, should thoughts of massed ranks and a people rising from its slumber enter his head at all, when it is only a matter of an item on the Council agenda which could prove troublesome, and why should he use such rhetorical language? Hovstad and Aslaksen are not in the wrong, in retreating instinctively from him.

This is interpreting the play in the expectation that it will be an interesting study in the relationships between the compromisers and the complete radical. Ibsen clearly sees the danger of presenting Stockmann without a suggestion that he is at least half in jest, yet the play is constantly running the risk of spilling over into solemn earnest. As it goes on, doubt increases because of the way in which Ibsen seems more intent on carrying a flag for Stockmann himself than with drama. The question of the artist's degree of control over his projected *alter ego* is close under the surface.

Stockmann's outburst in Act Three was based on ignorance, and completely reversed his euphoric vision of the society in the town in Act One, based on equal ignorance. He ended the argument between himself and the Mayor, Hovstad, and Aslaksen with an even more sweeping generalisation: finding that he would get no support from them, he declared that everybody was against him 'because all the men in this town are nothing but a lot of old women – like you [his wife]'. This in its turn completely reversed his expectation, if it really was one, that there could be the very large degree of dissatisfaction that would be needed to provide support for a revolution in the town. In Act Four, however, his last diagnosis seems to be proved correct. There is next to nobody – only his family and Captain Horster, in fact – who will stand by him.

The public meeting, summoned at Captain Horster's house since all public halls are denied to Stockmann, is addressed first by

Aslaksen and Hovstad, who rightly point out that Stockmann is not now so much concerned about the Baths as about revolution. Their withdrawal of support is understandable, though in Aslaksen it looks more convenient than principled. Stockmann goes on, not improving the situation, to insult his audience:

> I have said I am going to speak about the tremendous discovery I have made in these last few days...the discovery that all the spiritual sources of our life are poisoned, and that our whole civic community is built on a foundation teeming with pestilential lies.   (Act 4) (VI. 93)

'These last few days' is worth noting. The euphoria of Act One was not play-acting, and it is in fact only since then that Stockmann has changed his mind. But he has in reality discovered so recently nothing more shattering than that three men are unwilling to support him, and certainly he has not learned enough to justify him in what he goes on to say:

> If there's anything I can't stand at any price – it's leading men. I've just about had enough of that kind of people in my time. They are just like a lot of goats in a young plantation – there's mischief everywhere they go. They'll get in the way of any free man at every move he makes. If I had my way I'd like to see them exterminated like any other pest.   (Act 4) (VI. 95)

This language of exasperation is not a momentary outburst, it is part of a coherent philosophy, partly anti-democratic, as Ibsen's own philosophy generally was, partly aristocratic, partly violent and massively intolerant. Stockmann is not the man to mean seriously his talk of exterminating the opposition, yet this leap from critical objection to total and ruthless contempt makes Stockmann one of Ibsen's more childish egoists – no ordinary distinction – and reduces the political interest considerably.

It is not only the leaders whom he attacks:

> The worst enemy of truth and freedom in our society is the compact majority. Yes, the damned compact, liberal majority.   (Act 4) (VI. 96)

This soon extends to what, as Hovstad rightly points out, amounts to a declaration that the whole community must be destroyed. 'Who cares if it's destroyed? I say it should simply be razed to the ground. And all the people living by these lies should be wiped out, like vermin', is Stockmann's answer to that, and he goes on to say he would not mind if the population of the whole country were wiped out, if it ever came to be similarly infected. He regards the majority as mongrels and asks how they could be trusted to rule at all.

People inquire if Stockmann is drunk; someone wonders if there is insanity in his family, others oddly suppose he wants a rise in salary. So Ibsen plants the suggestion of a different view of Stockmann than the one taken by the Doctor himself; yet his sympathy with him remained strong, as we know from his own words. The result is chaos and uproar, – the people become a mob, half-mad themselves – while Stockmann seems unaware that he has said anything outrageous and declares he has simply done his duty. His reversion to the calm of a just man resting in the conscience of a good job done is another volte-face after this burst of bad temper.

Ibsen's concern with symbols needs to be kept in mind here. Stockmann's reactions to the sewage report are incredibly far-reaching and cannot arise reasonably from the negative response of the three men who have actually seen it. It is rather because the sewage symbolised corruption in Ibsen's mind – not Stockmann's, since he knew nothing of corruption until a few days before his outburst – that he let the play develop as it does. Ibsen's knowledge of the world, particularly of the way in which *Ghosts*, his own 'report', had been received, entitled him to say things about its corruption which needed greater foundations in the play itself than he troubled to provide, if Stockmann was to appear more than an opinionated ranter. He did in fact share some of Stockmann's views. He told Georg Brandes that he would join a revolution that promoted the abolition of the State (though Stockmann is not so precise about what his revolution will lead to). He opposed the dramatist Bjørnson for saying that the majority was always right and retorted, as Stockmann does, that it is on the contrary the minority which is always right: which minority, he did not say. Ibsen even confessed, in a genial mood, that he and Stockmann got on excellently with one another:

We agree about so many things, but the Doctor is more muddle-headed than I am, and apart from this he has a considerable number of other traits that make people more willing to hear certain things from him which, if I myself had said them, they would not perhaps have taken quite so well.

What Ibsen privately thought is only relevant to the play if there is any doubt about its interpretation, and even then is not authoritative. Only the play can ultimately answer for itself. Still, it is clear from these remarks that Ibsen did suppose there was some value in Stockmann's vague ideas, and that his audience would not be put off, as the stage audience is, by Stockmann's wild exaggerating, his lack of self-awareness, his paranoid tendencies, and his fondness for exterminating as well as leading vast numbers of people. 'In ten years,' Ibsen wrote in another letter, 'the majority might possibly have reached the point where Dr Stockmann stood at the meeting. But during these ten years the Doctor has not been standing still; he continues to be at least ten years further on than the majority...As far as I personally am concerned, I am always conscious of continually advancing.' From this, it must appear that, despite his muddle-headedness, Stockmann really has Ibsen's admiration, that Ibsen really supposed him to be saying something valuable, ahead of his time, and that occasionally Ibsen could come close to identifying himself with him.*

Stockmann is seen in the last Act back at home on the morning after the riot, with all his windows smashed in, and of course indignant at such treatment from the mob, which confirms his

---

* Ibsen turns to dramatic account what his contemporaries outside the theatre were able to formulate in a more balanced way. J. S. Mill places the matter in perspective, when he writes: 'Like other tyrannies, the tyranny of the majority was at first, and is still regularly, held in dread, chiefly as operating through the acts of public authorities. But reflecting persons perceived that when society is itself the tyrant (Stockmann's objection)...its means of tyrannizing are not restricted to the acts which it may do by the hands of its political functionaries ...Protection against the tyranny of the magistrate is not enough: there needs to be protection also against the tyranny of the prevailing opinion and feeling... There is a limit to the legitimate interferences of collective opinion with individual independence; and to find that limit and maintain it against encroachment is as indispensable to a good condition of human affairs, as protection against political despotism.' Abraham Lincoln, another contemporary, was equally clear: 'A majority held in restraint by constitutional checks and limitations, and always changing easily with deliberate changes of popular opinions and sentiments, is the only true sovereign of a free people. Whoever rejects it does, of necessity, fly to anarchy or despotism.' Ibsen, on the other hand, expressed a preference for the despotism of Tsarist Russia, on the grounds that it intensified the desire for freedom. It was not only in the theatre that his political ideas sounded naive.

opinion of them all, and leads him to say that things would be exactly the same 'out West', that is, in America, where he has never been. He still cannot conceive that there could be any allies in his struggle, and the next events all bear him out in this. Ibsen, who as author directs these events, now shows how Stockmann's daughter is dismissed from her job, how Captain Horster loses the command of his ship, and how the Ratepayers' Association urges all respectable citizens to sign a list declaring they will boycott Stockmann's medical practice. Sympathy for Stockmann among the audience is actively enlisted by these means.

The fundamental innocence of the doctor is then suggested by the device of having the Mayor express the obviously unfounded suspicion that Stockmann has made this fuss about the sewage only because he hoped to ingratiate himself with his eccentric father-in-law by vilifying the leading members of the community, and thereby gaining a personal share in the bequests of the old man's will.

It appears that, though Stockmann knew nothing of it, the father-in-law, Morten Kiil, is a wealthy man. (Stockmann must have known at least that he owned one of the tanneries whose effluent caused the pollution.) Stockmann also denies having known that a large part of Kiil's fortune was to be left to his children, while he and his wife were to have the interest on the capital during Stockmann's lifetime. This strange ignorance on both counts does, it is true, enable Stockmann to play the injured innocent to perfection when the Mayor makes his fantastic suggestion, that the attack on himself and the others could have been 'part of a bargain', by means of which Kiil was induced to make over such large sums to the Stockmann family. Ibsen's exaggerated self-identification with Stockmann seems the more probable here, as he digs into his imagination for means of arousing even stronger sympathy for his *alter ego*.

At this point, in fact, his invention breaks down. A moment later, Kiil himself enters to give yet one more diabolical twist to the lion's tail. He has in his wallet a large number of shares in the Baths, which he has bought up while they are extremely cheap, using for the purpose the money he had intended for the Stockmanns. The Baths thus in effect belong to Stockmann himself (the shares belong to Kiil, while he still lives), and if Stockmann goes on saying that the water is polluted he will ruin himself and his children financially. Will he, Kiil demands, now withdraw his accusations? Stockmann is neatly placed on the horns of a dilemma at a climactic point in the play.

How Kiil has come by the shares so cheaply is a mystery. The whole point of the rejection of Stockmann is that nobody is willing to believe in the pollution for fear of losing money. It now appears as though the shareholders already believe the report and are ridding themselves of their useless holdings as cheaply as possible, without waiting to see what remedy could be applied. Ibsen, for the advantage of his plot, is having it both ways, and shortly turns the new revelation to still more account. Hovstad and Aslaksen have heard the rumour that Kiil and Stockmann are buying up the shares cheaply, and have put two and two together even more preposterously than the Mayor did. They seem to know nothing about Kiil's will, but are convinced, and insinuate the point with the slyness of regular villains, that Stockmann is a party to the purchase because he wanted to get control of the Baths himself. When Stockmann pretends, ironically, to agree, and suggests he intends to make merely a brief, inexpensive show of putting things right, without costing the town a penny, Hovstad is heartily with him, and promises the support of the newspaper, as Aslaksen promises that of the Ratepayers' Association.

This is an eye-opener. In the earlier scenes Hovstad was represented as a genuine Liberal, who gave in perhaps too readily under pressure, but all the same a man really concerned to see the pollution made public. Now he takes the most cynical view of Stockmann's motives, an extremely improbable one to anyone who has seen the naivety of Stockmann in action, and for no better reason than that the newspaper is 'a bit shaky at the moment; it just can't quite make ends meet.' In other words, Hovstad is replying to Stockmann's pointed question, 'What do *you* get out of all this?', that he would be glad of some money from Stockmann in exchange for his help with spreading any better news about the Baths that seems expedient.

The argument has thus developed to a confrontation between an innocent, righteous, truth-loving champion and a despicable, insinuating, bribe-taking hypocrite. The full chord of Victorian melodrama has been struck, and there remains only the determination of the hero to go on undaunted against overwhelming odds. It might almost be a preposterous joke at Stockmann's expense. Perhaps from time to time, in Ibsen's thoughts, it was.

The overwhelming odds come next. Stockmann's sons return early from school – the final blow – because the other boys harassed them and the master has sent them home. Stockmann himself is nearly penniless, having been dismissed from his job, and having refused to accept Kiil's shares in the Baths, but he decides to make independent and decent-minded men at least of his own children. He proposes now to run a school in Horster's house in which he can teach them along with a few others: 'at least a dozen boys to start with.' Who will patronise the school, who will pay fees, is not discussed. He will fetch in 'some of the street-corner lads...the real guttersnipes', or rather he blithely tells his son to 'get hold of one or two for me': the authoritarian voice is in that, as the would-be aristocrat is in this: 'Just for once, I'm going to try an experiment on these mongrels. You never know what you might find amongst them.' Stockmann has had a low regard for humanity so far, and 'mongrels' is more or less his name for the town in general, though he has on the whole had a better opinion of youth. The attitude he now takes is not promising, but the words, said with a smile (if Stockmann were capable of saying, by means of that smile, that he was never too serious about the depravity he found), could sound bold and cheerful.

Still, the prospects are dim: no job, no money, and as yet no school and no pupils. These are the circumstances in which Stockmann chooses to make his final dramatic stand, and declare himself 'one of the strongest men in the whole world, *now*':

MORTEN (*his son*). Honestly?
DR STOCKMANN (*dropping his voice*) Sh! You mustn't say anything about it yet. But I've made a great discovery.
MRS STOCKMANN What, again?
DR STOCKMANN Yes I have. (*he gathers them about him and says confidentially*) The thing is, you see, that the strongest man in the world is the man who stands most alone.
MRS STOCKMANN (*smiles and shakes her head*) Oh, Thomas, Thomas...!
PETRA (*bravely grasping his hands*) Father!   (Act 5) (VI. 126)

There is a note of irony in these final words – Mrs Stockmann is unconvinced, though condoling – but Petra, the daughter, ends with the right tone of heroic admiration, the 'My Master Builder!' touch. There may be a certain paradoxical truth, too, in what Stockmann says, though not a new one, for it was said by Schiller a hundred years earlier. The trouble is, it clearly does not apply to him. With his amiable ignorance and naive arrogance he may be strong in that he is unassailable, but he is not strong in the sense that he can expect to gain anything. He has made himself an enemy of the people, but the consequences Ibsen hoped for from the play are improbable: no public is likely to reach Stockmann's position within ten years or a hundred. Only a play on a different level, the level at which it seemed for a time, up to Act Three, that this one could become, could achieve that result, and that was a play Ibsen never wrote. As Edmund Gosse, one of his foremost champions, observed as early as 1889, he had taken his revenge (on the critics of *Ghosts*) in an 'interesting novelette in dialogue form' (p. 109). The allegory was, Gosse concluded, rather transparent, and 'the play is really a piece of rather violent personal polemic'. It cannot be valued on any other grounds. The really surprising thing about it is that Ibsen was capable, as an artist, of reproducing so starily, and on the whole naively, the tantrums which he sometimes displayed as a man. If, on the other hand, Stockmann is taken as representing rather Ibsen's view of Bjørnson, the naivety still remains in the construction of the play, in the way that it turns into melodrama and heroics (or somewhat sour farce, if the play is produced that way) what might have been both tragic and real.

6

The Wild Duck

The pairing of Ibsen's plays is nowhere easier to see than in *An Enemy of the People* and *The Wild Duck*, the one about a man who seems to have a degree of justification in his demand that the truth be told, the other about the fatal consequences of a similar demand. The man who seems to sum up the main trend of *The Wild Duck* is the cynical Dr Relling, with his doctrine that no man can live without illusions, without a 'life-lie' to sustain him. The two plays are curiously like two of Goethe's, in this pairing. Goethe's *Egmont*, like his *Iphigenia in Tauris* of a few years later, is about having the confidence to reveal the whole truth, even to those who may use it against one. Egmont is executed for his presumptuous trustfulness, Iphigenia succeeds in converting her captor to tolerance. (A similar dialectical pair, though on a different theme, is Brecht's *He Who Said Yes* and *He Who Said No*.) Like Goethe, Ibsen divides his dramatic analysis of truth-telling into two separate plays with contrary conclusions. Also like Goethe, however, he simplifies each part so much as to inspire some scepticism, so far as any general 'message' may be intended. It may be that he had in mind, as Goethe possibly also had, a dialectical demonstration, an affirmation of both a positive and a negative – though, like all dialectical pairs, neither side would totally exclude the other. If that is so, *The Wild Duck* turns out to be little more convincing than *An Enemy of the People*. Yet there is a matter of real human concern at stake: the play could have depth in treating the tragic and comic consequences of conceit and attempts at devotion. The chief hindrance is the symbolism. But technical awkwardness occurs too.

An initial weakness shows as early as the exposition. Ibsen starts traditionally enough with the device of a conversation between two servants, one permanent, the other hired only for the evening, and therefore needing to be told who everyone is. Tennant calls this clumsy (p. 90), but it is acceptable, however well-worn, as a swift means of sketching in the background. It is in the scene between Gregers Werle and Hjalmar Ekdal, later in Act One, that more serious difficulties become noticeable.

There is a complex situation to be divulged: first, that fourteen years ago Werle senior has had a child, Hedvig, by his former housekeeper, Gina, and has arranged for the mother to marry Hjalmar, whom he has set up in business as a professional photographer. Then it needs to be explained that old Werle has also – perhaps for confidential reasons of his own connected with a business deal – looked after Hjalmar's aging father, that Hjalmar has no suspicion of the reason for this, or for his own specially favoured treatment. It also has to be brought out that the son, Gregers, is beginning to believe that his father is motivated by a certain self-interest.

These events may pass well enough as credible at a performance, when there is no time to consider them. As on other occasions, Ibsen gains by not presenting them as staged action. Reflection shows that the story depends on some considerable degree of naivety in Hjalmar, and a willingness in old Werle to gamble on very long odds. We are asked to believe that after Werle discovered Gina's pregnancy he first dismissed her from her job as his housekeeper, then arranged matters so that Hjalmar took up lodgings in her mother's house, and finally waited until Hjalmar not only fell in love with Gina but married her before her pregnancy became obvious to him – and then failed to notice that she gave birth rather soon after their marriage. Given that Hjalmar is extraordinarily naive, or very willing to be deceived, this is not impossible. But with only four or five months for all this to happen – Hjalmar could hardly have failed to notice if Gina had given birth within three or four months of marriage – the time-scheme is rather tight.

A greater awkwardness arises from the needs of the exposition. Gregers, who describes Hjalmar as his 'best and only friend', must be brought into conversation with him in such a way that Hjalmar reveals all the facts about his engagement and marriage, and, while suspecting nothing himself, causes Gregers to see the hidden hand

of his self-interested father in all the ostensibly generous bene-
factions intended to hush up the past. This is dramatically useful:
the audience hears just what Gregers hears, and puts two and two
together just as he does: its interest is actively engaged. The question arises, though, how Gregers can be so completely uninformed
about the affairs of so close a friend. He has been away, it appears,
for sixteen or seventeen years, working 'up at Høidal', 'slaving
away like any ordinary clerk', and in the whole of that time he
has never been back to town or heard any news except what his
father chose to tell him in postscripts to business letters. He did
learn that Hjalmar Ekdal's father had been in prison on account of a
dishonest business deal, which almost involved Werle senior also
(hence the elder man's only apparently charitable care for old
Ekdal), but this did not induce him to write to Hjalmar, despite
his own father's involvement. And Hjalmar did not write to
Gregers because Werle senior told him that Gregers was offended
with him, old Ekdal having nearly brought his own father into
disgrace:

GREGERS And you think I was against you on that account? Whoever gave you
that idea?
HJALMAR I know you were, Gregers. It was your father himself who told me.
GREGERS (*amazed*) My father! Indeed. Hm! Was that the reason you never let
me hear from you...not a single word?
HJALMAR Yes.
GREGERS Not even at the time when you went and became a photographer?
HJALMAR Your father said there was no point in writing to you about any-
thing.   (Act 1) (VI. 135)

Ibsen has covered every conceivable objection that a critic of the
Scribe school could make. As an exposition this cannot be faulted:
there is an explanation for everything. But the demands of the
exposition have required the characters to seem naive or unintelli-
gent to a degree that makes them in themselves less interesting.
The exposition has taken precedence over the character-drawing.

It is, again, not impossible for such a man as Gregers to leave
his parents' home – even when his mother, to whom Gregers was
devoted, was still alive – and to seclude himself in some remote
part of the country for years on end, never inquiring about his
best friend, learning nothing of events from his mother, not

returning for her funeral, not getting in touch with his best friend when the friend's father is jailed (a fact which Gregers knew), and maintaining himself on a pittance. But such a hermit seems eccentric to a degree that can damage the play. One wants to know why he acts so queerly, and Ibsen gives no sign of interest in that question.

It is not impossible for a man, marrying a woman in the circumstances in which Hjalmar married Gina, to remain unsuspicious, and not to tell his close friend either that the marriage had taken place or that a daughter had been born, simply because he had been given a rather unlikely reason why the friend should be offended. (What offence could Hjalmar have given Gregers by virtue of old Ekdal's business deal having come near to incriminating Werle senior?) But such simple-mindedness and gullibility are too frequent a feature of Ibsen's characters for one not to feel that the sheer technical difficulties have prevented the portrayal of characters possessing more subtle qualities, or else that Ibsen was little interested in the real complexities of behaviour.

There is here not merely a technical question of an unlikely exposition. It is not the creaking revelation of the dramatist's labour caused by Hjalmar's repeated questions – 'Surely you know that?', 'Gregers, didn't you know?', 'Maybe you didn't know anything about that either?', 'Don't you remember she was called Gina?', and so on – that matters most. Hjalmar himself is one of those many characters in Ibsen for whom it is hard to find a more charitable name than 'booby'. Ibsen seems to parade him for the audience's scorn. He is made to ask at Mrs Sörby's party whether the vintage makes any difference to wine, and having learned that it does, to show off his knowledge at home to his wife and daughter. He is mockingly asked by the Fat Guest to recite some poetry, which he 'used to do so prettily', and has at the time no retort to this insult, but again boasts at home as though he had put everyone in their places. There is in all this a psychological interest, in seeing Hjalmar turn his defeats into satisfactions. He is a sort of prim and unbending Micawber. When his daughter Hedvig asks if he has remembered to bring her home a titbit from the dinner-party, he has not – which might happen to anyone – but offers to show her the menu and tell her what the courses tasted like. Only after she has shown her unquestioning devotion, offering to bring him first his flute, then some beer, does he show any sign of being aware of her, but then he goes straight into his rôle as hagridden but loving father of the family, plays his flute 'with much "feeling"', and declares there is no place like home. Hedvig kills herself, in the end, to please him, and the play means to show how his falsity drove her to it. As with Helmer Torvald, the demonstration is laid on with a trowel.

Gregers is equally near to a caricature, though again not altogether incredible. His absence of curiosity about his old friend need not be taken as a mark of his character, rather as a distortion caused by technical considerations. The difficulty about being moved by the play comes from his unreasoning and fanatical insistence on opening Hjalmar's eyes to the truth. The need for this is never discussed. Gregers merely speaks of freeing Hjalmar from 'all the lies and deceit that are causing his ruination,' and is never challenged to say what that ruination is. So far as the play shows us, Hjalmar is comfortably off in his marriage, and it might be more to the point to ask him to show consideration for Hedvig and his wife, rather than to insist on his knowing his daughter is illegitimate. Gregers never reflects on the likely consequences of telling Hjalmar the truth about the past, but assumes the results can only be good, and this blindness in both of them is not offered so that we may understand it: it is the mainstay of the play.

As Relling says, Gregers is 'an acute case of inflamed scruples'. But he is precisely that, a 'case', not a man with whom one feels any degree of affinity, such as Relling implies when he goes on to say Gregers' disease is 'a national illness'. If the issue could be presented in those terms it might well have that extension of meaning from the individual to the more general which a play needs for real success. A Norwegian 'national illness' is likely to be shared by other nations too: there can be few people with no desire at all to remove splinters from other people's eyes. But the objection is not that in *Ghosts*, by contrast, the Norwegian disease is rather hushing things up than revealing them. It is rather that the deep need most people feel to get at the truth is not adequately represented by Gregers' bald-headed rush at it. We suppress the truth about ourselves for reasons of which Gregers is ignorant; we have more inhibitions than his puritan zeal comprehends, and Ibsen, in showing the results of zeal of that order, is plugging away at the obvious. The place for such a grotesque is farce.

Gregers' proposal to Hedvig that she should show her love for her father by sacrificing the wild duck, her dearest possession, is a crux of the play: without it there could be no catastrophe. But this is based on no better grounds than Gregers' revelation to Hjalmar about Hedvig's parentage. In his first wild reaction to that news, Hjalmar turned on Hedvig in a fit of bad temper and said he would like to wring the duck's neck. There was no reason to take this any more seriously than other unthinking things he says throughout the play. But as though grateful to the dramatist for giving him a cue, Gregers reminds Hedvig in Act Four that her father used such language, and turns it into a pretext for sacrificing the bird for Hjalmar. At this point, when Gregers says, 'Supposing you offered to sacrifice the wild duck for *his* sake... Suppose you were ready to sacrifice for him the most precious thing you had in the world,' the play ceases to be about any desire for truth and becomes at best – but it is not really this – a study of a man slightly crazed. (The number of characters whose sanity one begins to doubt increases from here on.)

Gregers is surely not meant to be crazed, despite the remarks to this effect which his father makes about him. One indication of that is his similarity, on this particular point, with other Ibsen characters, so many of whom expect their relatives or friends to behave as Gregers suggests Hedvig should. Nora supposes her husband will quite certainly destroy his own reputation to preserve hers, and is astonished when he does not. Rosmer accepts willingly Rebecca West's idea that she should drown herself to restore his faith in mankind. Hedda suggests suicide to Løvborg. Oswald takes it for granted that Regine will end his life if he asks her to. The sacrifice Gregers proposes is nothing like so great as some of these, which are not presented as acts of madness, and in some cases seem to be seen as great, tragic necessities. (A parodistic version of the Ten Commandments was current among some radical thinkers in late nineteenth-century Norway, including a Commandment to take one's own life. But Ibsen does not have such modern Albigensians in mind.) Besides, Gregers' case is not studied by the dramatist; it is simply the means by which the plot is furthered, and this puts an end to any serious pretensions. Gregers, again, gives no account of how he thinks his proposed course of action will help anybody. With the zeal of a leech he fastens onto the idea of self-sacrifice, as he does to the idea of truth, and is astounded by the results of his inspirations.

With two such men as Gregers and Hjalmar at the centre the play is bound to remain at a crude level; humanly speaking it does, however, also introduce a new kind of play, in which symbolism is more important than in any previous work of Ibsen's. Hitherto, symbolism had generally been only apparent here and there. Bernick's leaky ships, Nora's forgery, Oswald's disease, Stockmann's sewers all had at least a metaphoric value. But so far no play had made the symbol so predominant, or so interrelated with all the characters' lives, as the wild duck is, and on this account it is possible to discuss here the question of Ibsen's achieving a *poésie de théâtre*.

The bird is certainly an image with many potential meanings. It can expand with something like the iridescence of poetry, by virtue of its ambiguity, for it never stands for any one thing. In some places it seems to be associated with despair: it is compared implicitly with 'some people in this world that dive straight to the bottom the moment they get a couple of bullets in them, and never come up again,' and is thus linked, sometimes explicitly, with the despair of old Ekdal and Hedvig. They are the people who have, like the duck, dived to the bottom of the river or sea, and clung fast there, or so the explicit parallels suggest, though it is not clear how this can be said of Hedvig: the symbol is forced upon her, yet she is not remotely like her shattered grandfather. Gregers' self-imposed task, as he sees it, is to dive down like a well-trained dog, and save both Hjalmar and Hedvig, who to his way of thinking have gone down to die in the dark. (It really is not true: Hjalmar is too self-centred for despair, and Hedvig is spirited in her difficult situation.) Yet the bird also stands for the opposite of despair. In one sense it is the creature that tried to commit suicide when it was only slightly hurt, in another, it is, as Hedvig says, the most important thing in the room, 'because she's a *real* wild bird'. The place where it lives is also the place where the clock does not work, which leads Gregers to say, with the disclosure of symbolism characteristic of him, that 'time stands still in there... beside the wild duck'. We may be chary of accepting this offer of a symbol at face value – the metaphor is so pressed into service – but the suggestion is surely that there is something of eternity about the duck. Is it that total freedom Skule dreamed of, and Brand, and Julian, perhaps? But if we choose to think that, the attribution is tacked on. There is nothing more timeless or eternal about the duck than the fact that the clock in the same room has stopped; the duck has no function in the play that could be described in this particular symbolical way.

Other ambiguities include the fact that, though the bird symbolises the depths, it lives in the highest part of the building, and that, though 'wild', it lives cooped up in the attic, even though it is often said to have been saved. (This relationship between imprisonment and freedom will seem more notable still in Hedda Gabler's desire to liberate Løvborg.)

The rôle of the dog which rescues the duck is equally ambiguous. The purpose of the dog which belonged to Gregers' father was not to save the duck's life by refusing to let it bite fast to the weeds on the sea-bed, but to bring it back to the hunter, who for some reason kept it alive where he would normally have killed it. (What was old Werle doing, sending a duck with two slugs in its body and a damaged neck as a pet for Hedvig? Presumably he shot it in order to eat it.) Gregers, however, when he says that he would like to be a dog, speaks as though his purpose would be to rescue the duck, or people in a similar situation. His lack of success, indeed the bungled job he makes of the whole operation, is related to this confusion in the symbols themselves. Gregers does not know what he intends by 'liberating' Hjalmar and Hedvig; he plunges in and brings Hedvig, at least, straight to her death.

These are not poetic images: the ambiguity is not enlivening but confusing, both to audience and to characters. Yet it almost seems at times as though Ibsen were aware of this, as though he were presenting in Gregers a parody of himself. That he is to a degree such a parody, so far as Ibsen was a man continually concerned with 'the claims of the ideal', is self-evident. That he is a parody of Ibsen's 'poetic' character needs more showing, and cannot be said so definitely in every case. Yet the hint is often proffered.

In *The Wild Duck*, more than in any other play, Ibsen seems to ridicule the habit of talking in a double sense, in inappropriate metaphors, as when Gregers is asked by Hjalmar what he would most like to be, if not himself.

HJALMAR (*laughs*) Ha! ha! And if you weren't Gregers Werle, what is it you would want to be?
GREGERS If I could choose, I should most of all like to be a clever dog.
GINA A dog!
HEDVIG(*involuntarily*) Oh, no!
GREGERS Yes, a really absurdly clever dog, the sort that goes down to the bottom after wild ducks, when they dive down and bite fast on to the seaweed and the tangle down there in the mud.
HJALMAR You know, Gregers...I don't understand a word of what you are saying. (Act 2) (VI. 172)

Yet the possibility of a certain self-ridicule by Ibsen looks more remote when he at once follows this dialogue with another in which Gina's hard-headedness turns to a kind of awe, only increased by the comments of the innocent child Hedvig:

GINA (*staring into space, her sewing on her lap*) Wasn't that funny, him saying he wanted to be a dog?
HEDVIG I'll tell you what, Mother...I think he meant something else.
GINA And what else might that be?
HEDVIG Well, I don't know. But it was just as though he meant something different from what he was saying – all the time. (Act 2) (VI. 171-2)

This heavy underlining, of a symbolical sense which must already be thoroughly clear to the audience, might well be a mark of Ibsen's involvement with his symbols to the point of not realising how obvious they are. Yet he also provides a contrast in the character of Gina, one of whose chief rôles is making a down-to-earth, crudely commonsensical interpretation of every metaphor used. If Gregers speaks of a poisoned atmosphere she at once protests that she aired the place this morning, and when Relling speaks of 'inflamed scruples' she almost thinks they are physiological. Uncertainty about the irony comes from the fact that Gina's misunderstanding is so gross: a 'poisoned' atmosphere is not so very unusual an expression, and we half sense that the joke is on her, for what it is worth.

Yet there must surely be irony in the scene in which Hedvig's dead body is discovered, however movingly it may be staged. For Gina this is an instant when she is desolated; her response is pure motherly grief. For Hjalmar his daughter's death is something to be denied, for Relling it is an occasion to reprove Hjalmar for his sentimentality. For Gregers, it is a symbol:

HJALMAR Well, Relling... why don't you say something?
RELLING The bullet hit her in the breast.
HJALMAR Yes, but she'll be coming round.
GINA (*bursts into tears*) Oh my little one!
GREGERS (*huskily*) In the briny deep...   (Act 5) (VI. 240)

Gregers' line is grotesque, not only because of the fact that he speaks symbolically, but because of the particular words he uses, which could hardly make the symbolism more obvious. I have quoted here James McFarlane's translation, which may slightly overdo the exaggeration: it is difficult to say, but perhaps 'the vasty deep,' being a Shakespearean quotation, has something to be said for it. What is certain is that in Act Three Ibsen has deliberately drawn attention to the oddity of these words. When Gregers uses them for the first time, Hedvig at once asks why he uses that particular phrase. It is true that the alternatives she proposes are closer to one another in sound than 'the briny deep' is to 'the seabed': where Gregers says *på havsens bund*, which uses a slightly archaic and 'poetic' form of the genitive, she suggests as more natural *havets bund* or *havbunden*, and clearly his phrase, though only slightly different in Norwegian, sounds out of place to her. When it is repeated after Hedvig's death, the oddity must strike us, and the incongruousness of Gregers' response must be brought home to us. (On the other hand, Hedvig admits that she herself uses the archaism for the room of the wild duck, so that the repetition of it reflects on her also.)

Ibsen, then, wanted the moment of Hedvig's death to be tinged with criticism of the man whose blundering way of speaking has helped to bring it about. Gregers has implanted in Hedvig's mind the idea that she herself is the wild duck who must be sacrificed, and now he is refusing to face the consequences. But it is the symbolical mode, rather than the idealism, which is criticised through the 'poetic' words, and that same mode is the chief feature of the play Ibsen is presenting.

He had no real need of a symbol at all, in order to cope dramatically with the shattering of illusions. Gregers could simply have humiliated Hjalmar to the point where Hedvig would do anything, even kill herself to demonstrate to him that he was still loved. The device of the duck seems to give a greater scope to the play, to hint at Freedom in a more than local sense, but only serves to produce a less moving, more confusing work. The duck is a mere *fait divers*, and the play would be more telling without it.

Any resistance we may still feel to the idea that Ibsen is ironically detached from such symbolising probably comes from the awareness that for his own part, as a dramatist, he continues to use symbolism, both now and in later plays, in exactly the same way. There is comedy in the moment when Gregers asks Hedvig whether she is so certain the loft is really only a loft, as there is in his prim retort to Relling's accusation that he carries the 'claim of the ideal' around in his back-pocket: 'It is in my breast that I carry it.' Yet it is Ibsen who makes Gina say that Gregers has lit a stove and then damped it too much, and finally thrown water all over it and the floor too. Gina cannot herself mean that symbolically, but Ibsen means us to understand it so, and to see in it an epitome of all the mess that Gregers causes throughout the play. Ibsen is by now incapable of writing without some degree of symbolism, and that is precisely what prevents *The Wild Duck* from being deeply moving. Take, for instance, the actual moment of Hedvig's death, which is as artificial as anything Ibsen wrote:

HJALMAR ...Suppose the others [Mrs Sörby and old Werle] came along, their hands loaded with good things, and they called to the child: 'Come away from him. With us, life is awaiting you...'
GREGERS (*quickly*) Well, what then, d'you think?
HJALMAR If I then asked her: 'Hedvig, are you willing to give up life for my sake'? (*Laughs scornfully*) Oh yes! I must say. You would soon hear the sort of answer I would get!
(*A pistol shot is heard within the loft.*) (Acts 5) (VI. 237)

Such appropriate coincidences are not uncommon in Ibsen's plays.

Whether Hedvig has heard what Hjalmar has said and mis-
interpreted it is uncertain. She may have understood 'life' to mean
not life with Mrs Sörby but life of any kind, and the pistol shot
may be an answer saying that she does love Hjalmar, enough to
sacrifice herself, or that she is in despair at his (only recently and
unexpectedly expressed) doubt about her love. The indisputable
point is that the pistol-shot is, metaphorically, an answer, and that
same fact is what makes the moment stagey. It is also a quality not
of any particular character but of the play.

The final touch is given in the conversation between Gregers
and Relling, just before the curtain falls. They have been discussing
whether Hedvig's death will have any notable effect on Hjalmar,
or whether he will be ennobled by it or return to wallowing
deeper and deeper in self-pity. Gregers is convinced that some
good will come of the sacrifice he has unwittingly caused:

GREGERS If *you* are right and *I* am wrong, life will no longer be worth living.
RELLING Oh, life wouldn't be so bad if we could only be left in peace by these
    blessed people who come running round to us poor folk with their claims of
    the ideal all the time.
GREGERS (*staring into space*) In that case I am glad my destiny is what it is.
RELLING If I may ask – what is your destiny?
GREGERS (*turning to leave*) To be thirteenth at table.
RELLING The devil it is! [Literally 'Devil believe that'.]   (Act 5) (VI. 242)

Gregers' portentousness still leaves some doubt about the significance of this exchange. He is still talking in a symbol, and rather an
obscure one. Whether he means merely that it is unlucky to be
thirteenth, or that he is the Christ-figure among the twelve others,
or the Judas-figure, is disputable, and no doubt Ibsen intended
ambiguity here as he did in the case of the wild duck itself: to himself Gregers is a Christ, to others a Judas. It is both good and bad
that the claim of the ideal should be presented – that might well be
Gregers' view. But Ibsen himself has carefully made that remark
possible, and given the symbol a basis in the reality of the play's
action. Gregers actually was thirteenth, or at any rate one of
thirteen, at table in Act One, as was carefully brought out at the
time, and this seems to lend a kind of weight to what would
otherwise be a remark out of the blue. On the other hand, Relling's
scepticism and his colloquial reference to the Devil (echoing the

same unintentional use of the word by Regine at the beginning of *Ghosts*, and several other similar uses scattered through the plays) suggest a final negative, or at least a doubt.

There is an intriguing quality here, tempting us to unravel the puzzle. In reality, though, there is no unravelling it: it is an indeterminate ending as well as a portentous one, and that is the most serious criticism that the play has to meet, at this point. In the final moment Ibsen is not really concerned about the death of Hedvig, any more than Gregers was. He is concerned to maintain the ambiguity of his position, both maintaining his symbolism and decrying the impulse which draws him towards it. In that comprehensiveness, he may have felt, lay the only full realisation of himself as an artist.

If Ibsen maintained his interest in nineteenth-century German philosophy of the kind he satirised in *Peer Gynt*, he might very well have seen a justification for such a train of thought. We are always in a difficulty here, since his reading was largely confined to newspapers, yet certain basic essentials were so much in the air that any intelligent reader, especially in Germany, would pick them up without recourse to the originals. In Hegel's thought, for instance, which Ibsen knew at least at second hand, the whole process of world-history is seen as the pure spirit's becoming aware of its own self 'phenomenalised', turned into the phenomena of experience, as though in a mirror. The paradox I discussed earlier (p. 59), that the condition of the world is to be brought about, is an instance of that same growth in awareness – what the 'world-historical man' produces is an image in the real world of what already exists in his own spirit, and it becomes accepted by others because they see, in the reality he has made for them, a mirroring of what already exists in the Spirit as they know it in their own individual spirits. Yet at the same time, this phenomenalisation, or realisation, of the Spirit is less than the fullest mirroring of it in all its progress through the whole course of history, and thus the claim to mirror the Spirit at any one moment must always be made ironically, in the awareness that it is not really so – or rather, that it both is and is not really so: paradox remains at the root of this type of thinking.

Hebbel's play *Agnes Bernauer* (1852) ends with a discussion in which ideas very similar to these are put forward. Ibsen might well have come across them there, or in any of Hebbel's rather less penetrable theoretical writings. They do not, however, quite express the idea which may have induced Ibsen to adopt the ironically affirmative negative stance of *The Wild Duck*. That is given rather by a remark of Friedrich Schlegel's about *Wilhelm Meister*, with which Ibsen is less likely to have been familiar, though he could well have drawn similar conclusions from the same basic system of thought.

For Schlegel, Goethe's novel was a work which was above criticism, which saved the critic the trouble of judgment, because it judged itself, and not only judged itself but, in a curiously Hegel-like phrase, 'represented itself'. In other words, *Wilhelm Meister* was both an Idea, and the realisation of that Idea, both a potential reality and the phenomenalisation of that potential. Moreover, since it judged itself – that is, since Goethe displayed throughout an ironical detachment from his own work, an awareness both of the importance and of the insignificance of what he had achieved – since it was produced by a mind in the state of perfect critical awareness concerning the nature of literature, and produced not despite such awareness but because of it, it had a special kind of perfection. It was not perfect as the Spirit which produced it is already perfect, or as the Spirit's self-phenomenalisation in the world will be perfect in the fullness of time, but it was perfect in itself, or its own right. For the Spirit had come to know itself perfectly as it was at that time when the novel came into being, and the negativity in the novel, the ironic awareness of its limitations, was one more feature of its perfection, its adherence to the facts about its own situation.

I have paraphrased Schlegel and in part taken over the commentary by Erich Heller which he uses in explicating Thomas Mann (*The Ironic German*, London, 1958, p. 185), since my purpose is not to maintain that Ibsen had read Schlegel, but only to suggest the kind of thinking which could have led to *The Wild Duck*. Ibsen had by now become very familiar with the alternating poles of negation and affirmation, following first one course, then the other, from play to play, and occasionally attempting a synthesis, as he did in *Emperor and Galilean*. By now, he had become more conscious of his method, and had a greater wish to take up a position with relation to that, rather than to the immediate content of the plays. Thus, although *The Wild Duck* is a negative, on the whole, to the affirmative claim made by Stockmann on behalf of 'the ideal', it is also a stock-taking, a reckoning up of the advantages and disadvantages of Ibsen's own mode of playwriting. A further coil of the spiral has been entered upon, a further refinement of the eternal affirmation and negation. What *The Wild Duck* shows is not merely the folly of Gregers' idealism and use of symbols – at the same time as it seems to allow the possibility that it was not folly, but necessary and beneficial – but also the folly of all symbolism, including Ibsen's own. It is true that we have to add to this, as we do for Gregers, the possibility that the symbolism may be fruitful after all. There is no end to the spirals, the dialectic continues indefinitely. Yet such an account could explain why Ibsen seems at one and the same time to condemn Gregers, while he himself uses an identical mode of approach to things and people. This is the perennial spin of the wheel of the polar opposites, and would seem to justify even the ambiguities about Christ and Judas in Gregers' final exchange with Relling. These merely continue the ambiguities in the wild duck, in the attic, in the ideal, and even in Hedvig's sacrifice. It is true that the ambiguities usually correspond to no particular realities. It is the system itself that counts, not the human beings involved, who are manipulated in this play as they generally are in all Ibsen's work, and this is a flaw, since in theory the system, the Idea, should become the phenomena of a real world. What the Idea does in Ibsen is to become the phenomena of an artificial world, which has only a superficial resemblance to the world of human beings. It is a world of art, but of an art removed from contact with reality, spinning its own cocoon, walking along the spider's filament thrown out by its own body, a fundamentally solipsistic affair. We are never likely to be touched by any humanity in it, unless by Gina's.

7

Rosmersholm and *The Lady from the Sea*

The opening of *Rosmersholm*, which was written in 1886, after what was becoming the regular two-year interval, is expertly done. The setting itself is made to tell – the old-fashioned furniture and portraits of Rosmer's ancestors on the one hand, the wild flowers showing Rebecca West's freshening influence on the other. The dialogue leads the audience into knowledge of the background without strain: the fact that Rosmer is unwilling to cross the footbridge, though we do not yet know why; that the person approaching the house is not Rosmer himself but the headmaster, Rektor Kroll; the suspicion that Kroll's sister, Rosmer's former wife, met her death mysteriously – all this is conveyed in speech which sounds naturalistic and yet is supplying essential details with every word. The established convention of the conversation between servants, used for the exposition of *The Wild Duck*, was not nearly so deft.

The same holds true for the pattern of the play as a whole. The five acts of *The Wild Duck* make it seem diffuse by comparison. *Rosmersholm* with its four acts is both more closely knit, and brings in a new issue, political reform, for the first time in Ibsen's work. (Stockmann has no reforms in mind, only total overthrow of the existing order.) In Act One, the general position is given in a leisurely way that allows the succeeding Act all the more impact. Rosmer is a clergyman who has lost his faith and is thinking of entering politics for the almost religious purpose of 'ennobling mankind'. His wife Beate has been dead for a year, but Rebecca is living with him, and opposes the conservative crusade in which Kroll wants him to join. As the end of the Act approaches, Rosmer declares himself against Kroll, which could be dangerous for his entry into politics, and the curtain falls on ominous remarks about the legendary white horses of the millrace claiming more victims.

Act Two then exposes Rosmer to attack from both right and left: both the conservative Kroll and the radical newspaper editor Mortensgaard know something of the events which led to Beate Rosmer's death, and threaten to use their knowledge against Rosmer if he does not conform politically. Act Three shows the mounting sense of guilt in both Rosmer and Rebecca, and Act Four sees them each resolve to atone for the past by ending their lives in the same millrace where Beate died. There is pleasure in seeing these manifold strands separated out and joined again.

Rosmersholm still suffers, like the preceding plays, from improbabilities in the account of the past. As before, it is not that these are impossible events; they could have happened, but, if they did, at least one of the characters must have been extremely naive. We are asked to believe, in short, that a nineteenth-century Norwegian pastor could – or even would – introduce a young, attractive unmarried woman into his household to live as a companion with himself and his wife, that she did so for 'years and years' – the period is never exactly stated – that she spent many evenings with him discussing intellectual matters, while his wife was elsewhere in the house – and that it never occurred to him at the time that his wife might object. Stranger still, Beate is said to have invited Rebecca herself, assisted by, of all people, her brother, the rigidly principled Kroll. This is not the Norway we saw through Mrs Alving's eyes, and it is unimaginable that Manders could have behaved as his counterpart Kroll does here. But even granting that this is a play set in a different world from *Ghosts*, there is still the question of how Rosmer could have been so blithely unaware. As usual, Ibsen manages these things only if we either concede that Rosmer is astonishingly innocent, or that the details of the past are best ignored in the interests of the immediate action on stage. The trouble is, they cannot be ignored completely. It is part of the whole plot that Rebecca not only lived under the same roof with the Rosmers, but also helped to destroy Johannes Rosmer's religious beliefs, intimidated Beate by suggesting that a barren wife is an unwanted burden to a husband, wounded her by suggesting that she, Rebecca, had conceived a child by him, and by similar means drove Beate into taking her own life in order to leave Rosmer a clear path to remarriage or some other fresh start.

These events are essential to the plot since it is because of them that Rosmer is unable to put into practice his ideals. As in *Ghosts*, the dead hand of the past reaches out to stifle the ambitions of the present. But again as in the other plays it is uncertain what the ambitions or ideals amount to. At times something socialistic seems to be implied – nothing more definite than that Rosmer says he stands on the same side as his nephew and niece, who have significantly embroidered a red cover in which to keep copies of Mortensgaard's periodical *Beacon*. Yet only a few lines later in Act One Rosmer says he supports 'no prevailing doctrine', or indeed either of the sides in 'the dispute'. Nor is it said what the dispute is about, only that Rosmer in some way places confidence in the people. (The crucial word in this exchange is *folkedømme*, a compound of 'people' and 'judgment' or 'discernment', (as it were, 'folk' and 'deeming') but rendered variously by Ibsen's translators as 'popular judgment' 'public opinion', and 'democracy'. It is not, however, the normal expression for any of these, and is very rarely used.

ROSMER ...I want to live and put all my strength into one thing – creating in this country a true democracy.
KROLL Don't you think *we* have enough democracy already? I for my part think we are all of us well on the way to being dragged down into the mud where as a rule only the *hoi polloi* feel at home.
ROSMER That is just why I want to set up for democracy its true aim.
KROLL What aim?
ROSMER To make every man in the country a nobleman.
KROLL Every man – !
ROSMER As many as possible, at all events.
KROLL By what means?
ROSMER Why, by freeing their minds, and purifying their wills.
KROLL You are a dreamer, Rosmer. Will *you* free them? Will *you* purify them?
ROSMER No, my dear fellow – I merely want to try and awaken them to it. As for doing it, that is their own affair.   (Act 1) (VI. 314)

There is a degree of vagueness in Rosmer's political ideals – which need do no harm to the play, since it has no political axe to grind. The harm comes rather from the ineffectuality of Rosmer's character, so little likely to have fired Rebecca's enthusiasm. When he returns in Act Four from another meeting with Kroll and announces he has given up the whole idea of political action he sounds casual and inconsequential, as though the ideals had never meant anything to him:

REBECCA ...How did you get on with Kroll?
ROSMER We made peace.
REBECCA I see. So that's what came of it.
ROSMER He gathered all our friends together at his house. They got me to see that working to ennoble people's minds – is simply not for me. – And besides it's all so hopeless anyway, you know. – I'm giving it up.   (Act 4) (VI. 367)

If Rosmer were not to give up so instantaneously what seemed to be a matter of great concern, the play could not proceed so quickly to its concluding suicide-pact. Yet his yielding to Kroll and his friends after only a few hours' conversation does not suggest the courage and tenacity which Rebecca found so invigorating. The volte-face is, it is true, on a par with Mrs Alving's sudden switch from abhorrence of incest to an unreasoning condemnation of herself for opposing it. Ibsen's characters generally move by these extreme swings, but that does not help the feeling that the construction of the plays is made so much the easier by such idiosyncrasy. The frequency with which these labile – though not therefore incredible – characters appear in central rôles not only makes them inwardly resemble each other but suggests a limitation in Ibsen's capacity to imagine firmer wills. He may have the dialectic more in mind than the portrayal of people.

In this respect, there is even a similarity between Rosmer and Rebecca, for what we see of Rebecca on stage is completely out of keeping with what she says of her own past, and she too seems to have undergone a total transformation. On stage, Rebecca is a considerate, thoughtful woman, deeply conscious of having a good mission in life, to be realised through Rosmer. Her ruthless destruction of Beate Rosmer's self-confidence, on the other hand, accords very little with the devoted, sincere, idealistic woman we now see in action. It is sometimes suggested that this idealism can be explained as a deliberate mask, intended to drive Rosmer to a suicide like his wife's, that Rebecca is impelled by a powerful death-wish of her own, in which she involves both Rosmer and Beate. Certainly there is something to be cited in support of this in the passage where Rebecca is confronted by Kroll with the evidence that she is an illegitimate child. It is Kroll who takes the view of her that she has Rosmer and 'everything else' in her power, and it is Kroll who accuses her of having a cold heart, and acting always with calculating deliberation. Yet her emotional response, her over-reaction to the charge of being illegitimate, seems to belie any such interpretation. She has been coldly calculating in the past, while Beate was alive, it is true. But that seems to be over, and we can only imagine her to be still calm and deliberate in planning the husband's destruction if we disbelieve everything she now says.

Such a reading 'against the current' is not out of the question. Rebecca's hot denial of her illegitimacy is surprisingly intense, and as Freud observed, there are some innuendoes in Kroll's charge, which could be understood by her to imply that he knows she was not only a stepdaughter to Dr West, but a mistress. On this interpretation, the added charge of illegitimacy, which she was not aware of, suddenly makes her realise that she has made love not to a stepfather but to a father. The intensity of her response is accounted for by the taboo on incest being much stronger than that on bastardy. And if her real motives can be as unconscious as that, when she confronts Kroll, they may be equally unconscious when she is bringing about Rosmer's suicide.

The difficulty about any such interpretation is that nothing can prove or disprove it. Rebecca has, for instance, subtracted a year from her age ever since she was twenty-five. Was this done from coquetry, as she says it was, or was it in order to conceal the fact that Dr West was living near her mother in the year when she was conceived? If she was in fact concealing her illegitimacy by altering her age, and if also she was Dr West's mistress, there is no surprise for her in Kroll's innuendoes, and Freud's case is seriously damaged. In any event, such speculation, where the meaning of the words spoken is constantly capable of interpretation in the opposite sense, is endlessly unfruitful. We would have to say, for instance, that, although Rebecca's conduct seems idealistic, she is not deliberately and consciously plotting against Rosmer, as Kroll implies, but unconsciously, with no preconceived design. Or we would have to say that her unconscious self is plotting, without any awareness of this in her consciousness.

On the other hand, no plotter, conscious or unconscious, could carry out a plan involving two people so unaccountable as Rebecca and Rosmer turn out to be. What Ibsen intends by Rebecca is clear enough: she is the 'pagan' woman of his early plays, the Furia of *Catiline*, the Viking woman of *The Vikings at Helgeland* in a new guise, but also a woman who has been converted by the atmosphere of the Rosmer household into adopting a more Christian attitude. In terms of Hegelian 'polar opposites' that is perhaps intelligible; it is much less so in terms of a real woman of Ibsen's or any other day. Her dialogue with Rosmer puts the theoretical position plainly:

REBECCA ... Yesterday ... when you asked me whether I would be your wife – I cried aloud for joy –

ROSMER Yes, you did, didn't you, Rebecca. I thought I understood you rightly.

REBECCA For a moment, yes. I forgot myself. Because that was the spirited will I had of old, on the point of freeing itself again. But that has no power any more – not in the long run.

ROSMER How do you explain what has happened to you?

REBECCA It is the Rosmer philosophy – or *your* philosophy at all events – that has infected my will.

ROSMER Infected it?

REBECCA And made it sick. Made it a slave to laws that used to have no validity for me. You – living with you – has ennobled my mind –

ROSMER Ah, if I could truly believe that!

REBECCA You can believe it. The Rosmer philosophy ennobles –. But – (*shaking her head*) – but, – but –

ROSMER But? What?

REBECCA – But it kills happiness, my dear. (Act 4) (VI. 371)

In terms of what is supposed to have happened, these speeches mean that Rebecca had never felt any compunction about driving Beate to her death, or about the lies and hypocrisies necessary to that end. The laws – presumably moral rather than legal – which condemn such conduct had meant nothing to her, and she was happy in the unreflecting exercise of her will-power.

That in itself is hard to believe, of a woman born in nineteenth-century Norway, or any other part of modern Europe. It is not the thoughtless harshness of an inexperienced young woman, but the deliberate and prolonged harassment, which makes Rebecca's protestation unpersuasive. Even harder to give credence to is her description of her present state of mind. She does not say she has become convinced that encompassing Beate's death was wrong, or that she sees the error of her ways in any other sense. Rather, her will has been 'infected' – as though the will could be subject to some disease – it has been made sick and 'enslaved' – this time as though it had been externally compelled to act without inner conviction. Moreover, this infected will cannot even feel joy at the prospect of marriage. Joy is something that the pagan in Rebecca could have felt, but from which the Christian or quasi-Christian is debarred.

Psychologically, this is perhaps impossible to comprehend. Rebecca's account of her motives will not bear examination, though we see well enough how it accords with some rough-and-ready classifications which Ibsen might have believed in – the clichés of some nineteenth-century thought, whereby pagan life is free, happy and untrammelled, while Christianity is sick, unhappy, repressive. Only a character in a play, manipulated by a desire to impose some such view, could speak in such terms as Rebecca's. A woman who had been converted to a belief in sin and repentance would hardly say she was infected and sick; it is Ibsen's mind which plants that thought. On the other hand, a woman who could hold such a belief to be infecting would be unlikely to knuckle under. The notion of infection adds to the difficulties, for while it would occur naturally to the author of *Ghosts*, it makes poor psychological sense in this new context.

Imagine, all the same, that Rebecca does not mean what she says here: that she is not, and does not believe herself to be, infected, but is still deliberately plotting against Rosmer as she had done against his wife, and you are still left with the unpredictable behaviour on his side. Rebecca could not reasonably expect Rosmer to act as he does in the final Act; no conceivable plot could be meant to make him take his life in the way that he does take it.

The effect on Rosmer of Rebecca's confession is at first to deprive him of all remaining hope for mankind. Already vacillating after the conversation with Kroll and his friends, he now fails to see that he has 'ennobled' Rebecca, although she reminds him of it with some justice, since the repentance she now shows is presumably within the meaning of his vague word. When she insists that she really is ennobled, and asks what more she can do to prove it, she is still behaving in accordance with his expectations, though there is something embarrassing in the way they bandy the word about. Rosmer regards the whole business as a kind of mathematical calculation – he is perfectly serious when he says ('as if impelled against his will', as the stage direction has it):

Let us see, then. There is a great love in you, you say. That through me your soul is ennobled. Is it true? Are you sure you have reckoned things out right? Shall we see if it adds up? Eh? (Act 4) (VI. 378)

The expectation that someone else will commit suicide is not abnormal in Ibsen, but that makes it no less extraordinary in real life. If anybody is doing any deliberate plotting one might think it was Rosmer, but for the stage direction. He takes things a good deal further than was suggested by Ulrik Brendel on his fleeting return visit. Brendel suggested only that Rebecca would need to cut off her finger or her ear before Rosmer could succeed – and that perversity sounded like a piece of advice from an old troll, better ignored than followed. Rosmer, however, seems to think that he is proposing only what Brendel suggested when he asks Rebecca to throw herself in the millrace at the precise spot where Beate died.

This 'tooth for a tooth' philosophy of retribution is commented on by Hjalmar in *The Wild Duck*, when he observes that old Werle, who has 'blinded' many a trusting fellow human being, is now going blind himself. Similarly poetic justice is dealt out, or nearly dealt out, to many of Ibsen's characters. Consul Bernick nearly loses his son in one of the very ships he was ruthlessly sending to sea in an unseaworthy condition. The 'lie' represented by Mrs Alving's Orphanage burns down, just as her son 'burns down': the affliction of Oswald seems, at least, to be directly related to her hypocrisy. Hedda Gabler, having failed to induce Løvborg to shoot himself in the temple, shoots herself in just that place. But for a lover, as Rosmer appears to be, to demand such a sacrifice not as a retribution but in order to reassure himself that human beings can be strong enough to kill themselves, to prove their repentance, is more eerily perverse than Brendel was.

That is still not to say that Rosmer is incredible. What makes him strain one's suspension of disbelief to the uttermost is his next idea, which is that if Rebecca dies he must die with her. Since the whole point of her dying was to prove to him his capacity for ennobling people, this is pointless, and not only pointless, but expressed in the baldest language, as though the whole thing were again a kind of arithmetical demonstration (as indeed Rosmer has just suggested it should be):

REBECCA Suppose you were deceiving yourself. Suppose it was only a delusion? One of the white horses of Rosmersholm.
ROSMER It might well be. For we never escape them − we of this house.
REBECCA Then stay, Johannes!
ROSMER The husband shall go with his wife, and the wife with her husband.
REBECCA Yes, but tell me *this*. Is it you who are going with me, or I who am going with you?
ROSMER That we shall never completely fathom.
REBECCA Yet I would so much like to know.
ROSMER We two go together, Rebecca. I with you and you with me.
REBECCA I rather think so too.
ROSMER For now we two are one.
REBECCA Yes. Now we are one. Come! Let us go gladly.   (Act 4) (VI. 380)

Again the thought behind this is more important than the human actions. The problem of who is following who may interest a philosopher of the Hegelian school, who may just see in its solution a kind of 'synthesis' − it is neither the one nor the other of them that is the thesis or the antithesis but both act as in a synthesis; their decision is taken simultaneously and spontaneously, and as they neatly put it, 'now we two are one'. No doubt the idea in Rebecca's last words, that they should go gladly, has a connection with something like Hegel's notion of 'the Affirmative' − or it may be with Nietzsche's 'Yea-Saying'. Whether one can arrange one's feelings to suit the book so readily is no more a matter of concern to Ibsen than it is in the remainder of the scene.*

Rosmer and Rebecca die like other Romantic lovers, distantly like Tristan and Isolde. The distinctive feature of Ibsen's play is the bareness of the language, and the incongruity of the debate.

---

* John Northam, in his Judith Wilson lecture of 1976, drew attention to the echoes in this dialogue of *St John* 17, 21−23, which are not irrelevant, although many mystical works about the uniting of 'I' and 'Thou' could provide similar ones. The echoes matter less than the stilted questioning, which is not an echo at all.

Romeo and Juliet dispute for several lines whether it is the nightin-
gale or the lark they can hear, but the effect is not of an ornitho-
logical discussion. Ibsen's characters introduce the question of their
precedence in such prosy terms, and solve it by such an off-handed,
bald reference to their unity-in-duality, as though it were in fact
a matter of numbers to be added up, that the moment is deprived
of all serious content. There is nothing of the rapture of Wagner's
music in the *Liebestod*. The fault with Ibsen lies not in the matter,
but in the presentation: he seems to imagine that what Wagner
shows as a mounting climax of irresistible passion can be presented
as a decision taken on the spur of the moment, with no emotional
power, entirely schematic.

As the two leap to their deaths, off-stage, they are seen by Mrs
Helseth, the housekeeper, who fancies she sees in the foam of the
torrent the 'white horses' of Rosmersholm (which were to have
given their names to the title itself in an early draft). These have
been referred to from time to time as the traditional harbingers of
doom; even the emancipated Rebecca has thought of them with a
shudder. But the reference to them is purely superstitious – they
have less presence in the play than even the Furies in Eliot's
Family Reunion, and belong rather to the Romantic Fate-tragedies
of the early nineteenth century than to the world of which Ibsen
was writing. Nothing in the play suggests that they influence
events, nor is Ibsen himself committed to anything the characters
in his play may believe. Yet since the horses are so completely unconnected with the action, they can do no more than provide a
dramatic *frisson* for the final curtain. The monster which comes
out of the sea in *Phèdre* – though also a little difficult to appreciate
in modern terms – is much more closely integrated in a play
dealing with an ancient world where Neptune can still be thought
of as punishing offences against himself by such means. In *Rosmersholm*, the terror of the housekeeper is adventitious. It is as though
Othello were to end with a servant blaming the deaths on the
sorceress who embroidered Desdemona's handkerchief. The play
thus ends with another of Ibsen's stagey 'curtains'.

There is, it is true, one final remark of Mrs Helseth's, after she
has spoken of the white horses: 'No, no help there...the dead
woman has taken them.' This has more relevance than the horses

have, since it suggests that it was Beate who did the deliberate plotting, rather than Rebecca or Rosmer, and it is true that Beate was perhaps not blameless in divulging to others her suspicions. That she confided in Kroll, her brother, was understandable enough. That she also told Mortensgaard her suspicions, at a time when Mortensgaard was Rosmer's open enemy, looks more like a malicious intention to be revenged on Rosmer after her death by spoiling his chances of living at peace with Rebecca. But even Beate could not have foreseen or intended that Rebecca and Rosmer should both do away with themselves, least of all in the way that they choose. The relationship between her action and their deaths is too remote to carry conviction, and the concluding mention of her is really no more than a baseless reiteration of the idea of retribution represented by the horses.

Rosmersholm has no clear link with the plays preceding it, except that, like all Ibsen's plays, it is concerned with the possibility of freedom, or rather of total independence from all responsibilities of living in society. With *The Lady from the Sea* it is linked so closely that the later play can be seen, if one wishes, as a companion piece, with a positive instead of a negative ending. Both plays are about a woman living with a man whose first wife has already died. Ellida Wangel is married to a doctor, where Rebecca West lived unmarried with the clergyman Rosmer, but neither Ellida nor Rebecca is a wife in the full sense. Both women feel an elemental attraction to a terrible danger, represented for Rebecca by the millstream, for Ellida by the sea. Both end with the reconciliation of husband and wife, as Rosmer and Rebecca finally become, though theirs is a reconciliation in death, where Ellida's with Wangel is a reconciliation for life. Ellida is able to cast off the hypnotic fascination of the water and turn her mind to the freedom which Rebecca also desired.

The parallels are closer than those, for instance, between *Ghosts* and *An Enemy of the People*, which similarly present reversed consequences, though of a different kind. In none of the preceding plays is the pattern of one so imitated by the pattern of the next. The question remains, of course, how this reversal is achieved, and here there si reason to think the process too mechanical, too much dictated by the intention to reverse.

Ibsen is moving now towards a more metaphysical level. The attraction of Ellida to the sea is the central thing about her, it is what makes her bathe in it daily, frustrates her desire to be a happily married wife, and haunts her with terrors, whereas Rebecca does not make up her mind to drown until quite late in *Rosmersholm*. But we are aware very soon that Ellida's fears are more than fears of the real sea, and are not merely caused by her vow to the Stranger, made years ago, wedding her with him to the sea. Rebecca dies in atonement for her guilt; Ellida's death, if she were to die within the play, would not be on account of anything so specific. Both she and the Stranger are said to be like or actually to be the sea, as is her child by Wangel, and the suggestion is that for them the sea is what it was for many Romantics, Leopardi being the most notable, the symbol of the quenching of all individuality. As Ibsen said on one occasion, man came from the sea, and could never be happy in his separation from it. It is a longing for self-immersion in the whole that Ellida experiences, the feeling which Freud called 'oceanic', and which terrifies at the same time that it attracts, by requiring the individual to relinquish all hold on selfhood. We might think here of Nirvana, or Schopenhauer's 'Naught'. By comparison, Ibsen's earlier plays, from *Pillars of Society* onwards, had been social dramas, with only a hint of the wider sense which the idea of freedom now has.

In strong contrast to *Rosmersholm*, the setting of Act One is in the open air, on a warm and brilliantly clear summer morning. A painter is at work in a leisurely way; Bolette brings in a huge vase of flowers; the sun which Oswald called for is present at full strength, and is matched by the happy teasing of Lyngstrand by Hilde and Bolette, Wangel's two daughters by his first marriage. The exposition begins in a way familiar enough with the arrival of Arnholm, an old friend, and former admirer of Ellida, who has not visited the family recently and so needs to be told of her and Wangel's child, which died in infancy. The fact that the flowers are for the celebration of Wangel's dead wife's birthday, also brought out by Arnholm's presence, underlines Ellida's remoteness from the family, and begins to account for her lonely visits to the seashore. But the essential point, the revelation that Ellida is threatened, comes up more awkwardly. Ibsen entrusts this to

Lyngstrand, the only character in this play except the Stranger to behave with the naivety of such men as Hjalmar in *The Wild Duck*.

Lyngstrand, a sculptor, announces his intention of creating a sculpture which, if realised, would be a comic monstrosity: the young wife of a sailor who lies dreaming in strange unrest, while the figure of her drowned husband, to whom she has been unfaithful, returns to her bedside as an apparition. The possibility of creating this essentially literary idea in sculpture need not concern us: Lyngstrand is not intended to appear even a modestly competent artist, and the only point of his idea is that it introduces his memory of an occurrence which gave rise to it. This, related directly to Ellida, is both portentous and melodramatic: the whole exposition is poorly done. Lyngstrand relates that some years ago he was returning from America in a ship whose American boatswain entertained himself with reading a pile of old Norwegian newspapers. On one occasion the American started up from his reading with a shriek, and tore one of the newspapers into a thousand pieces, adding in perfect Norwegian, 'Married — to another man. While I was away.' Ellida at once draws attention to the significance of this by closing her eyes and saying, half to herself, 'He said that?' Lyngstrand continues:

Well, now the remarkable part is coming — that I shall never forget as long as I live. For he added, and that quite quietly, too: 'But she is mine, and mine she shall remain. And she shall follow me, even if I have to come home and fetch her, as a drowned man from the dark sea.'   (Act I) (VII. 48)

The menace is quickly seen to apply to Ellida herself, though the gloating malevolence, and Lyngstrand's providentially coincidental hearing of it, make a ham-fisted piece of exposition. (Incidentally, Lyngstrand builds on to this memory by speaking of the American as an 'avenger', which turns out to be completely misleading.) Ellida soon remarks to Arnholm that it may not be so mad a story as he evidently thinks it, and the revelation of the following Act is prepared for.

Unlike many of Ibsen's curtains, the one that follows is almost completely undramatic, as indeed most of the curtains in this play are. It is altogether a leisurely work, and the climax of Act One has already been reached with Lyngstrand's narration, well before the curtain falls. What is surprising is that a craftsman of Ibsen's reputation should bring in the menace of the Stranger in such an awkward, roundabout way. One explanation could be that when he does appear the Stranger is far less tenacious and vengeful than Lyngstrand's account would lead us to believe. It is as though Ibsen were seeking to impress this menace on us all the more determinedly, since it was not deeply in him to provide it when the time came.

The mention of the Stranger having murdered the captain of his ship is an attempt at impressing us in a similar way. Ellida is quite clear about it – the Stranger confessed to her that he had stabbed the captain, and this lends a certain grimness to his character, even though he protested, without explanation, that he had acted justly. Nothing more specific is ever said about the killing, and when he does appear grimness is one of the last qualities one would associate with him.

Meanwhile, however, the whole of Act Two has to pass. There is indeed very little development of the main subject, and perhaps there could be none. It needs to be established that Ellida has had a child by Wangel, that she swore fidelity to the Stranger before her marriage, and that she is cut off from her family, from Wangel and his children. Once this is done, there remains only the confrontation with the Stranger, managed in two meetings, at the second of which Ellida rejects him, whereupon the play is essentially over. There is no complication of the situation, once it is revealed that the Stranger is back. All that can be provided, dramatically, is the progress of Ellida's fear, an inward feeling not constantly provoked or altered by new incidents. It is also essential to show the family life from which Ellida is excluded, so that her decision to remain with Wangel may carry some weight. For this reason, no doubt, the episodes with Hilde and Bolette, Lyngstrand and Arnholm are introduced, though they are not needed for the furtherance of the plot and take up too much time for the sustaining of dramatic interest. Every act begins with several minutes of their casual conversation, and two-thirds of Act Five is devoted to them before the brief appearance of the Stranger at the end.

At his first appearance, in Act Three, the stage directions require the Stranger to be got up in a surprisingly unprepossessing way. It is hard to know whether a man with bushy red hair and beard, wearing a tam o'shanter, would look terrifying to a Norwegian audience of the late nineteenth century, though one would have thought not. In fact, Ibsen gives the impression, not that he means any ludicrous quality in the Stranger, but that the Stranger should act in a harmless way, without the least sign of a threat. When he first addresses Ellida he speaks in a low voice, and, though he makes clear that he has come to take her away, he continues to speak gently, if imperturbably. Her overwrought reaction seems to be caused by her imaginings, rather than his actual presence: she stares at him, staggers backward, and utters a half choked cry, pleading with him not to look at her with his terrifying eyes, but nothing he does could in itself produce terror. When she persists, recoiling again in fear, holding her head in her hands, and groaning in her anguish, he merely asks whether she does not want to go with him, and when she replies 'in despair', 'Don't look at me like that,' though he does at this moment climb over the fence, which produces a paralysis of terror in her, his advance is only in order to tell her one thing before he goes. He approaches her 'cautiously', telling her repeatedly not to be afraid, and merely reminds her, still without violence of tone or action, of the vows they made years ago to be faithful to one another. He does not even accept Wangel's interpretation, that he is laying a 'claim' to Ellida. For him there is no claim: he is merely reminding her of how she once felt, and affirms that if she is to come at all she must come freely. All this is as far from the former murderer and avenger presented by Lyngstrand as it is from the elemental force which at other times the Stranger is made to represent. Ellida's reaction appears exaggerated, in this encounter, and we are left wondering whether she has any real cause for her terror at all.

The difficulty of reconciling the Stranger, as a man, with the symbolical overtones he is required to carry is at the root here. To suit the tremendous cruel and vindictive force which Lyngstrand's words suggest, a man more akin to the Heathcliff of *Wuthering Heights* would be appropriate. The sheer incongruity of a Heathcliff in the cosy atmosphere of Wangel's home is a mark of the difficulty with which Ibsen was faced. The Stranger as we see him from the text is more akin to an enlightened, liberal and selfless lover than the figure we were led to expect. The horror is all in the eyes, rather than in the rest of the face or body, and so can make no visual impression on the audience.

The result is that, when the Stranger returns a second time to ask Ellida to make her final decision, there is no correspondence between what he is and what he stands for. If Ellida were merely called upon to choose between a former lover, even one with whom she had performed a kind of marriage ceremony, and Wangel, she would be in a different situation. She is not in love with the Stranger, though she is frightened of him. She has no prospect of any future with him, no home, no country even to which she can go. All he offers is a cabin on the ship, now in the fjord and about to leave, whereas she loves Wangel – or so she said in Act One, though she seems to forget that now – and has a good deal of comfort to expect from staying with him. If she felt any personal attraction to the Stranger, there would be a genuine choice, realisable in terms of the people on stage. But she has not, she has only what Wangel explicitly calls – there is not much mystery about its nature after all, it is all too literally defined – 'the craving for the boundless, the infinite, the unattainable', 'the concentrated power of the sea'. Ellida has no craving for the Stranger as a man. So the genuine choice which Wangel tries to offer her is not what it seems. Ibsen clearly has in mind a husband at the opposite extreme from Nora's Torvald, a man who does not dominate his wife, but who unselfishly offers her a complete freedom to go her own way. As an offer from a husband to a wife, to free her to go back to another lover, this could be moving, and Ellida's decision to stay with Wangel might be a telling moment, as gratitude and recognition of his real love for her conflicted with her earlier passionate attachment. But Ellida has no passionate attachment to the Stranger, only a fear engendered, not by what he is, but by his symbolical implications.

The Stranger still remains the almost passive, and certainly un-assertive figure that he was on his first appearance. It is true that, then as now, he steps over the dividing fence into the garden, which can in performance, for all its simplicity, be a thrilling representation of what his threat might be. The defending palisade is no obstruction to him. Yet as soon as Wangel – not a man of very strong purpose, or so Ellida complains earlier on – intervenes to threaten him with arrest for the murder of some years before, the Stranger draws a revolver not to shoot either Ellida or Wangel, but himself. The attraction of the sea for Ellida is supposed to be much more powerful than that action of the sea's representative suggests. And finally, when Wangel repeats his offer to Ellida to 'choose in freedom and on your own responsibility', Ellida's decision to reject the Stranger does not throw him into confusion, or cause him to renew his plea: he simply gives up.

ELLIDA ...I shall never go with you after this!
THE STRANGER You will not?
ELLIDA (clinging to Wangel) I shall never go away from you after this.
WANGEL Ellida, Ellida!
THE STRANGER So it is over?
ELLIDA Yes. Over for all time.
THE STRANGER I can see it. There is something here stronger than my will.

(Act 5) (VII. 121)

With that he vaults over the fence and disappears once and for all. The 'avenger' has never put in an appearance: the Stranger represents a suitor as fair-minded as Wangel, and given the clear advantages of remaining in her own home, Ellida's decision is not surprising. Emily Brontë's Cathy could not have given up Heathcliff so easily. We are surely driven to conclude that this smoothly achieved victory for marriage and simple happiness is no more telling than Rebecca West's defeat. Ibsen has turned the tables, but just as there was no real reason why Rebecca and Rosmer should have killed themselves, so there is too easy a conquest for Ellida over her man of straw. The endings are contrived with little concern for intelligible motivation, rather for the sake of the contrast than out of any necessity arising from the terms of the plays themselves.

8

Hedda Gabler

Of all the plays, *Hedda Gabler* is the one on which those critics who are generally favourable to Ibsen seem most in accordance. It is an exception among his works – there is no possibility of supposing him to be setting a social problem for solution, and symbolism plays only a subordinate part, in comparison with *The Wild Duck*. The ruthlessness of the central character was strong enough for at least initial comparison to be made with the starker tragedies of traditional theatre, even classical tragedy, and it has been praised by critics whose views are not easily disregarded. Henry James, for instance, wrote of 'the firm hand that weaves the web, the deep and ingenious use made of the material' (p. 252):

Wrought with admirable closeness is the whole tissue of relations between the five people whom the author sets in motion and on whose behalf he asks of us so few concessions. That is for the most part the accomplished thing in Ibsen, the thing that converts his provincialism into artistic urbanity. He puts *us* to no expense worth speaking of – he takes all the expense himself. I mean that he thinks out our entertainment for us and shapes it of thinkable things, the passions, the idiosyncrasies, the cupidities and jealousies, the strivings and struggles, the joys and sufferings of men.

There are generalities in that, it is true, which may give rise to doubt: James was adept at not committing himself irrevocably, when courtesy was a large consideration, and he had reasons for going cautiously where *Hedda Gabler* was concerned. Disconcertingly, his whole account of the play tended to reverse his opinion of Ibsen expressed only a few weeks earlier (see p. 204 below). A closer look reveals that he has concentrated at first on the closeness of the tissue of relationships, and then moved by a hiatus to praising Ibsen for taking all the expense himself: there is admiration for technical accomplishment, but not a deeply considered judgment of what counts in drama, while at the same time a reference to 'provincialism' has been allowed to slip in. Still, so far as these words go, they are clearly laudatory, and James, we may assume, did not mean to imply any serious qualification. Even Mary McCarthy, whose criticism of Ibsen in the 1930's was strongly worded, still called *Hedda* a 'near masterpiece'.

James does, however, go on to say things which prompt one to question him a little further. He observes of Hedda herself that she is a character 'complicated, strange, irreconcilable, infernal'; she is 'infinitely perverse', and, blame indeed, 'a perfectly ill-regulated person'. Yet within the same page James goes on to say that 'one isn't so sure she is wicked, and by no means sure...that she is disagreeable. She is various and sinuous and graceful, complicated and natural; she suffers, she struggles, she is human.' The change of front is startling, and when James does not explain how infinite perversity can be reconciled with naturalness, 'infernal' with 'human', or ill-regulatedness with grace, we have some reason for withholding assent. Was James thinking at times more of the actress herself than of Hedda?

The wickedness and perverse cruelty of some of Hedda's actions is undeniable. If Ibsen had any model for her in mind, it might well have been Medea: as Medea kills her lover's child and exults in the destruction, so Hedda destroys the child of Eilert Løvborg's brain, his manuscript. Yet even Medea is less perverse than Hedda, since Medea carries out her revenge with an exultant relish, releasing her whole hatred of the injustice done to her by Jason. Hedda artificially creates ground for despair in Løvborg, though he has done her no wrong, and then drives him to what she thinks of as a 'noble' suicide. It is calculating, not emotional, perverse by contrast with the all-too-natural flood of passion that Euripides' Medea lets loose. Even Iago, whom Hedda also resembles a little, has jealousy, spite, and enjoyment of his own cunning to spur him on. By comparison with him, she is petty and mean.

That Hedda was 'corrosive' was admitted by Elizabeth Robins, the actress whom James knew as the chief interpreter of Ibsen on the stage in his day, and who may well have tempered the edge of James's comments about him. Miss Robins gave in fact one of the best defences of Hedda that are to be had, one to which James could properly have paid respect. What struck her first was the same point as the one Ibsen had stressed in his private notes, that Hedda was 'in...revolt against those commonplace surroundings that the bookworm she had married thought so "elegant"'; she had an 'unashamed selfishness', a 'scorn of so-called womanly qualities', and 'above all, [a] strong need to put some meaning into her life, even at the cost of borrowing it, or stealing the meaning out of someone else's'. Hedda had first thought to find such a meaning in Løvborg and, though his accounts of his debauchery had repelled her, she was still sufficiently aroused, when he returned, to want his company again. The course of the play shows her disappointment: she was destined never to have for herself 'the man whose faith in his own genius, faith in life, had given Hedda the one respite she had known from mean standards, mean fears' – the standards and fears of the Tesman household and its comfortable mediocrity. The loss of Løvborg, and the prospect of being reduced to living not only with a husband like Tesman, but also in the embraces of a blackmailer like Brack, drove Hedda to the one gesture which still had any meaning left for her: the killing of herself 'beautifully' with a bullet through the temple. On such terms, Elizabeth Robins was able to see Hedda as pitiable in her hungry loneliness, to see her as tragic: 'Insolent and evil she was, but some great celebrators of Ibsen have thought more meanly of Hedda than the text warrants.'

This is not far from Ibsen's own view of Hedda in his preliminary notes. 'The pale, apparently cold beauty,' he wrote. 'Great demands on life and happiness,' and again, 'Hedda's desperation is a conviction that life must offer so many possibilities of happiness, but that she can't catch sight of any of them. It is the want of a goal in life that torments her.' This, if the play gave more weight to it, would be convincing. The difficulty is that Hedda herself never makes any 'great demands': paradox lies at the root, and, as Ibsen says, the conviction that there *must* be happiness is not a source of strength, it *is* her desperation. The only conceivable expression of her need for a meaning or for happiness that we see is in Act One, when she hears Tesman saying goodbye to his aunt; the stage directions read:

(Miss Tesman goes out through the hall door. Tesman follows her. The door remains half open. Tesman can be heard repeating his message to Aunt Rina and thanking her for the slippers.)

(During this Hedda is walking about the room. She raises her arms and clenches her fists as though in a frenzy. Then she draws the curtains open, at the French windows, and stands there looking out.)   (Act I) (VII. 182-3)

When Tesman asks what she is doing, she is calm again, and observes how yellow and withered the leaves on the trees are.

Hedda's private frenzy is partly caused by Tesman's cosiness at this moment. But it is also caused by the knowledge that she is pregnant, and of the two it seems the latter that gives her the most pain, perhaps disgust. (As Peggy Ashcroft played her, she was continually sliding her hands down her belly, as if to thrust out the unwanted child.) So it is not exactly a demand for happiness that we see, it is the life-denying mood at which she has already arrived. Both the loss of summer, and the expected child, as well as Tesman, make her unhappy, but we see no spirit of rebellion in her, only frenzy.

Later, Hedda confesses to Løvborg (in Act Two) that what he thinks of as 'our common lust for life' was not really that. Still unmarried, she was curious about his erotic adventures, but unwilling to offer him love herself. His stories were intriguing, but 'there was an imminent danger that the game would become a reality'; his offer of caresses she calls 'violence'. Thus even before she bound herself to Tesman she made no demand, and suffered no externally imposed frustration, but felt an imperative need to stifle pleasure. Nowhere do we hear of any positive wish she has had, at any time, until the end of Act Two.

For the rest, most of Hedda's actions are uncontrolledly trivial, like a spoilt child's: she deliberately insults her husband's dear old aunt or pulls Thea Elvsted's hair. It is by such actions, and by pretending to shoot at Brack, by shocked revelling in the accounts of Løvborg's earlier libertinism, that any demand for happiness she may have reveals its existence, if Ibsen's paradox is accepted. That is not to say that the demand does not exist. It is believable that it does, not only because Ibsen says so, but because human motives are infinitely complex, and in real life one might never be certain of the contrary. The difficulty is that there is not one word or gesture or action of Hedda's, until her apparently Dionysian ideal for Løvborg is expressed, that directly reveals it: it all has to be surmised. In short, there is no dramatic realisation of her need for a meaning. If James had been right, Ibsen would have put the audience to less expense than this. As the play stands, the spectator is continually obliged to shape the character for himself, looking in vain for the clues to what after all, as the private notes reveal, was the author's intention.

Hedda is commonly seen not as a frustrated seeker after happiness, but as a rebel against conventionality. In Ingmar Bergman's production, she was placed within earshot of Tesman and his aunt in their initial conversation, and could be seen by the audience raging at their stupidity. This is a means of making unparadoxical sense; a criticism of it might be that Ibsen himself did not provide for it, but it illustrates the way in which producers and commentators fill in his void. On the other hand, the conventional characters are themselves drawn so conventionally, with so little insight, as to make Ibsen seem to identify himself with Hedda in opposition to it. Tesman is so entirely a booby, a bookworm, a nincompoop, in everything he does. His ignorance about marital relations, and apparent unawareness that Hedda may be with child after their honeymoon, is heavily handled. By comparison with his counterpart in *Uncle Vanya*, Professor Serebryakov, or with Anna Karenina's husband, Tesman is a stereotype, with no degree of sympathy or awareness. Mrs Elvsted is simply a lady of prim devotion to ideals, a bluestocking, and Brack almost a moustachioed villain, in spirit, without thought for anything but his own advantage. Chekhov presents more subtly a roughly similar society – *Uncle Vanya* reads very much like a restatement of the situations of *Hedda* in less cut-and-dried terms – with a great deal more compassion, and intelligent interest in all parties. Ibsen's people are like grotesques in the rigidity of their personalities. Hedda may see the world in such a monotone; in a play a greater balance is needed.

The monotone is so pervasive that it affects even events before the time of the play. Løvborg's life before he met Hedda, and at the time of their first acquaintance, is usually referred to by them both as a time when the 'joy of life' was at its height. The action itself depends on the idea that Hedda will regain that time for him by challenging him to be a man again. Yet his 'lust for life', which shocked and intrigued her so much, is given no more definition than that he would be 'out on the razzle for days and nights on end'. Even Løvborg's enjoyment was of a kind that is conventionally recognised, rather than a liberation from what people like Brack might consider exciting. This curious turning back to the standards of the very people for whom Hedda displays contempt becomes a weakness of the play as a whole.

The mainspring of the action is Hedda's decision to try and bring Løvborg back to what he once was. Since those earlier days she has married Tesman, and Løvborg has gone off to the North, where Thea Elvsted has proved to be a new inspiration to him. He has written his masterpiece, the new book which now threatens to install him in the university chair Tesman was hoping for. (A piece of unreality, this, if there is any in the play: Løvborg's book sounds like a best-selling work of popular philosophising on the future state of Man; it has nothing to do with Tesman's line of country, which is mediaeval technology, and could not be regarded by the university as a claim to any chair Tesman might hold.) Yet although Løvborg was never capable of writing this masterpiece while he was with Hedda, she does not see in the fact that he has now written it any evidence of his present 'lust for life'. That is lacking, it appears, despite his success, and the play turns on Hedda's experiment, aimed at restoring it to him. She seizes the occasion of Brack's inviting Løvborg to join him and Tesman with some other friends at dinner. If Løvborg can accept that challenge, and return from it successfully, Hedda will be satisfied. But the demands on life which she thus makes prove to be ambiguous in every way. There is nothing in her challenge that shows a desire that does not thwart itself in the moment it appears.

It is unclear why Hedda stakes such hopes on such an occasion. There is to be a dinner at Brack's, starting at about seven-thirty, and Løvborg is to retire to a private room with Tesman to read his manuscript to him. Brack assures Løvborg, however, that they intend to have a 'lively time' – a phrase which he means Hedda to understand in an erotic sense – and at first Løvborg declines. There is a difficulty for him here, since he is a reformed alcoholic, and is not inclined to start drinking again. But for Hedda his initial refusal to accept even one drink, in her own house, is a sign of the degree to which Thea Elvsted has destroyed his courage; he must go to the party at Brack's, to prove himself a man.

Again Hedda behaves conventionally, asking Løvborg to act entirely in accordance with what Brack and perhaps Tesman, when they are not being respectable citizens, most believe in. (It is true that Tesman does not go on to the soirée at 'Mademoiselle Diana's', and possibly Brack does not go there either, on this occasion.) Exactly the same association between debauchery and exultant living is made here as in *Ghosts*, in relation to Captain Alving, and with a similar ambiguity. For it is not very clear what Hedda expects to happen, whether she expects Løvborg to drink moderately, exercising due self-control – but she has just seen how he took one drink after another as soon as he succumbed to her temptation to drink one – or whether she expects him to take part in the 'liveliness' too. The difficulty is that she both sees him as a kind of wine-god, and as a good boy who will be back home inside two-and-half hours:

HEDDA Ten o'clock – then he'll come back. I can see him now. With vine-leaves in his hair. Splendid and confident.
MRS ELVSTED Yes, if only he were to.
HEDDA And then, you see – he will have gained control of himself again. Then he will be a free man all his days.
MRS ELVSTED Oh, God, yes – if only he would come just as you see him.
HEDDA He will come as I see him and in no other way! (*getting up and drawing closer to her*) You may doubt him as much as you like. I believe in him. And now we shall see.
MRS ELVSTED There's something underlying all this, for you, Hedda!
HEDDA Yes, there is. For once in my life I want to have power over a human destiny.   (Act 2) (VII. 230)

If Hedda is serious about the vine-leaves, she can hardly be serious about Løvborg returning at ten. Indeed in Act Three, when she and Mrs Elvsted are thinking, early next morning, where the three men can be, Hedda implicitly mocks the idea that Løvborg, as she puts it, is 'sitting, with vine-leaves in his hair, reading his manuscript'. At that moment she is clearly aware of the incongruity. Yet she can hardly be expecting any liberation for him out of a night spent at some such place as Mademoiselle Diana's –

vine-leaves are equally incongruous there. Either way, what she expects must turn out to be a very bourgeois Bacchus.

Ibsen fails again to supply events which correspond with the ideas his play is supposed to be concerned with. By the end of Act Three, when the second instance occurs, Løvborg has been to the party, got drunk, lost the manuscript of his book, which Tesman has found and left with Hedda, and has returned to Hedda in despair. Hedda's plan has failed: he has no self-mastery, no confidence, no vine-leaves. But again ambiguity is the keynote. Like the party at Brack's, the manuscript has a value that changes from instant to instant. In the first place, it is not self-evident that the manuscript is the masterpiece they all say it is – it sounds like something more commonplace, though the audience does not seem meant for certain to draw that conclusion. But then again, though it is the great achievement of Løvborg's life, a work of genius far beyond Tesman's range, it is also the fruit of his 'unworthy' collaboration with Thea Elvsted. It is both a manifestation of his regained energy, his 'lust for life', and a proof that he has never had any such energy since he left Hedda.

Løvborg's reactions to the loss of the manuscript are equally hard to understand. This is how he relates it all to Thea Elvsted:

LØVBORG I've torn my own life to pieces. So I might as well tear up my life's work as well.

MRS ELVSTED And that's what you did last night!

LØVBORG Yes, I tell you. Into a thousand pieces. And scattered them out in the fjord. A long way out. At least it's fresh salt water. Let them drift in it. Drift with the current and the wind. And after a while they'll sink. Deeper and deeper. Just as I will, Thea. (Act 3) (VII. 247)

All this is untrue. Løvborg has not torn up the manuscript, he has merely lost it, and there is no reason why he should not tell Thea this. The reason he does give, to Hedda, for the deception is unconvincing – he compares the loss of the manuscript with the loss of a child, and says that if he were a father coming home to announce that he had lost his child (in a brothel, he implies), he would do far better to say that the child was dead – the mother would prefer that. This is absurd, for it is surely better, with a child as with a manuscript, to believe it lost rather than at the bottom of the sea, so long as there is any hope of finding it again, and Løvborg lost his manuscript only a few hours ago. If, on the other hand, he were to tell Thea it was lost, she would look for it, and Hedda might hesitate to burn it; more important, he would not have the motive for suicide he now seems to have, and the play would be unable to proceed with the neat economy Ibsen contrives for it. But it is contrivance. Løvborg and Thea have no occasion for such despair; Løvborg is simply serving the dramatist's overriding purpose when he misinforms Thea, and since Løvborg knows perfectly well that the manuscript is not destroyed, only lost, we believe in his suicide rather because we too have accepted his story than because we see him in a desperate situation. This one backsliding on the path of temperance and the one moment of carelessness about the manuscript are comparatively trivial, and we have seen nothing in Løvborg to make it seem that it would take so small an upset, as the temporary loss actually is, to make him end his life. Like Rosmer, Løvborg falls from idealising enthusiasm to total despair on very little compulsion.

The same ambiguity, which allowed Elizabeth Robins to interpret Hedda sympathetically as a woman who needed a meaning in life, allows James McFarlane to see her above all as a woman who is determined to control others. Professor McFarlane too has evidence from Ibsen's private notes for this, as Miss Robins had for her interpretation. 'The demonic thing about Hedda,' Ibsen observed to himself, 'is that she wants to exert influence over another person.' Of this there is evidence in the text itself, when Hedda explicitly claims to want to control Løvborg. It is the savagery of her failure, as Professor McFarlane puts it, that drives Hedda to kill herself, and Ibsen is inviting us not to find Hedda tragic, as Miss Robins did, but rather to join him in a kind of Flaubertian analysis. Hedda's attempt on Løvborg's freedom is

an aspect of existence that had always roused Ibsen to fury: any interference of this order in other people's lives, any tampering with their liberties or their efforts at self-realization, particularly if done under the guise of altruism or in the name of righteousness, at once drew his anger...Whereas Ibsen's clergymen... stand by ready to direct their fellows into orgies of self-denial, Hedda is a pagan priestess, driven by a vision of Dionysian beauty, whispering of vine-leaves in the hair and the thrill of beautiful death. The sources of their interfering zeal are very different, the relentlessness of it is common.

McFarlane, *The Oxford Ibsen* (III. 14)

McFarlane sees all the characters as involved in the same search for the power to dominate – it is for him the theme of the whole play.

This can be readily admitted, in a sense. It is one of the weaknesses, already mentioned, that the characters are so one-sidedly presented that sympathy, and awareness of the general situation, scarcely enter their heads. (Some exception may have to be made for Mrs Elvsted, but McFarlane makes out a case against any supposed altruism in her.) This is an aspect of living that Ibsen is particularly aware of. At the same time, one essential issue of the play is the possibility of freedom. Though Hedda says, in the passage just quoted, that she wants to feel for once in her life that she can control a human destiny, she also says, only a few seconds before, that she wants Løvborg to be free – 'Then he will have gained control of himself again. He'll be a free man for the rest of his life.' Here is the same ambiguity once again – Hedda controls only in order to liberate, and one cannot call her interference an attempt on Løvborg's freedom without explaining that. Ibsen, having left motivation unexplained, provides scope for many interpretations, but warrant for none. The same is true of the final scene, the scene of Hedda's suicide.

Ibsen's contemporaries were bewildered by this final scene. Halvdan Koht relates that in Norway the most common words used to describe Hedda herself were 'puzzling', 'improbable', 'incredible'. No meaning or purpose was apparent, simply a suicide ending an absolutely pointless life. This is a normal unthinking reaction. Yet a diametrically contrary view is possible. Eva le Gallienne, for instance, an actress who has translated the play and published a long commentary on it, sees in Hedda's suicide a Romantic fulfilment, a finding in death of beauty which Hedda was unable to find in life. There is something to be said for this view too, seeing the play through Hedda's own eyes. Hedda does urge Løvborg to kill himself beautifully and, when she hears that he has shot himself or been shot in the abdomen (whether by accident or not is never apparent), she has only one other person from whom she can expect a beautiful death, herself. Ibsen meant, if we take a Romantic view, to make a double statement: Hedda's life was pointless, yet she chose at least the beauty of shooting herself in the temple. (When Maggie Smith played her, she shot herself in full view of the audience, admiring herself in a mirror as she did so. There was no doubt there about the aesthetic value as Hedda saw it, and as Maggie Smith did.)

But these are matters of interpretation, not of realisation. The play could have infinite ambiguities without being impressive as drama, and the critical crux is in the fact that, all through the final speeches, people speak more to further the climax intended by Ibsen than in realisation of their own characters.

A few moments before the final suicide, Brack reveals to Hedda that he knows she gave Løvborg the pistol with which he shot himself, and at once Hedda, like all Ibsen characters subjected to blackmail, sees herself completely trapped, with no recourse but to yield or to kill herself:

HEDDA But all this revolting business has nothing to do with me.
BRACK No. But you will be obliged to answer, under interrogation, the question why you gave Ejlert Løvborg the pistol. And what conclusion will be drawn from the fact that you gave it to him?
HEDDA (*lowers her head*) That's true. I didn't think about that.
BRACK Well, fortunately there is nothing to fear so long as I keep quiet.
HEDDA (*looks up at him*) And so I am in your power, Mr Brack. From now on I am at your beck and call.
BRACK (*whispers more softly*) Dearest Hedda...believe me...I shall not abuse the position.
HEDDA In your power, all the same. Subject to your will and your demands. Not free! Not free! (*she gets up violently*) No! That's a thought I can't bear. Never! (Act 4) (VII. 266)

Like Pastor Manders, threatened by Engstrand, Hedda immediately sees that her position is impossible, even though nothing is said to show why it should be so. What inference might be drawn from the fact that her pistol may be found by Løvborg's body is open to guessing. Unless Hedda voluntarily admits that she gave it to him to kill himself with – and she has seen no difficulty in lying about the manuscript – it might well be supposed by the police either that he took it without permission, or that she lent it to him for some purpose which she supposed harmless. Hedda need not see any danger here at all, despite her instant acquiescence in the idea that there is a threat to her married life. Such crude motivations were the stuff of French intrigue-drama.

Ibsen is generally said to have progressed beyond them.

In draughts, a move requires an immediate response, on pain of being 'huffed'. A piece moved forward into jeopardy has to be taken, or a penalty is suffered. In chess, on the other hand, a more complex development becomes possible by virtue of the rule that pieces may be taken or not taken as the player thinks best, so that, when several pieces are threatening or *en prise*, a situation laden with suspense is built up. Ibsen here in effect plays draughts. He presents a new situation about which the characters are not given time to reflect, but to which they are made to respond instantly, so that, whereas in situations off-stage such circumstances tend to be weighed up at least a little, and people in a situation of conflict test each other out, in his plays a gesture of blackmail, however implausible, has to be instantly accepted. One can agree with Raymond Williams's phrase about 'the mechanical logic of Hedda's destruction', but not that it is 'completely convincing'. A crude mechanism is its only strong feature.

The decision to commit suicide is made to seem more imperative in the next piece of conversation. Tesman suddenly and very conveniently shows no concern about Hedda, and positively thrusts her into Brack's arms. For a convention-respecting academic he is surprisingly untroubled by thoughts that from now on he will be spending every evening with Mrs Elvsted, piecing together the notes for a reconstitution of Løvborg's book, while Hedda will be entertained in her own home by the other man. (Equally conveniently, he still does not reveal that he knows Hedda burned the manuscript.) The lack of interest in her could only come from a character as devoid of awareness as the characters in this play generally are:

HEDDA ...But how shall I get through the evenings out here.

TESMAN (*turning over the leaves of the notebook*) Oh, I'm sure Judge Brack will be so kind as to come out and keep you company, anyway.

BRACK (*in the armchair, calls out gaily*) Glad to, every single night, Mrs Tesman. We'll have a rare old time together, the two of us!   (Act 4) (VII. 268)

The purpose of Tesman's acquiescence − he was anxious, earlier, at the idea of Løvborg spending even one evening alone with his wife − is to channel Hedda's course to suicide. The blackmailing position of Brack is, at its absolute best, not enough to force

Hedda to that, so long as she remains able to arrange her life so that she and Brack are never alone together. If that becomes impossible, as Tesman's nonchalant remarks indicate it will be, suicide becomes increasingly her only way out. Ibsen serves his overriding purpose by making Tesman so extraordinarily compliant.

The suicide is not a free act, as one theory would require. Though Hedda's first reaction to Brack's blackmail is to realise she is 'not free', she does not achieve freedom by killing herself. She dies as much because she is afraid of scandal and detests sexual love, as because she is brave enough to pull the trigger. But again one notes how Ibsen is more concerned with directing his audience than with the human aspects of the situation. Nobody shows any interest in Løvborg's death by grieving for him, not even Thea, and they all go on with their affairs very promptly. But the moment of Hedda's death, too, is not presented as something about which one has feelings. In its general outline, the scene resembles a Victorian melodrama in which the maiden takes her life rather than suffer a fate worse than death. If it does not ultimately make that impression as a whole, that is because it is not designed to be moving in any way. It might be supposed, for instance, that a husband's feelings on unexpectedly discovering his wife's dead body would be food for a dramatist's imagination. No such idea enters Ibsen's mind. His principal concern is with making the audience see the contrast between her death and Løvborg's, and Tesman's only function is to bring that out.

'Shot herself! Shot herself in the temple! Think of that!' 'Think of that', Tesman's stock phrase, is all he can muster even at such a moment. For the rest, the audience is presumably making a series of mental reflections, on such lines as these: 'So whereas Løvborg killed himself (if it wasn't an accident) by destroying himself basely in his physical self, Hedda has gone one step further and destroyed her brain, the seat of the mind, the higher self. Løvborg's way was only a minor death, the major death is to let the bullet destroy one's thinking powers altogether.' Any death-wound would in fact destroy them, but the symbolism is interpretable in no other way.

It is important too, for Ibsen's purpose, that Tesman should use the same word as Hedda used, earlier. The natural expression for him would be to say that Hedda shot herself in the head – which he does, in Michael Meyer's translation. All other translators make him say 'in the temple', which has the loftier associations of Hedda's own word, and is in any case accurate. But, in doing so, they help to stress once again how Ibsen's main purpose is not only to make Tesman reveal where the bullet struck (why should Tesman mention it at all?), but to make explicit that it has symbolical significance. Ibsen's detachment is further emphasised by what Jens Kruuse calls the 'farcical stage directions, such as Hedda "putting out her head between the hangings" and aping Jørgen Tesman...' (p. 56). There is indeed something of the Punch-and-Judy show, if not of 'grand guignol', in this appearance of Hedda's as she uses words which clearly reveal to the audience her intention to kill herself. The doll-like head gives a touch of grotesqueness to the Romantic pretensions of Hedda's suicide, and is not untypical of Ibsen in the later plays. There is a similar black humour in the scenes with Irene, for instance, in *When We Dead Awaken*, but the detachment which gives rise to it is often, as with Tesman, rather a lack of concern with the characters as human beings.

Thus Brack's final comment is also not meant to reveal his feelings so much as to make a point for the dramatist. 'But, good God Almighty...people don't do such things' – that is a dig at 'comfortable bourgeois assumptions': people do do such things, when they live as much in opposition to conventionality as Hedda does – some such thought is likely to enter one's head. Once again, we are left to suppose that Brack is incapable of any other emotion.

These simple thrusts at unamiable characters are shared by Ibsen with Flaubert, who is capable at times of equal callousness, and equal indifference to subtler differentiation. Yet we do not have the sense, in *Hedda Gabler*, that Ibsen is anything like so involved as Flaubert was (however ambiguously) with Emma Bovary. Flaubert may mock Emma's romantic fancies with pitiless savagery, yet he is still partly identified with her, and this shows.

Where Ibsen presents Hedda's desperation as an accomplished fact, Flaubert shows the process that leads to Emma's. Emma's demands for happiness are explicit, even too explicit for Léon and Rodolphe, and her keen erotic pleasure is never stifled, only corrupted by lack of sufficient response. Hedda, by contrast, has never had more than a prurient interest in erotic love. Emma's dissatisfaction with her husband is comprehensible, yet Charles is never a Tesman: he is a good country doctor, apart from his one blunder, a man respected by the peasants, and with such touching devotion to Emma that there are times when she even warms to his goodness of heart – only to realise more bitterly, it is true, how unsatisfying to her that is. Such a combination of perversity and goodness as Emma shows may have been what James thought he saw in Hedda. But it is not there. She is the most null of all Ibsen's characters.

Yet in Hedda Ibsen is drawing yet another *alter ego*. By the time he came to write about her, the repeated failure of almost all his characters to achieve anything at all (Ellida Wangel is the sole exception) must have been borne in on him. Their supposed ideals were always vague, they were frustrated by failure of nerve, by their own passivity, or even by their own insistence on failure. At best, they slammed the door and sought for what they wanted elsewhere. The nullity of vision this implies is reflected in Hedda. Ibsen said of her that she made great demands, and yet gave her none that she did not contradict in the moment of making them. Realising that, he saw there was nothing left but suicide, which through Hedda could be arranged. But his own self still remained, and like Peer he could still peel one more covering from the onion, stand by and watch Hedda's death from a yet deeper point of ironic vantage. It was not his own suicide, and there were voids beyond for contemplation, through Borkman and Rubek. The process need never end till natural death.

This coldness distinguishes Ibsen from Flaubert. He feels as coldly towards Hedda as he does towards the rest; what distinguishes her from the ordinary 'bourgeois' characters is that she simultaneously desires and detests, so that neither her life nor her death can be called a desire or a fulfilment, a despair or a defeat. She is poised constantly on the pin-point where the opposites coalesce, and perhaps it is on that account that discussion can spin on endlessly round her. The company in which she lives, on the other hand, is almost all without nuances (Løvborg is an exception who comes nearer to Hedda's synthesis): straightforwardly drawn pawns, who allow the bourgeois to be mocked without hindrance. Ibsen includes no idealists in the Chekhovian spirit, no Astrov, no positive reformer with practical aims, however unrealisable they prove. The absence of any particular goal produces a sense of fatuity: of course a woman in Hedda's position is likely to take her life, but there has been no strong contrast to her, and the dismal prospect of the book Tesman and Thea are probably going to concoct is like a *coup de grâce*. This comprehensive cynicism, coupled with the one-dimensional characters who are made to serve its turn, is the reason why *Hedda Gabler* comes off poorly in any comparison with *Uncle Vanya*, or *Phèdre*, or *Medea*. A meanness of spirit runs through the play from beginning to end.

The comparison with Chekhov, in particular, can tell us a good deal. Though it is impossible that *Uncle Vanya* should have been originally conceived as a counterpart to *Hedda* (the original version, *The Wood Demon*, was first conceived two years before *Hedda* appeared, but was recast in 1890, and not finally completed with its new title till 1896), the similarities are remarkably close. In both plays there is a character at the centre, frustrated by the humdrum life he or she is forced to lead. However much Hedda and Vanya differ in their humanity and power to attract our sympathy, their situations are closely similar. Almost all the remaining characters echo each other, despite the differing interrelationships. Hedda is married to the pedantic Tesman. Vanya used to venerate the equally pedantic Serebryakov, though it is Helen who is married to the Professor. Hedda seeks release from her frustration through Løvborg, Vanya through Helen, and both speak of a Dionysian liberation: where Hedda expects 'vine-leaves in the hair' for Løvborg, Vanya urges Helen to 'plunge into the sea and become a mermaid' (but he means it – he genuinely wants her to let her hair down.) The resemblance between Astrov and Brack is purely formal – in character they have nothing in common – but both are 'outsiders', and, while Astrov and Vanya compete for Helen's love, Løvborg and Brack are rivals in Hedda's eyes. Finally, Sonya and Thea Elvsted are serious-minded, dedicated women, devoted to idealistic aims. Again they differ in their relationships, but both plays end with a scene in which they are seen trying to piece together the broken lives and almost ruined work of the men they love. A basically similar pattern runs through both works.

The essential difference lies in the ending. *The Wood Demon* had ended with the suicide of the character who later was named Vanya, though even in this earlier version the suicide took place in the last Act but one, not at the climactic position where Ibsen places Hedda's. As time went on, Chekhov was less and less inclined to round off with a suicide, and in this the modern spirit of his plays begins to show itself. Ibsen is still thinking in terms of the debased drama that resulted from the nineteenth-century's veneration of Shakespeare. Despite his realistic or even naturalistic settings, he is still imposing a scheme that requires startling curtain-falls, and is willing to sacrifice characterisation and realistic probability to this end. Chekhov is the more realistic in the sense that he will not allow himself the artifices of earlier theatre – climax, peripeteia, stark confrontation, dénouement – so much so that Tolstoy demanded, 'Where is the drama? What does it consist of? The play just doesn't move anywhere.' *Uncle Vanya* does move, of course, but not with the dynamic rise and fall of *Hedda*, rather with a series of lapping advances, like a slow tide, which gradually engulf the audience and achieve that 'breaking down of dykes' which Yeats thought of as essential to tragedy. Chekhov succeeds better in *Three Sisters* and *The Cherry Orchard*. *Uncle Vanya* ends on too sentimental a note for comfort, and the actress who speaks Sonya's final words of consolation has an immensely difficult task. Yet the steady advance of the ripples is detectable all the same.

At the same time, Chekhov often insisted that his plays were comedies, even 'gay farces', and though that probably has to be understood rather as a counterbalance to over-solemn productions than as precise description, there is a familiar note of comedy in all Chekhov's plays, contrasting with Ibsen's grim purposefulness, alternating with a 'grand guignol' or raillery which is always difficult to gauge. Humour in Ibsen never amounts to more than the guying of simpletons like Tesman, and is never in his mind except as an occasional sarcasm when Hedda or Rosmer or Mrs Alving occupy the centre of the stage. Shakespeare can let Lear be mocked, without damage to his power to move us. Ibsen is too primly concerned in Hedda's isolation to risk letting that happen.

Similarly, Chekhov is less rigid than Ibsen in his treatment of minor characters. The treatment of Tesman is unrelenting, he is never allowed to arouse sympathy for a moment. His counterpart Serebryakov, by contrast, is not only petted and comforted by the servant Marina (whose conventional wisdom is allowed sympathy, while Aunt Julle's is not), but is aware of the contempt he arouses in others by his valetudinarian ways, whereas Tesman is totally blind to the impression he creates; we see, too, how Serebryakov has come to deceive himself in his self-esteem as a scholar and critic – he is intelligible, where Tesman is an object of ridicule. Again, Brack would come off better in any comparison with Astrov if he showed anything but a determination to possess Hedda's body, regardless of her inclination. Astrov is powerfully attracted to Helen, and would seduce her if he could, though blackmail would be beyond him. Brack shows no interest in Hedda beyond forcing her into bed, yet even so powerful a sexual urge could have been shown struggling against a more personal consideration for her. A different kind of play would result. The chief virtues of *Hedda*, its sharp dramatic outline, its swift movement and repeated climaxes, would have been harder to achieve with such care for the ordinary complexities of people's relations with one another. But the comparison with Chekhov serves to show how much Ibsen sacrificed to the dramatist in him, to the neglect of the observer of the human comedy.

9

The Master Builder

The new feature for Ibsen in *The Master Builder* is an uncertainty about the motives of the characters, and about the degree of reality of the events, at least those recounted from the past. There is no doubt of this kind about *Ghosts* or *A Doll's House*, though the possibility of doubt arose in *Rosmersholm*, where Rebecca could conceivably be carried by some unconscious undertow. Again, although Oswald ends in insanity, and this is related to his 'demand for the sun', that demand is not represented as paranoiac, any more than was Julian the Apostate's; in *An Enemy of the People*, on the other hand, there are signs of what might be called megalomania, and people in the crowd ask whether Stockmann is off his head. But if there is any megalomania or paranoia in *Rosmersholm* it is in the eccentric Ulrik Brendel, who is evidently included in order to contrast an extreme form of idealism with that of Rosmer and Rebecca. Brendel's grip on reality may be weak: we are not explicitly led to believe that Rosmer's is.

There is some question of insanity even in *Lady Inger*, as in several early plays. All the same, it comes more to the fore in the later ones, as perhaps was natural, seeing that Ibsen's constant theme of extreme individual freedom was always capable of developing into a total disregard of other lives and other views of reality, not wholly unlike madness. Ellida Wangel comes from a family with a history of mental illness, and Ibsen represents her decision to stay with her husband as a kind of cure.

Master builder Solness begins the play with a display of egotism that is still not egomania. His rejection of potential clients merely because they want to move into a place of their own, rather than have a home – the difference is unexplained – does not sound rational, and may be better understood from his remark that he wants nothing to do with these 'strangers' – which is no more rational in itself, but may come closer to revealing what is really in his mind. There is something neurotic about this way of conducting an architect's practice. There is also something abnormal about his fear and jealousy of young people, typified in his relation with his assistant, Ragnar Brovik. Solness is a man not yet old – 'of mature years', to quote the stage directions – and has no grounds that we can detect for feeling so insecure. Yet he is at an age where doubts about his sexual power may worry him more than formerly, and this could account better both for his apparently professional jealousy of Ragnar, and for his flirtation with Ragnar's girl friend Kaja Fosli.

Yet that flirtation is not necessarily infatuation. When Solness's family doctor, Herdal, taxes him with it, he explains that his loving behaviour towards Kaja is part of a calculated plan, intended to keep Ragnar from handing in his resignation and starting up in business on his own. We may suspect that Solness is partly deceiving himself about this. It is surely at least pleasant for him to be stroking Kaja's hair and hearing her endearments addressed to himself; and, after all, if Ragnar were to set up on his own, he would presumably either employ Kaja in his own office, or expect her to stay at home bringing up their children: Solness can hardly expect to retain Ragnar by this scheme. It is true that Ibsen prescribes reactions for Solness, when alone with Kaja, which do suggest he is thinking mainly of his prospects of keeping Ragnar. Yet the pretext is so slight, and the likelihood of sexual attraction so strong, that once again Solness's account of himself has to be doubted. It is at least on the cards that he is flattering himself both as to his astuteness, and as to his continuing capacity to attract a pretty woman. Indisputably, his motives are ambiguous.

These self-deceptions do not amount to a neurosis. What begins to point in that direction is Solness's suspicion, openly admitted to Dr Herdal, that Herdal has only begun the conversation in order to sound him out, medically, and that both Herdal and Solness's wife, Aline, come to believe Solness is mad. It is no confirmation of that diagnosis, of course, when Solness confesses that Aline may have good grounds for believing so. But the possibility has been raised, and will be explicitly raised several more times in the course of the play.

It is at this point that Solness's expectations are, in a way, reversed. He has just confessed to Herdal his 'real' fear, which is of being supplanted by a younger man, and has just said that one of these days youth will come knocking at the door, when Hilde Wangel does knock at the door. The simultaneity of the knock is unimportant, merely one of Ibsen's rougher touches. But the significance of Hilde's arrival is to provide Solness with re-assurance. Youth is not hostile. As represented by Hilde Wangel (seemingly the same person as the stepdaughter of Ellida in the slightly earlier play), youth is very much in favour of Solness, looks to him for inspiration, expects him to perform miracles of new architecture, and has come to fire him on, not to rob him of power and prestige.

It is almost too good to be true. Though Solness never strokes Hilde's hair or has any overt sexual relation with her (the erection of the tower is another matter), she provides just that femininity he needed, and in a positively encouraging way, just at the moment when he was confessing both his fear of impotence and his 'real' motive for engaging the affection of Kaja.

The question begins to arise, though, by the end of Act One, how much of all this is in fact real. Hilde herself is real, she is recognised by other characters and so on. But the past of which she comes to remind Solness is less obviously so. To begin with, she has to force him over several minutes of conversation to remember it at all. The repeated phrases 'Are you very forgetful?', 'Surely I don't have to remind you about *that*?', 'I might have known you'd say you'd forgotten that, too', together with Sol-for the sun', that demand is not represented as paranoiac, any ness's real or assumed astonishment. 'But did I really say all this?', and 'What on earth did I do after that?', and 'What happened then?' accumulate to the point where it might look as though Ibsen were making heavy weather of the exposition. The events were so unusual, and Solness's memory is so selective – he does remember clearly the ordinary events of that time – as to suggest either that he is ironically leading Hilde on (but why should he?) or that Ibsen is determined to put the audience in possession of the facts without regard to probabilities.

Neither of those explanations is needed. It is true that the story Hilde relates is partly contradicted by the memories of other characters. It is generally said by them that Solness does not climb towers in order to 'top-out' the buildings with a wreath, in accordance with custom, and if his wife is to be believed he has never climbed a tower in his life, and scarcely dares stand on a first-floor balcony. By his own account, the occasion when Hilde was present at such a ceremony, as a schoolgirl of twelve or thirteen, was the only one at which he did top-out the steeple, and perhaps Aline was not there or has forgotten it. The fact remains that Ibsen includes Aline's denial, and thus puts the whole story into some doubt. As for the rest, that Solness could be heard singing at the top, and that there was a sound like harps in the air, Hilde's need for a symbol might be sufficient explanation. Solness himself, however, grows 'thoughtful' at the idea, which does not sound as though he were ironically intending to see what else she will dream up, but rather as though he found her impressive, despite himself, and despite his avowal that he has never sung a note in his life. The later events, when he was invited to Hilde's home and was left alone with her, are less likely to have escaped his memory. He told her, according to Hilde, that she was a princess, promised to come back like a troll in ten years' time and carry her off to his 'Kingdom', took her in his arms and bent her backwards and kissed her many times. It was all light-hearted and gay, in her version, and Solness had just come in from a swell dinner. But he never admits to remembering, and if Ibsen had not implied it was fantasy we would probably think it was in any case. The process of Solness's thought is given as, at first, a protest that Hilde must have dreamt all this, then an acquiescence in her dream, then, as the italicised verbs show, a fervent acceptance of it:

All this you've just told me – it must be something you've dreamt. [...] Listen, now [...] Or... wait a moment! There's more in this than meets the eye, I tell you. [...] I must have *thought* it all. I must have *willed* it... *wished* it... *desired* it. And then... Mightn't that be the explanation? [...] All right, damn it...! So I *did* do it then!   (Act 1) (VII. 384)

With this speech, the ground is prepared for the half real, half symbolical mode in which the rest of the play remains, till the final curtain. (It appears later that even Hilde's name was given her on that day ten years ago by Solness; it is a solipsistic world, like Joseph K's in Kafka's *Trial*, who appoints the location of his

own courtroom. Or it may be that something like Schopenhauer's Will, forcing the world to embody its own reflection, was
in Ibsen's mind.)

Ibsen had become conscious of the problematic nature of his
symbols, at least as early as *The Wild Duck*, if only in the sense that
to say one thing while meaning another might have disastrous
consequences, as it does in the case of Gregers Werle. Symbols, in
the way that Ibsen normally uses them, can too readily be used to
state a general case which has only a limited, particular relevance.
This was true in the case of Stockmann's revelations about the
sewers, which became in his mind, if not in Ibsen's, a revelation
about the corruption of all humanity. *The Wild Duck* might have
been written in the awareness of the unpredictable results of taking
the part for the whole, or at least of attributing so many meanings
to a single object that the wrong one is understood. On the other
hand, Ibsen has often been praised for the very reason that his
words and his dramatic symbols work hand in hand. Thus John
Northam says, 'from the beginning the verbal and the visual co-
operate', although as his art matures 'the co-operation of the two
kinds of imagery becomes integration' (p. 7). It is one of Ibsen's
claims to fame that he married naturalism and symbolism so
successfully. Yet all the evidence of the later plays goes to show
that the symbols are useless additions, attempts at giving greater
portentousness, distractions from the human relations with which
he seems to be concerned.

In *The Master Builder*, Act One concludes with a dialogue in
which the relation of the symbol to reality scarcely seems to
matter. Convinced, now, that Hilde is his ally, Solness takes up
her words about having been promised a kingdom as though they
were based genuinely on his own, and at once opens a vista on to
many other plays of Ibsen's. We are back again with Earl Skule
and Brand and Peer Gynt, Julian and Oswald and perhaps Stockmann, and the old pattern begins to reassert itself more strongly
than it had ever done from *Pillars of Society* onwards. Yet there is a
greater degree of unreality, now, when there can be no proper
talk of kingdoms ('it doesn't have to be an ordinary, real kingdom', as Hilde helpfully says), and when the symbol has to be
conveyed in terms of a nineteenth-century architect's practice. In

such realistic terms, there is something ludicrous about Solness's conversation with Hilde; reality and symbol have parted company:

SOLNESS No, I don't build church steeples any more. Nor churches either.
HILDE What do you build now?
SOLNESS Homes for people.
HILDE (*thoughtfully*) Couldn't you put a sort of – a sort of steeple on the homes too?
SOLNESS (*startled*) What do you mean by *that*?
HILDE I mean, something that points – that points straight up in the air. With a weathercock at a great dizzy height.
SOLNESS (*thinking it over*) Strange you should say that. Because that's what I want to do more than anything.
HILDE (*impatiently*) Then why on earth don't you?
SOLNESS (*shaking his head*) No. People don't want that.
HILDE Fancy them not wanting it!   (Act 1) (VII. 387)

A translation can mislead a little here. Solness quite clearly means 'steeple', not 'tower', though *kirketårn* can be used for either, and when abbreviated to *tårn*, 'tower', used in some versions, is less obviously incongruous. Solness's idea of supplying extremely tall steeples for private houses is more symbolically meaningful than practical, and it is small wonder that clients reject it. Even so, what is symbolised remains vague. Solness has abandoned religious belief, and yet is dissatisfied with his programme of humanism – 'houses for people to live in' – somehow, his purely architectural ambition must be to supply a spiritual meaning to ordinary life without involving himself in any traditional religion. But the symbol never receives closer definition, and remains architecturally something of an absurdity.

A certain autobiographical element may well be present. At the time of *The Pretenders* Ibsen had been the rising contender in the theatre, against Bjørnson. By 1892, the year when *The Master Builder* was published his own position was being challenged by Strindberg, writing in Swedish it is true, but aiming at a European reputation. *The Father*, Strindberg's play published in 1887, was about a man who, like Solness, had fears of being accused by his wife of insanity, and who ended by being inveigled into a straitjacket. It would not be surprising if in some degree *The Master Builder* were Ibsen's response to Strindberg, or perhaps even more to another rival, his own fellow-countryman Knut Hamsun, who had begun to challenge him openly. The play also includes, of course, a reflection of Ibsen's devotion to young women, which increased with age.

Ibsen's play, unlike Strindberg's, makes it clear that no one takes really seriously the suspicion of genuine insanity. Aline is bewildered by Solness's suspicious interpretations of her remarks, unlike Strindberg's Laura, who confirms her husband's fears all too well. Ibsen had no such fears as Strindberg's to contend with. Yet the degree of his personal involvement is shown in Act Two, which soon turns to one of his perennial themes in a way that does not greatly help the development of the plot, though it gives it a sinister turn. When Solness first spoke to Hilde about the day ten years ago, of which this is the anniversary, he called the schoolgirls, screaming their enthusiasm at the foot of the steeple, 'little devils', and remembered one little devil in particular, who turns out to have been Hilde. This is an awkward piece of symbolism, though hardly to be understood as anything but a symbol. References to the devil are made in this colloquial way quite often by Ibsen, with a clear possibility of being taken in a double sense. In this particular context, the parallel with the monk who offered to take Skule up to a high place and show him all the riches of the world inevitably joins itself alongside Hilde's demand for a kingdom, and her new proposal that Solness should climb the spire of the house he has just had built for himself. Hilde has nothing else diabolical about her, it is true, nothing purposefully and unambiguously destructive. In terms of realism she is merely rather reckless in urging such a climb on a man who is not up to such things. Like Rebecca West, another 'woman from the North', Hilde might conceivably be concerned, without overt intention, to egg her man on to destruction, but she too shows no such conscious purpose. The diabolical element is all in the colloquial phrase about the schoolgirls.

As Act Two develops, more of Ibsen's personal preoccupations recur. Solness needs to build a new house for himself because the old house has burned down, and not only for that reason, but because his children died as an indirect result. (His wife, we learn later, lost her own 'children' in the fire itself; but they were dolls. The real children died from her inability to suckle them after the shock of the fire.) Here the Orphanage in *Ghosts* and many similar fires and losses of children come to mind. (See above p. 75). This does, it is true, afford a reason for the building of Solness's new home, which is so important in Act Three, but that could have been achieved without introducing either the fire or the loss of the children. In part, Ibsen is reiterating here the Romantic view of the artist who must yield up all expectation of marital happiness for the sake of his art, the view of Kierkegaard and Grillparzer. In part, he may have had the Faust legend in mind, or have been influenced indirectly by it, for it is related in the sixteenth-century Faust-book, not only that Faust was obliged to forswear marriage, but that, when he tried to circumvent this clause, the house was destroyed by fire; it is also related that the one child he did have was removed from him.

Some such mythical idea may account for Solness's strange remark that in order to build homes for other people, ignoring the church, he has had to renounce – 'for ever renounce' – any hope of having a home of his own. It is not a question of his wife being past child-bearing, or of any impotence of his own. It is a deliberate renunciation, or, as he also puts it, a penalty exacted for all the beauty, security, comfort and magnificence he has been able to create in his houses. He gives no explanation of this conviction – indeed Hilde herself begins to say he must be 'ill', after all. But he does go on to say that he longed for the house to go up in flames so that he might become successful as a builder; he even left a crack in the chimney unrepaired, so that it might result in a fire, though the cause was not that – and he does see now that the fire afforded him the land on which to build his 'homes for human beings'. We are a long way, here, from any normal account of behaviour and motive, and the mythical element is reinforced when Solness adds that ambitious men like himself need 'helpers and servants', who have to be summoned inwardly. He even suggests that it was his ability to call on such helpers that caused the outbreak of fire: as though the house of his rival, old Brovik, would never have been consumed so conveniently, since he had no such ability.

Solness is, in effect, accusing himself of a kind of wizardry. The circumlocution of 'helpers and servants' is soon replaced by 'devils', and the everlasting guilt Solness feels is caused by his conviction that he has, through deliberately summoning diabolical aid, not only caused the fire and the death of his children, but destroyed his wife's essential life too. He is ready to believe even that he has inwardly summoned Hilde, including her, so to speak, among his diabolical servants, though she still shows no sign of deserving such an inclusion beyond her capacity for flattering his ego.

All this makes better sense mythically than in terms of the situation in the play. It makes better sense in terms of Ibsen's life than it does in terms of Solness's, for Ibsen may well have felt that he owed his success as a dramatist to his having abandoned, 'burned', his earlier mode of writing in order to concentrate on the more ordinary edifices of his 'social' plays, and, though he did not renounce children, and his son even outlived him, he may well have felt that his career as an artist isolated him from his family. Solness, by contrast, was only able to profit in his business as an architect through being able to build other houses on the site of the ruins of his own house, and there were surely ways of obtaining building plots without sending for agents from hell. Ibsen is visibly looking here for some 'real' correspondence between the architect's practical life and the symbolism, and the strain shows. Myth and reality gape further apart as the Act proceeds.

By the end of Act Two, the myth has gained a good deal in coherence, all the same. Though Hilde is still not diabolical, she begins to assume a rôle which, in Solness's terms, could take on the aspect of a Luciferan rebellion, as the conversation takes a turn towards the Nietzschean self-assertion which figures in almost all the later plays. The talk of Vikings, of plundering and burning, and killing and carrying off women who were only too glad to submit to he-men is part of Solness's fantasy, like so much else. He fancies the idea of such brutality, and Hilde ministers to it by suggesting she might be captivated herself by anyone who would display a little of it towards her. Thus it is Hilde who plants in Solness's mind the idea which does eventually lead to his death. There is no essential connection between the ability to climb a tall steeple and the ability to behave like a Viking, though the play develops as though there were, as though courage required brutality. But for Solness Hilde presents a challenge to his manliness, and by the end of Act Two he has made up his mind to place a wreath over the weathercock at the topping-out ceremony, despite his fear of heights. The personal challenge in this is clear. The symbolical purport is vaguer. There is a sexual meaning as well as a spiritual one, a consummation in achieving self-mastery, and an expectation of praise from Hilde. Nothing architectural is involved, but Solness's fantasy will live itself out to the full in this endeavour.

The stage-setting for Act Three describes the view from Solness's present house, which includes some dilapidated cottages, presumably the houses he has previously called magnificent, since they seem to be on the part of the garden now 'taken away', as Mrs Solness puts it. There is no certainty about this, though Ibsen surely mentioned the cottages for a purpose, and may even have wanted to denigrate his own 'social dramas', which the 'houses for people' represent. But this ambiguity in values is typical of much else in the play. Not only is the division between reality and illusion hard to draw; Solness speaks also of 'good' and 'bad' devils (though the goodness of a devil is an ambiguity within an ambiguity), and even his immensely strong feeling of guilt is matched by his remark that he 'may be completely innocent'. (This ambiguity is repeated by Borkman.) With such rapid veering between one pole and another it would be wrong to expect any greater certainty about the meaning of Solness's ideal, what it is that he hopes to achieve through his act of daring. Essentially, he is playing Løvborg to Hilde's Hedda.

There is a coy note in the dialogue between Solness and Hilde when they come to speak of his kingdom, and the 'castle' she expects him to build for her. Both of them treat it as a joke, in a way: Hilde bangs on the table and demands her castle at once, and then addresses him as if he, not herself, were the child:

HILDE (*banging on the table*) Fetch the castle! It's *my* castle. I want it *this minute*!
SOLNESS (*more seriously, leaning towards her, his arms on the table*) How have you imagined this castle as being, Hilde?
(*Hilde's expression becomes veiled. She seems to be gazing deep into her own self.*)
HILDE (*slowly*) My castle shall stand high up. Very high up it must stand. And with a view on all sides. So I can see far, far away.

SOLNESS And it will have a tall steeple, I suppose?

HILDE A terribly high steeple. And at the very top there shall be a balcony. And that's where I shall stand, out there –

SOLNESS (*involuntarily clutching his forehead*) How you can enjoy standing at such a dizzy height –

HILDE But of course. That's where I want to stand and look down on the others – the ones who build churches. And homes for mother and father and the children. And you shall come up and look at them too.

SOLNESS (*in a low voice*) Will the master builder be allowed to come up to the princess?

HILDE If the master builder *will*.

SOLNESS (*more gently*) Then I think the master builder will come.

HILDE (*nodding*) The master builder – he'll come.

SOLNESS But never build again, poor master builder.

HILDE (*animatedly*) But he will! We two shall be together in that. And we shall build the most beautiful – the most beautiful thing in the whole world.

SOLNESS (*tensely*) Hilde – tell me what that is.

HILDE (*smiling at him, shakes her head and pouts as though talking to a small child*) These master builders – what very, very stupid people they are.

(Act 3) (VII. 430)

There is a curiously ironical quality in this exchange, a strong suggestion that neither Hilde nor Solness is conscious of doing more than indulge in a dream. Yet they are also apparently in earnest, despite the pouting and the childlike pretence:

SOLNESS But tell me, what is it? This most beautiful thing in the world? That we two are to build together?

HILDE (*remains silent a moment and says, with an enigmatic expression in her eyes*) Castles in the air.

SOLNESS Castles in the air?

HILDE (*nods*) Castles in the air, yes! Do you know what that is, a castle in the air?

SOLNESS It's the most beautiful thing in the world, you say.

HILDE (*rising abruptly and making a kind of dismissive gesture with her hand*) Yes, of course, yes! Castles in the air – they're so easy to take refuge in. And easy to build, too – (*looking scornfully at him*) – especially for master builders who have – a dizzy conscience.

SOLNESS (*rising*) After today we two will build together, Hilde.

HILDE (*smiling half doubtfully*) A *proper* castle in the air?

SOLNESS Yes. And with a solid foundation. (Act 3) (VII. 431)

No more is said by either of them to define this still vague ideal. The symbolism implied does not seem to differ from that of the steeples attached to ordinary houses – a general combination of the real and the ideal must be intended, but nothing more enlightening than that is vouchsafed.

It is still possible, at this stage, to go on believing that the play is to be about something more than the failure to realise an inchoate dream. The ascent of a steeple is, after all, rich enough in its possible associations – it is not the richness which creates dissatisfaction. But accepting the symbol as one of aspiration in a very broad sense, there is still the question why Solness fails. It would not be enough, for instance, merely to say that he is a man spurred on to new courage in an attempt at self-mastery, which fails, without saying something of why it fails. Merely to assert that it does is too easy a form of pessimism. If we look solely at the actions, we see Solness climbing the steeple of his own new house, and crashing to destruction. Has he lost his nerve after all, as everyone except Hilde predicted he would? Has she, devil or not, willingly or not, spurred him on to do this, to him, unnatural act, and so been the agent of his destruction? Did he himself, willingly or not, desire that destruction, conjure it up for himself as he perhaps conjured up Hilde out of his own longing, or is he the victim of her machinations? Some spectators will be content to leave it at that, in an inconclusive state; others will expect more certainty, or at least something of an indication. What Ibsen provides is virtual certainty, though in a way which the conditions of the theatre, by their very nature, do not permit. At the climactic moment, after Solness has placed the wreath over the spire, and Hilde at least has seen him disputing with someone, and heard a mighty song in the air, the stage direction reads:

(*The ladies on the verandah wave their handkerchiefs, and cheers are heard from the street. There is a sudden silence, and the crowd lets out a shriek of terror. A human body, together with planks and poles, can be dimly glimpsed plunging down between the trees.*)

The significance of the planks and poles is explained by Solness's earlier remark, that he feared a second climb because he feared retribution: on his first climb he had stood at the top of the steeple and hurled defiance at the Almighty; now, he fears the wrath of God will exact vengeance for his earlier pride. But in the test of conscience and courage he has no fair chance. Some hand, human, diabolical or divine, loosens the knots which hold the scaffolding

together, or in some equally strange way the poles break, and he
falls to his death not because of any failure of his own courage or
of his conscience, but because of an act of malice – if it was not
sheer accident, as might after all still be the case. (Muriel Bradbrook, ignoring the stage-instruction, says that it is Hilde who
'finally brings him down' (p. 131), but that is quite unsubstantiated.
James McFarlane, by contrast, says that 'the ascent proves too
much for him' (VII, p. 20), but for this again the text provides no
substance.) All that stands firm is the fact that Solness did not
break under his self-imposed task. So much Ibsen clearly intended.
Yet to convey that in terms of stage production is a practical
impossibility. Ibsen's craftsmanship is the real failure in this ending,
his inability to state his conclusion except through the vain
expectation that the audience might see the poles and planks, far
upstage, distinguish them from the falling body, and grasp their
significance. He was asking more than any stage-manager could
provide.

For all that, *The Master Builder* is in some ways more satisfying
than *Hedda Gabler*, whose situation it sees from a different aspect.
It corresponds to this immediate precursor, but with Løvborg as
the central character, so to speak, and with Hedda appearing as a
much more positive figure in Hilde. Thea Elvsted, Løvborg's
pallid love, now appears as Kaja Fosli, who is just as incapable of
providing her man with real inspiration as Thea was. But the
stereotyping of Brack and Tesman has no counterpart in *The
Master Builder*, which is, on the contrary, full of surprisingly subtle
nuances. Much of this is due to Ibsen frankly allowing Hilde to
be seen, if we choose, as Solness's own fantasies coming from the
outside world to meet him. Much that would seem improbable in a
real context becomes much more easily acceptable in a world of
wish-fulfilment, ironically portrayed as such. Yet Ibsen does seek
to come out of the fantasy-world again, and this is where the
ending fails to satisfy. Fantasy requires here the death-wish:
Solness must come to grief at the final moment, yet nothing in the
action requires it. If we suppose for a moment that Solness, having
had the nerve to climb to the tip of the steeple, found the nerve
also to climb down again, the arbitrariness of the ending becomes
obvious. It is only because, for reasons that are far from clear and

certainly not inherent in his act of self-reassertion, he perishes, that the play achieves a kind of impressiveness at the end, hollow as it turns out to be. The fact is, we may take to a sad ending more readily than to a happy one. In that respect, at any rate, Ibsen has provided an image of our own wishes. But the ending remains, in view of that vital stage direction, no more than a fortuitous frustration of Solness's vague dream of a heaven-challenging synthesis. Pattern and symbol rather than creative observation still predominate at a crucial moment.

IO
Last plays

The plays written between 1894 and 1899 take up, especially at their endings, a more tender note which had only been struck once, in the last twenty years or so, since Peer Gynt returned to the loving arms of Solveig. In almost all the 'social' plays there is little room for the kindlier qualities in human nature: gentle characters tend to be presented as examples of the weakness engendered by Christianity, and are stimulated, usually without success, to adopt pagan virtues; if they are minor characters they are targets for ridicule like Aunt Julle, or timid unfortunates like Kaja Fosli. Not until *The Lady from the Sea* had Ibsen shown traditional virtues succeeding against elemental opposition; in this play, for the first time, he shows a married couple defeating disruption from outside, and a similar, kindlier, humanitarian scene ends *Little Eyolf*. In this play love, tolerance and patience are given an unaccustomed emphasis in Asta Allmers, and even in the stark drama that followed it, *John Gabriel Borkman*, some of the same qualities are detectable, without satirical detraction, in Ella Rentheim. The final line of the last play of all, *When We Dead Awaken*, is a benediction, uttered with the sign of the cross: 'Pax vobiscum', words which seem to sum up the hope Ibsen felt for the most desperately ambitious of all his creations. At the same time, the last four plays introduce more clearly religious elements than Ibsen had used for many years. The challenge to the Almighty, or some similar Faustian quality, is made more evident, even while it is still being partly concealed. 'Problem play' is no longer a term that anyone would be likely to attach to these works, in which the cosmic symbolism latent earlier sometimes comes surprisingly close to the surface. Muriel Bradbrook sees the distinction most sharply: 'the four last plays are as sharply divided from his earlier works as the four last plays of Shakespeare', and the parallel suggests a correspondence with that period of Olympian calm which some say Shakespeare entered in the period of *The Tempest*, and Goethe after his Italian journey.

This is where the view that Ibsen's real reputation must rest, not so much on his dramatic craftsmanship or on his social influence, as on his ability to create '*poésie de théâtre*', admits the widest range of comparisons. Ibsen is scarcely writing in a 'social' vein at all, now, and the introduction of almost supernatural figures like the Rat-Wife or the Sister of Mercy shows how far his mind had moved away from what his followers in other countries were by now practising, though his settings remain Naturalistic and are remote from Strindberg's experiments. It becomes thinkable to place him, as Kenneth Muir and David Grene do, alongside Sophocles, Racine and Shakespeare in their final years, and to find in the greatest dramatists of all time a common pattern. In all of them there is a tendency – to summarise Professor Muir – to repudiate past work, to undergo something in the nature of a religious conversion, or to reconsider old themes in the light of a new vision, and the seal on Ibsen's greatness seems to be set by the similarity.

It is true, as Muir goes on to say, that the 'last plays' of the major dramatists tend to be less dramatic than their earlier works, and less obviously effective on the stage. Characterisation is generally weaker, and action is often slight. Yet there is a wisdom in them, Muir finds, which 'Shakespeare and Ibsen finally achieved and expressed' (p. 115), and for which we do well to listen in the theatre.

So far as poorer dramatic quality in the later plays of all four is concerned, all this is undeniable, whatever balance may be struck in the fullest account. What is also needed, however, is some appreciation of the quality of Ibsen's work in particular. It is one thing to accord him greatness by association, yet the case for associating him with the other three at all has still to be convincingly made, and the fact is that the first of the plays we need to be concerned with has never had much success with critics, and is not often performed.

Little Eyolf is the only play of Ibsen's in which there is a clearly positive ending (*The Lady from the Sea* ends on a note in which some irony is still audible): it is the only one in which the characters reach a solution of their difficulties which seems to be endorsed unreservedly. Disaster there is, but it strikes at the end of Act One, with the death of the child of Rita and Alfred Allmers, and the ending is a victory over the sorrow caused by that loss. If portrayal of reconciliation were the guarantee of the dramatist's success, *Little Eyolf* would rank high. Yet, on the contrary, it has until recently scarcely attracted any critical acclaim. In the whole of the anthology of Ibsen-criticism edited by James McFarlane there is not a word of solid praise for it, though there are a number of passing references, and the only two longer passages about it, by Henry James and Muriel Bradbrook, are disparaging. James Stephens was moved by it to write a letter of vituperation. On the other hand John Northam gives it pride of place: it is the only one of Ibsen's last works to be treated by him at length, and the praise he gives it suggests a supreme achievement.

The difficulties standing in the way of anyone who would be glad to see Ibsen vindicated here are hinted at by Henry James, who found the play 'dramatically, *representably* speaking...strangely and pitifully meagre' (Robins, p. 159). The action is all in Act One: here we see the unhappy state of Alfred's marriage with Rita, the strange attraction that he seems to have for his half-sister Asta, and the absurd ambitions he cherishes for his crippled son Eyolf; in these scenes also we see the mysterious but intrusively symbolic Rat-Wife, who lures Eyolf to his death and thereby makes possible a dramatic act-curtain. After that, it is all conversation; there is none of the build-up to tenser and more desperate situations such as we associate with Ibsen generally, and for a curtain at the end of Act Two we have the only potentially dramatic revelation that Asta is not truly Alfred's half-sister after all, although the possibility this opens up, that he may at last declare the passionate love he evidently has long felt for her, is not allowed to come to anything. No Ibsen play is so devoid of dramatic incident for so much of the time.

For Henry James, the difficulty lay in seeing how the ending arose: 'My objection is,' he wrote in a letter to Elizabeth Robins, 'that I find the solution too simple, too immediate, too much a harking back, and too productive of the sense that there might have been a stronger one.' Some of this surely carries weight with all spectators and readers of the play. Up to the last few pages we have seen in Rita and Alfred two not very impressive characters. As John Northam says (p. 191), Alfred generates from the beginning 'an indistinct smell of inauthenticity', he has a 'remarkable egotistical involvement' in his sense of his own place in the scheme of things, and even his grief for Eyolf sounds like affronted egotism. His language is full of inflated religious terms, all the more hypocritical in a man of his humanist leanings. Rita, on the other hand, though less of a thoroughgoing egotist, indulges in some 'wild talk' about the child Eyolf's evil eye, and shows, all through the first two acts and well into the last, a possessiveness in her love that seems almost irremediable. Northam's argument is that there is a gradual process of regeneration, beginning at the moment when Rita first speaks of the hard lives led by the children in the village who mocked at Eyolf and did nothing to save him from drowning: here Rita begins to grow in stature over her husband: 'she at least has broken out of the bond of egocentricity that once confined her' – and when she leads, Alfred begins to respond. Soon he too 'is no longer clad in the armour of callous self-righteousness', and there is a real achievement for them both, a 'breaking out into direct relationships with life'. It involves loss, too, Northam takes care to add, 'yet achievement it is for these two people'.

Modest as this claim is – and Northam's account is remarkable for its attentive listening to the moods of the play from moment to moment – it does not stand in the way of a claim, made within a page, that 'the play succeeds in expressing the inexpressible' (p. 213). What that inexpressible may be, remains, naturally, undefined, but it seems to advance a much greater claim than that an extremely egotistic man and woman have at last resolved to do something for other people. Put in terms suggesting such ineffable fulfilment, the value of the play might appear very great indeed.

Before looking at the greater claim, though, the practical ambition of Rita and Alfred Allmers deserves attention. It is, at first glance, a decision for good, though the suspicion of mere do-goodery cannot be dismissed. Northam attempts to dismiss it when he writes that Rita does not now intend to feed her 'devouring egotism' by 'using the local boys, willy-nilly, as substitutes for her lost son.' But that is just what Ibsen leaves obscure, and even allows us to suspect to be the case. The possibility that there might be any such remainder of that devouring egotism in Rita's new unselfishness, which is after all likely enough, is never allowed to come up within the play: the goodness of Rita's action is thus never 'placed', it is presented very much as she, and eventually Alfred, like to see it.

Rita's aim is not very different from Stockmann's (one remembers, too, that Mrs Alving founded an Orphanage, and that Solness was greatly concerned about 'children', in a not entirely real, somewhat symbolical sense: Ibsen's persistent preoccupation shows through once again). Like Stockmann, and perhaps with about as much chance of success, Rita means to 'bring all the poor neglected children home with me. All the mischievous boys,' and to take them to her heart. As Alfred remarks, he does not know anyone in the world less fitted than she is for doing anything of the kind – and that he says it at all might suggest that the ambition is 'placed' to some extent. Yet since in an instant he himself is persuaded to join her, the objection seems unimportant, uttered only to be forgotten. This, surely, is the moment that Henry James found 'too simple, too immediate'. For when one looks at the whole situation, it seems that Rita is taking for granted that the children will come, that they will live in, and not merely visit Eyolf's rooms, read his books, play with his toys and, significantly, take turns to sit in his chair at table: the intention is that each shall feel himself an Eyolf. How she will persuade their parents to let them come, on these terms, is left unsaid. Perhaps, like Mrs Alving's beneficiaries, all the children are orphans, but that is unlikely, in such a small community; the impression given is rather that they are all suffering from drunken, violent fathers and from mothers helpless to save them. The picture of the village below is, in fact, of a wicked place, and Alfred is still talking of the need to sweep it away only a few moments before he decides to save it instead. He is like Stockmann in his almost simultaneous rôle as total destroyer and merciful helper.

The whole errand of mercy is still based on the notion that Alfred and Rita are superior to the people in the village, that they are capable of enlightening the children, 'ennobling' them even, and that he and she only need to become aware of their responsibilities in order for this to become a possibility. The thought of what ennoblement the couple we have seen so far in the play might achieve is daunting. And in these terms, the gesture with which Alfred goes to the Norwegian flag which Rita has had flown at half-mast, and hoists it to the top, seems to confirm his over-solemn, self-congratulatory dedication. So does the way Alfred looks – he still keeps 'fixing his eyes upon her', 'gazing straight before him', and they both have a way of speaking softly, with great emotion, that argues some great self-consciousness in them. They love themselves in this new rôle:

RITA You'll see. A Sabbath stillness will fall on us now and again.

ALFRED (*quietly moved*) Then perhaps we shall be aware of the visit of the spirits.

RITA (*whispers*) The spirits?

ALFRED (*as before*) Yes. Perhaps they will be about us – those we have lost.

RITA (*slowly nodding*) Our little Eyolf. And your big Eyolf too.

ALFRED (*staring ahead*) Perhaps we will still, at times along life's way, catch a glimpse of them.

RITA Where shall we look for them, Alfred?

ALFRED (*fixing his eyes upon her*) Upwards.

RITA (*nods in approval*) Yes, yes – upwards.

ALFRED Upwards – towards the peaks. Towards the stars. And towards the great silence.

RITA (*giving him her hand*) Thanks!   (Act 3)*

John Northam comments that, after his conversion, Alfred's language begins to swell again with the old kind of elevation – the biblical language that earlier looked suspect – but that 'the vague and evasive grandiloquence' of the earlier scenes is not now being repeated. It is true that Alfred is no longer speaking of 'feeling nearer to the stars and in communion with them,' only of moving towards them. But to say that he 'stands on prosaic but solid ground at last' is greatly to exaggerate what Alfred is now doing. There is nothing prosaic in these portentous final words, and it is for that reason alone unlikely that he is standing on solid ground, and all the more unlikely if one thinks of the drunken fathers and defensive mothers he is likely to have to meet when he joins Rita in her project of turning their home into a kind of boarding-school

* For the last three plays there are no references to *The Oxford Ibsen*. (See Preface.)

or reformatory. In practical terms, one can see him giving up at the first raised fist, not to mention an intimation of a law-suit, or a truancy. Rita's pipe-dream, however well-intentioned – and we do not really know what is prompting her – has nothing in it to warrant Alfred's grand and (for an Ibsen play) surprisingly patriotic gesture as the curtain falls.

It may be that in terms of what the play meant to Ibsen the conclusion seemed to have more justification. Here we have to be more speculative, yet there are persuasive pointers towards the personal interpretation he may have made.

The strikingly unusual feature of the play is the theme of incest, which seems irrelevant to the main theme of the conversion of the two Allmers from their original undiluted egotism. To quote James again, 'I don't see the value or final *function* of Asta [the sister]; that is, I don't in the *presentation*. . . and it's the presentation that constitutes the play.' (Robins p. 159). Many audiences must have felt something like that. Yet Asta clearly is very important to Ibsen, and it seems less than enough to point to his doubts about the legitimacy of his own sister Hedvig. Incest had occupied him before, in *Ghosts* and in *Rosmersholm*: it seems to have had a personal significance for him, and its inclusion in *Little Eyolf* cannot be fortuitous.

The puzzling presence of Asta begins to become more intelligible when one recalls that in childhood Alfred used to call her Eyolf, and treat her as a boy. His ambition for his own son Eyolf is that he shall be 'the complete man of our race': the expression is surprising, especially since Eyolf is a cripple, but it seems to imply a totality of capabilities such as Goethe's Faust aspired to, a kind of self-identification with the whole of humanity. The child and the sister are thus representatives of Alfred's own desire, not so very far from Brand's, the desire to achieve fellowship with the cosmos. It is, as John Northam remarks, a 'remarkable egotistical involvement', for it means that a single individual imagines himself coterminous with the whole of existence. For the moment, all that needs to be observed is the paradox that combines self-fulfilment with a cosmic realisation.

Alfred has returned, at the beginning of the play, from a walking-tour in the mountains, the real significance of which we only learn in Act Three. He has determined, as a result of the deep spiritual experience that he had there, to give up his own project of writing his great work on Human Responsibility, for the sake of concentrating all his efforts on Eyolf, of making his son the complete man. But this decision has come about after a moment of total dereliction: Alfred walked with death in the mountains – 'Here went death and I, it seemed to me, like two good fellow-travellers' – and thought never to see the face of man again.

There was a paradox, however, even here. The point of Alfred's story of the walking-tour is that he wanted to get to the other side of a lake and was forced to make a detour. It was only when he 'rejoiced in the peace and luxury of death' that, quite suddenly, he found himself where he wanted to be, on the other side of the lake, and the point of this seems to be that he only succeeded after he had given up all hope. He lost himself and found himself, as it were: the element of cliché can, however, be smoothed over in production.

The episode with the Rat-Wife enacts the same paradox. That she also represents death is clear enough, but there is an ambiguity in every aspect of her. Eyolf shrinks in horror from her dog: 'I think he has the horriblest countenance I ever saw,' yet a moment later he adds 'but he is lovely – lovely all the same.' The Rat-Wife speaks of crossing over to the islands to rid them of rats, but adds, gleefully but unaccountably, that the people on the islands did not like her coming, as though the good she was doing them were somehow also undesirable. Presumably Ibsen's attention was more on the ambiguities than on realities, in writing this speech. The wish to be rid of real rats is unambiguous; with symbolical ones it is a different matter. The rats themselves are full of life, swarming with activity, but their secret wish, as the Rat-Wife presents it, is to plunge into the water after her, where 'all is as still, and soft, and dark as their hearts can desire,' and where 'they sleep a long, sweet sleep'. All this creates an ambiguous expectancy, early in the play, and contributes to the feeling that to seek death is to seek life, and vice versa. It is in keeping with the commonplaces of German philosophy of the period.

Alfred's decision to renounce his own ambition in favour of Eyolf's future is ambiguous in the same way. He reaches the decision after a moment of self-loss which also brings him just where he wants to be. The decision is itself ambiguous in that he knows Eyolf, as a cripple, can never be the complete man (just as Hedda Gabler might know that the freedom she seeks for the alcoholic Løvborg cannot flourish in the place where she sends him to find it, Brack's party: Ibsen launches characters in pursuit of the ideal from very unfavourable premises). At the same time, it is a decision to realise Alfred's own ambition by another route. In a sense, Eyolf is himself, and by renouncing in favour of his son he is also affirming himself all over again. Though Alfred speaks of himself pretentiously, as though he were a John the Baptist, he has already undergone the Christ-like sacrifice of self, or so he seems to think.

Similarly, Alfred does his best to persuade Asta, and perhaps the audience too, that there is some deep identity between himself and her. Some of his words in this connection sound enigmatic, even when spoken half jestingly, as when he reminds Asta of how often he and she spoke of their family having only vowels for their initials. The kind of identity between members of the Allmers family which Alfred seeks to suggest is in fact of a superficial kind – they are all equally poor, he says, and all have the same colour of eyes. True, as he confesses, Asta is not the least like the rest of them, and yet Alfred believes that living together 'has, as it were, stamped us in each other's image – mentally, I mean'. This is another of the biblical echoes, on which John Northam comments: the suggestion of 'God made man in his own image' is present, and yet the purpose in this case seems to be to suggest a certain crossing of effect. It is not self-evident, in fact, how each could have stamped the image of himself or herself on the other, yet the intention is more or less clear. Alfred wants to establish a sameness between himself and his sister, more than words can express.

Alfred needs Asta as he needs his own self. That is, possibly, why he invites her to live with him and his wife even after he becomes aware that Asta is not his sister. She is the woman with whom he can live in a 'pure' relationship. He talks several times of being 'ennobled' by her, and this can only mean, in the context, that she has no physical attraction for him, whereas Rita goes out of her way to captivate him with her beauty. For one can have no sexual relationship with a woman who is as much part of one's own self as Asta seems to be of Alfred's. The incestuous love he has for her seems pure, that is asexual, and is worth so much to Alfred, because it involves him in no contact with the outside world. To love Asta is to remain within the single identity of his own family, of his own self; it is not to become involved with another life, as it is when he lives married to Rita. Ibsen's extreme reticence about erotic matters in his own relationships could well find its explanation in a similar preoccupation with self. It is the Hedda in him coming to the fore.

The distrust of sexual love shows itself in the strange story Rita and Alfred tell one another about the cause of Eyolf's deformity. Though they are never explicit about it, they imply that the child fell off the table while they were making love, and they seem to see the act of love as evil on that account. 'In that hour,' says Alfred to Rita, 'you condemned little Eyolf to death.' He almost relishes the paradoxical coincidence, though there is nothing inherent in making love that should kill a child already born. The recriminations between the father and mother here are based not on reality but on the necessity, for the play as a whole, to let sexual passion appear unacceptable in comparison with the bond between two lovers who are really one and the same person.

If there were no such emphasis, it would be a simple thing for Alfred and Rita in the final scene to agree to beget another child to take Eyolf's place. That would afford Alfred more chance of success than the unrealistic proposal from Rita which he adopts. But to beget a child would be the fatal second step outside his self-encirclement that Alfred is not prepared to contemplate. What Rita conveniently proposes, on the other hand, though in a way it involves other people, can be represented symbolically as a genuine substitution for the loss of Asta, and one that still remains within the self's palisade. When Asta leaves Alfred in Act Three, he loses 'Eyolf' a second time. But just as he 'lost his self' in the mountains only to find he was on the other side of the lake, where he wanted to be, so here he loses self to find it again not through the 'evil' way of sexual love, but through all the children who will take Eyolf's place. This is why the solution comes in the particular form we see: to go down into the village and teach – a simpler solution in every way – is a course Alfred never considers and which would not suit him at all, nor can he afford to take any stock of his real chances of persuading village boys to come up to his house. But by imagining them coming up as Rita describes them, actually living in the house as Eyolf did, in his rooms, with his books and his toys, taking it in turns to sit in his chair, they become not only wider substitutes for Eyolf, but extensions of his own self such as he has always seen in the child and in Asta, his 'Eyolf', as he calls her. He has lost both her and Eyolf, and found them again in the children.

But this is only another form of fulfilment of Alfred's ego, a means of imagining a yet further extension of it. He is not interested in any particular child, or in the practicalities of Rita's suggestion. The fact that he can use them symbolically is the important thing for him, and it is also the only justification to be found for the orotund melodrama of the final words of the play, already quoted. A mere intention to run a boys' home would not warrant all those references to 'upwards', and the hieratic solemnities of the threefold repetition: 'towards the peaks. Towards the stars. And towards the great silence.' It is his own, extended dominion that Alfred, like Brand, is seeing, when he says that in the company of the boys (who are Eyolf, who is himself) he will perhaps 'be aware of the visit of the spirits' – the spirits, that is, of Eyolf and Asta, as his wife at once interprets. As the inflation in the final dialogue suggests in itself, there is no altruism here, even of the limited kind Northam suggests. And the 'positive' ending is merely allowed by Ibsen to stand, for this occasion. Before long, in *When We Dead Awaken*, there will be another avalanche, as in *Brand*, to sweep away the presumptuous searcher. But Ibsen has his way: Alfred is won over on the flimsiest of grounds, in the abruptest of ways, at the end of a play that has really been a fresh spinning of the same dialectical wheel we have seen in all his work. In his next, the pointer could be left lying in the opposite direction.

John Gabriel Borkman, though its catastrophic outcome is certainly a reversal of the ending of *Little Eyolf*, is, however, much more than that. If there is any comparison with Shakespeare or

Sophocles to be made, it is here more than in any of the other last plays: as Hedda suggested a parallel with Medea or perhaps with Lady Macbeth, Borkman seems to be conceived on the lines of Lear, so far as his stature is concerned, while his final moments recall the death of Oedipus. It is not that his situation is more than remotely like these others', but that his presence is clearly meant to have something of their over-awing power. As he paces up and down in the room above the stage set, working over and over in his mind the details of that moment in the past when he was about to bring off a great financial coup, the moment when he will reveal himself becomes an increasingly intriguing prospect. As a dramatic build-up for an imposing entry, the First Act has no parallel in Ibsen. (The germ of the idea can be traced back, though, as far as Captain Alving, who similarly kept to an upstairs room, but it had not been possible to make dramatic use of this in *Ghosts*.) The two sisters Gunhild, his wife, and Ella, who was once in love with Borkman, sit together reminiscing over the events of his bankruptcy, trial, and long imprisonment, like two Norns. The house is far from any town, ice and snow surround it, and the menace of a Northern winter can be felt throughout; it is this menance that finally destroys Borkman. The only hope lies in his son, Erhart, who in Gunhild Borkman's belief is destined to redeem the family, the house, and the name. But this too is a hope that will be defeated, or at best treated with cynicism. A heavy desolation settles over every scene. Borkman lives almost completely alone, never speaking even to his wife. It is as though *Lear* were to begin with no sign of the old man's earlier glory, but with his virtual incarceration in Regan's castle.

But it is also as though *Lear* were to be played with no indication of the fiery temper and inhumanity which cost the king his reason and his broken heart. Comparisons with Shakespeare tend to be against the interests of lesser dramatists, but if they are to be made, as in Ibsen's case they have been, then it has to be said that *Borkman* contains no figure comparable to Cordelia or Kent – all the characters are either embittered, or ruthless, or naive and even rather silly. The play is also surprisingly vague about some of the most central issues. That Borkman was condemned to five years in jail for his attempt at making a vast fortune on the stock-markets is

clear. Just what his speculations amounted to is, as so often with
past events in Ibsen, left in obscurity. By his own account,
Borkman intended to engage in operations which would have
brought benefits to millions of people, and only a betrayal by a
friend prevented him:

If I had only had another week to work things out! All the deposits would have
been covered. All the securities I had made use of with such a daring hand would
have been in their places again as before. Dazzling great companies were within
a hair's breath of being floated. Not a soul would have lost a halfpenny.   (Act 2)

According to Gunhild, his motives were less altruistic. He enjoyed
being fêted 'as though he were the king himself,' squandered his
money recklessly, but blamed her, in the law-court, as the initial
cause of his ruin. He also involved many other investors in what
were, for them, heavy losses. Yet the result of the eight years he
has spent since his prison sentence, searching his conscience, is to
leave him free – or so he says – of any sense of guilt. Though he
still remains shut up in this remote spot with all the outward
indications that he sees himself as a guilty man, his verbal declaration is that he is innocent.

The complete uncertainty about the past leaves us in too much
doubt about how to take John Gabriel. Has he any talent to
speak of? Is his pacing up and down all of a piece with his play-
acting (he stands with one hand in a Napoleonic posture at one
point), or has he something more than an indistinct fantasy to
support our interest? Is Ibsen writing about a figure of tragic
stature, or has he withdrawn him into a dream-world of the kind
master builder Solness often seems to be living in?

The contrast with a play on a very similar theme by Harley
Granville-Barker, brings out some of the quality of Ibsen's, so far
as concreteness of detail is concerned. *The Voysey Inheritance* –
surely written with some recollection of *Borkman* in mind – is also
about a man who has used other people's money to make invest-
ments they knew nothing of, and also about the possibility of a
son of the family restoring the family honour, as Erhart Borkman
seems meant to do. Barker's play lacks, it is true, the oppressive,
quasi-mythical power of Ibsen's. But it is concerned with a
recognisable and dramatic situation, existing in the present, and
demanding a crucial decision from the son. The elder Voysey has

inherited from his own father a complex variety of pooled accounts from which he is still able to pay annual interest to his clients, though any demand for capital repayment would be likely to reveal his secret, that the capital has dwindled considerably. The issue confronting Edward, his son, at the elder Voysey's death, is whether to continue this fraudulent, or at best dishonest, conduct of the business, or to make a clean breast of it, thereby destroying any possibility of the investors ever receiving back from him more than a fraction of their rightful due, and disgracing the family into the bargain.

Barker's piece is more than a problem play, and more than a naturalistic representation of an early twentieth-century dilemma. In naturalism it goes much beyond anything Ibsen ever tried, and in characterisation it is infinitely more complex and varied than Ibsen's one-dimensional Tesmans and Regines. In its wider implications, however, though it is quite without poetic power, it is suggestive about the possibilities of right and wrong conduct in a world which always has handed down evil situations from one generation to the next. Its most satisfying moments have something more appropriate to the novel than to drama, something distantly Chekhovian, and its conclusion has a touch of Shavian idealising. But there is no doubt about its ability to involve an audience in its moral issues, or to entertain with a broad range of minutely observed persons, in dramatic situations that arise with complete naturalness from the events of the play.

The absence of any such detail in *Borkman* leads to a vacuity in the action, an arbitrariness in the sequence of events. Borkman has ambitions, it is true, but he has no prospects. He is bankrupt; his only acquaintance is the humble Foldal, and there is no suggestion of any way open to him for a return to the scene of action. Nothing suggests that his dream of regaining power has the remotest chance of succeeding. His wife's hopes for their son, meanwhile, are equally insubstantial, and as the play progresses we become more and more conscious that the issues are not being embodied, enacted in real terms, but rather following a familiar pattern. As so often, Ibsen seems to be pursuing a guilt more nearly his own than Borkman's, without ever giving it such fictional reality as will allow him to face it fully.

The first hint of this comes when Borkman explains the circumstances which brought about his downfall. It would have been a simple enough matter, here, for Ibsen to have let him attribute this to some unlucky slump, some unpredicted change in market values. What Borkman alleges is more obscure, and less easy to understand as a cause of financial failure. It was through no mistake or mischance that he fell, Borkman says; it was rather due to the publication by his friend Hinkel of certain letters of Borkman's, about whose contents nothing is revealed. There is no intimation of how these letters could have damaged Borkman's reputation so severely, no hint of why he himself is so outraged. His reaction is out of all proportion to the bare statement that the letters were published: we are left merely speculating why he accuses Hinkel, on these grounds, of 'the most infamous crime a man can be guilty of,' or how he comes to say that a man who can do such things is 'infected and poisoned in every fibre with the morals of the higher rascality' (a phrase mysterious enough in itself, and which Ibsen declined to explain, when asked about it by William Archer). The exaggeration and mystery, together with, once again, a complete absence of clues to the real circumstances, suggest a devious self-defence, while at the same time they leave an undesirable gap in our knowledge.

All this, however, is only a prelude to the more forceful accusation which Ella Rentheim makes against Borkman, that he deliberately gave up his genuine love of her, as part of a bargain with Hinkel, in order to gain control of a bank. Borkman does not deny this: he even assents vehemently to it, and in terms carrying overtones which at least begins to suggest where, beneath the surface, the play is tending. The sacrifice of Ella to Hinkel is rather fanciful: only such a complete egotist as Borkman could imagine that a woman could be switched from one man to another, or that Hinkel could expect to gain anything from such a bargain. In terms of Ibsen's recurrent preoccupations, the scene makes better sense:

BORKMAN I knew his consuming passion for you. I knew that on no other condition would he –
ELLA RENTHEIM And so you struck the bargain.
BORKMAN (*vehemently*) Yes, I did, Ella! For the love of power was so

uncontrollable in me, you see! So I struck the bargain; I *had* to. And he helped me half-way up towards the beckoning heights that I was bent on reaching. And I mounted and mounted; year by year I mounted –

ELLA RENTHEIM And I was as though wiped out of your life.

BORKMAN And after all he hurled me into the abyss again. On account of you, Ella.

ELLA RENTHEIM (*after a short thoughtful silence*) Borkman, does it not seem to you as if there had been a sort of curse on our whole relation?   (Act 2)

At this point, the brief reference in Act One to Borkman's having been addressed everywhere by his Christian names, 'as if he had been the king himself,' takes on a fresh significance. It is the merest of conversational phrases as it stands, and does not yet carry the weight it will have after Borkman's impassioned speech in Act Four, when he talks of 'my vast, my infinite, inexhaustible kingdom'. But the allusions are familiar from the time of Earl Skule, and earlier: what Borkman has in mind must be the 'great kingly thought', the Faustian dominion over the world; he also believes, as it turns out, that in order to achieve it he must, like Faust, make a bargain with the devil. In these terms, Borkman's relationship with Hinkel, however mysterious its effects may seem in financial terms, has a recognisable pattern. Just as the legendary Faust forswore human passion for the benefits that the devil was to bring him, so the bargain with Hinkel – aptly named, since *hinke* means to limp, or hobble, and Ibsen had used that defect before for diabolical people – requires the same sacrifice from Borkman.

The skeleton pattern goes some way to explaining why the play seems vague and unorientated, viewed as an account of human relationships. To Ibsen the Faustian model, or something akin to it, meant a great deal; he was seldom entirely free of it in his creative thoughts. Clothing it in dramatic form yet again must have presented problems, however, which he did not face. To be a Faust would be one thing – Goethe's character is literally provided, by magical means, with the possibility of ranging through time and space in search of experience. To be Borkman is another thing entirely. It is not merely that Borkman has no prospects. For much of the play his ambition remains as vague as so much else, and it is not really apparent until Act Four, when he speaks with such passion, what his steamship-lines really meant to him, how the fact that they encircled the globe seemed to put the globe in his grasp, and how they seemed to him a great benefit to countless millions, as well as an inflation of his own importance. Even then, however, Borkman remains crippled, like Eyolf, like so many of Ibsen's men of ambition: there is, in view of his bankruptcy and withdrawal, simply no likelihood of his ever succeeding, and this must detract from the force of the play. He is a Faust with no prospects, and with a devil who never puts in an appearance.

There are three strands in the plot: first the quarrel between Gunhild Borkman and her sister Ella Rentheim for the possession of the young Erhart, then Erhart's assertion of his own independence, ending in his departure with Mrs Wilton, and finally Borkman's own decision to leave the house at last, after eight years' self-confinement in it, to assert his own freedom.

The quarrel between the sisters, though Gunhild's coldness is contrasted with Ella's warmth, is remarkable for the egocentricity of both. With Erhart well into his twenties, it is egocentric enough for either woman to expect him to go on living with her, even though Ella believes she has only a few months to live. The point of the quarrel seems to be to show how grasping even love can be; though Borkman may have renounced love, there is just as much evil in continuing to love – so the emphasis seems to lie.

If the two sisters correspond to the two women in Skule's life, and to many other pairs of women in the plays, Erhart corresponds to Skule's son Peter, and to all those sons in Ibsen who embody the promise of the future. It is an ambiguous promise, and does not arise out of the elder Borkman's situation, as Edward Voysey's arises out of the elder Voysey's. Ibsen tacks on the sections of the play dealing with Erhart without concern for any general unity. Erhart is said by his mother to have a great mission in life (for what end, she does not say), though he himself does not believe he has one, but looks for freedom and happiness with the worldly Mrs Wilton. Yet the assertion of this freedom involves ruthless disregard of others. It chances to be the covered sleigh in which Erhart, Mrs Wilton, and Frida Foldal are driving away from it all that runs over old Foldal, Frida's father. That is life, and the quest for happiness, Ibsen seems to imply: the old suffer at the hands of the young.

Foldal himself, Borkman's modest friend from former days who still visits him in his shameful retreat, is made to represent charitableness as ludicrous. His reception of the news that his daughter has already left is piously submissive enough: as soon as he learns it is with Borkman's son that she has left, he has no more qualms, but beams with joy. When Borkman follows this revelation with the news that she was in the sledge that ran over his foot he is in ecstasy, and there is one further point to raise him to the highest pitch:

BORKMAN They took her away in that sledge which ran over you on the road.
FOLDAL (*clasping his hands*) To think that my little Frida was in that magnificent sledge!
BORKMAN (*nodding*) Yes, yes, Vilhelm, your daughter drives in her carriage now. And young Borkman too. Tell me did you notice the silver bells?
FOLDAL Yes, indeed. Silver bells did you say? Were they silver bells, you say? Real, genuine silver bells?   (Act 4)

There is a heavy hand in the satire here, which might have come from Borkman himself, rather than from Ibsen. But Borkman himself is treated in the same way. Ibsen makes him as absurd in his pomposity as Foldal is in his meekness. Thinking that Ella or Frida is about to enter, Borkman straightens his necktie in front of a mirror, and stands beside the writing-table with his left hand resting on it, and his right hand thrust in the breast of his coat. To ensure that the point is not missed, Ibsen makes Borkman compare himself shortly afterwards to Napoleon. His condescension to Foldal is extreme:

FOLDAL But he (Hinkel) rose high in the world.
BORKMAN And I fell into the abyss.
FOLDAL Oh, it's a terrible tragedy –
BORKMAN (*nodding to him*) Almost as terrible as yours, I fancy, when I come to think of it.
FOLDAL (*naively*) Yes, at least as terrible.   (Act 2)

To pursue the parallel with *Lear*, this is as though the King were reduced to scoring points off Oswald, Regan's servant. The sarcasm of the exchange is mean. Yet it could be an expression of Ibsen's masochistic realisation that his own achievements were as slender as Borkman's. He too had given up a good deal in personal relations for the sake of becoming a world-dramatist, and in his worst moments he knew it had not come off.

Shortly before his death, Borkman is touched with a moment of passion which could have transformed the whole work. Here at last we have a glimpse of the vision that has been keeping him going, as he finally makes up his mind to break loose from the self-imposed isolation of the last eight years, and climbs the hill with Ella to show her the kingdom he has been dreaming of. Everything comes to life again here:

BORKMAN Ella, do you see the mountain chains there – far away? They soar, they tower aloft, one behind the other! That is my vast, my infinite, inexhaustible kingdom!

ELLA RENTHEIM Oh, but there comes an icy blast from that kingdom, John!

BORKMAN That blast is the breath of life to me. That blast comes to me like a greeting from subject spirits. I seem to touch them, the imprisoned millions; I can see the veins of metal stretch out their winding, branching, luring arms to me...I love you, unborn treasures, yearning for the light! I love you, with all your shining train of power and glory! I love you, love you, love you!

(Act 4)

In these lines we hear also some of the power which drove Ibsen himself through fifty years of life as a dramatist, past all disappointments. The mountains which play such an important part in his own poetry are often in the background, a quietly looming source of strength, as they are in *The Pretenders*, and in the final scene of *Ghosts*. Their rôle in this present play is another matter. Borkman has made up his mind, it is true, and the decision is a fatal one, since the icy blast which Ella speaks of kills him by its intensity within a few minutes of his having greeted it. Symbolically, the implications are clear: the ambiguity which ends *Peer Gynt* and *Brand* and many other plays is here too, and what Borkman greets as the breath of life is the touch of death. But Borkman's purpose in going out into the night and darkness remains obscure. We know his tormented sense of guilt and his self-declared innocence, but we have not been led to expect that there is any way out for him, or that he is seriously thinking of one. He is shown with the ambition of a Skule, but with a merely deluded notion of how he might realise it. There is some moving quality, it is true, even in his delusion: the passion of his speech carries conviction and arouses sympathy. Yet the issue is never tragic, merely disastrous. The difficulty about feeling the play as a tragedy lies in seeing what hope of life Borkman might have had from these luring, subject spirits. He confuses the 'promised millions' with the millions of human beings whom he hoped to liberate; so much is clear. He also sees the metals as potential money which he could command. But there is nothing in his hopes except mastery that excites admiration, and the mastery here is of too vague a kind to sustain that admiration. 'Liberating' human beings is different from 'liberating' veins of metal, and in any case Borkman seems to want to dominate rather than free his subjects. Ibsen, unlike Wagner in the *Ring*, does not do enough to endow the metals with symbolical value; the reference to them occurs so late as to seem almost an after-thought, while the attempt at linking them with real values like human liberation is without sufficient correspondences.

Borkman has only a shadow to offer, a man who might, thirteen years before, have had an ambition to glory in, but who now can only summon up strength for a futile gesture towards what might have been. There is pathos in that, and the reconciliation of the two women over his dead body can be touching, and yet the play does not hold together, its premises are too vague, its conclusion too inconsequential. No major dramatist ever provided a theme so indistinct.

If any comparison can be made here, it is surely with *Oedipus at Colonus*, whose theme is very close to that of *Borkman*. The simple plot about a man who brought disaster on himself through his expectation of bringing good to a whole community parallels Ibsen not only in this, but in the conclusion, where Oedipus's fearful summons to attend the will of the gods, and his disappearance amid claps of thunder and lightning matches Borkman's death in the snow. (There is a similar parallel in *When We Dead Awaken*.) But Sophocles, like Shakespeare in *Lear*, is writing about compassion and loyalty, humility and frankness, the mystery of things. Whereas Borkman declares, for reasons he does not give, that he is really innocent of the charge on which he was imprisoned, and argues that people should not be accorded too much sympathy when all that they have lost through his actions is money, Oedipus states outright the circumstances of his parricide and incest; he challenges his audience to condemn him, as the gods have condemned him, for crimes which he did not know at the time were crimes, for a murder committed in self-defence, and incest committed in ignorance. Yet from an early moment in the play the seed of the thought is dropped, that he may be intended by the gods for a great destiny, despite their hostility to him. The ending, when he passes on alone, blind, to meet his death, is prepared for, though mysterious: but it is not vague. Oedipus in his rags and filth and with his empty eyesockets rises at the end to grandeur, he condemns the fratricidal war of his son and will not lift his curse from him so long as it continues, yet his last words are a blessing on Athens, spoken with the full authority of the sufferer, and he welcomes and reciprocates the love of Antigone and Ismene, as Lear eventually does Cordelia's. The moving quality of the play comes from the knowledge that so great a man as Oedipus now proves to be, and the compassion that goes to him from Theseus and the chorus, can do nothing to protect him from the ordeal prepared for him in the sanctum of the Furies:

Neither did thunderbolt descend nor storm come up out of the sea, but some messenger carried him away or the foundations of the earth were riven to receive him, riven not by pain but by love.   (transl. W. B. Yeats)

The ending is grief for the two daughters, but the inscrutable love which takes Oedipus into itself remains in the mind of the audience till the final line.

  Borkman has nothing comparable. John Gabriel cannot be seen to be innocent, as Oedipus can; his self-exculpation sounds like casuistry; his departure from the house is no more than a wild fling, and his final aim is still egoistic dominion which he manages to persuade himself is of benefit to mankind. His failures in the past, and ambiguous triumph in the present, have no social echo – there is no Chorus to take pity on him or show any concern – and they take place rather within his own mind than in any world of other men and women. As the final lines make us feel, this is a play about death-in-life, not about the life that wrestles with death:

ELLA RENTHEIM It was the cold that killed him.

MRS BORKMAN (*shaking her head*) The cold, you say? The cold – that killed him long ago.

ELLA RENTHEIM (*nodding to her*) Yes – and changed us two into shadows.

MRS BORKMAN You are right there.

ELLA RENTHEIM (*with a painful smile*) A dead man and two shadows – that is what the cold has made of us.

MRS BORKMAN Yes, the coldness of heart. – And now I think we two may hold out our hands to each other, Ella.

ELLA RENTHEIM I think we may, now.

MRS BORKMAN We twin sisters – over him we have both loved.

ELLA RENTHEIM We two shadows – over the dead man. (*Mrs Borkman behind the bench, and Ella Rentheim in front of it, take each other's hand.*)   (Act 4)

Ibsen makes no more of the situation than there is, here. These lines are moving because of the accuracy with which they state the deathly condition to which the three have come, and the faint flicker of reconciliation they foreshadow. But the play has never provided the setting from which anything more than this bare minimum of constatation could be achieved. Till this moment there has been too much hardness of heart on all sides for the reconciliation to evade all suggestion of a certain ritual formality, an echo of the endings of other plays, *The Pretenders, Emperor and Galilean*, in which the hero is spoken of with awe by the remaining women. Neither Gunhild nor Ella grieves over Borkman, in fact Gunhild is repelled by the thought of looking at his dead face, while Ella is wry and inscrutable. Ibsen is writing of a world that has never come to life.

From the realisation of the last lines of *John Gabriel Borkman* comes the impetus for *When We Dead Awaken*. It is Ibsen's last testament, consciously so intended, even though he was still thinking, up till the moment of his breakdown, of continuing with yet one more play. He was seventy-one when he wrote it, and as things turned out nothing followed this final declaration of a will to go on striving incessantly. Yet that striving, like Faust's, is the strongest characteristic of all Ibsen's dramatic work. It is because of it that Robert Brustein, for instance, is persuaded to take the analogy with the last plays of the great dramatists still further, and compare this play also with Beethoven's last quartets.

The comparison, or rather ranking, for Professor Brustein says nothing in detail on this particular point, is one more sign of the general tendency to create greatness for Ibsen by association, which R. G. Cox pointed out in an article in *Scrutiny*. So long as no actual comparison of the play with the quartets is made, the effect can be simply emotive; there is no end to the great last works of painters and sculptors and other artists which might be added. Brustein does, however, concede that *When We Dead Awaken* is 'full of minor flaws, and often inconsistent in plot and character,' and this allows us to look more closely at his claims on Ibsen's behalf, for he makes this concession while at the same time maintaining that the dramatist is 'prepared to fall into excesses in order to expand the possibilities of his art' (p. 79). The weakness of Brustein's case is that he mentions none of the inconsistencies specifically, and only one of the flaws or excesses. We do not get a real sense of the expanded possibilities, since we do not see what Ibsen had to sacrifice in order to gain them. Nothing Brustein says shows how Ibsen's dramatic art expanded, and his account of the purport of the play is in such general terms of 'total revolution', 'ceaseless aspiration', 'ultimate truth' as to leave us in doubt about what he really has perceived. If *When We Dead Awaken* is the great work Brustein sees, it must lead to some more interesting assertion than 'the tired artist has found his resting place.' We are still without an account which would show us this final work as a crowning masterpiece.

An account in words of the last movement of Beethoven's last piano sonata cannot do what a performer on the piano does, when he creates in the imagination an image, perhaps, of a spirit rising out of darkness into a new world of delight. The greater part of the last movement is, all the same, an enactment of that delight, a flight of sweeping grandeur over vast expanses, a plunging up and down the scales in long arpeggios, and at last an act of thanksgiving and benediction. We know from the whole of Beethoven's music with what demons he had to contend, but the final movement is not justified by that knowledge: it might, conceivably, have been written in pure innocence (though we can scarcely persuade ourselves that that could be so); the telling power of it comes because the music is itself the delight, it acts it, it is there once and for all, and would still be there if we knew nothing of the rest of Beethoven's work whatsoever.

It is something similar that Brustein claims for Ibsen when he writes that at the last, he had 'found his way back to the mountains where, free from the "taint" of man, liberation and revolt were pure and absolute' (p. 83). (That means, I take it, that it is a total rejection of all humanity, allowing not even Stockmann's or Almers' slight hope. But to carry weight, Brustein would have to show us something of that liberation, and this he does not do – in fact it is questionable whether he could, in terms of the language, structure, and form of symbol Ibsen used, though the first scene is evocative enough.

The play begins calmly, on a warm and sunny summer morning, with the aging Professor Rubek and his young, vivacious wife Maia sitting at their hotel breakfast table, in the open. Everything ought to make for contentment, the fountain and park, the fjord and small islands, the champagne and Rubek's velvet jacket – Ibsen sets the scene with his usual care for detail. The effect is not one of contentment, because of the total silence. For some time neither Rubek nor Maia speaks, and the first words are a sigh. By this simple means, Ibsen establishes with complete economy the initial ambiguous mood, the dissatisfaction with perfection, or what passes for perfection. We know this from experience – though it may not be all our experience – and he has merely to keep quiet to make his point.

For a while, the silence becomes the topic of conversation, as Rubek recalls the way the Norwegian train which brought them here stopped at all the little stations, where nothing was happening. A mood like Samuel Beckett's grows, as he reflects:

No one got out or in; but all the same the train stopped an endlessly long time. And at every station I could make out that there were two railwaymen walking up and down the platform – one with a lantern in his hand – and they said things to one another in the night, low, and toneless, and meaningless.

And Maia responds:

Yes, that is quite true. There are always two men walking up and down, and talking —
(Act 1)

But the men are talking of nothing, Rubek is persuaded, and

here for the first time a note is struck that has something of the eerieness which characterises a good deal of the play. There is not merely the beauty of the setting, with the silence undermining it, but a ghostly presence, still realised within a realistic frame. The railwaymen are perfectly real, only Rubek's haunting fears make him see in them the image of his own inner reality. By such means, Ibsen leads us from the 'real', external world into the internal one about which he is writing. The first crux for a production will be the moment when the correspondence between the two begins to look strained.

For the time being, Ibsen is perhaps willing to treat this with a degree of irony. We become aware that he is once again leading in to his familiar themes when Maia begins to speak in terms of the Biblical phrase about Christ's temptation on the mountain-top, but this is not presented as straightforwardly as it used to be in earlier plays. When Solness was reminded by Hilde of a similar occasion when he promised a kingdom to *her*, he denied all knowledge of it. Rubek fobs Maia off with a humorous shrug:

PROFESSOR RUBEK ... Well, what did I promise?
MAIA You said you would take me up to a high mountain and show me all the glory of the world.
PROFESSOR RUBEK (*with a slight start*) Did I really promise *you* that, too?
MAIA Me too? Who else, pray?
PROFESSOR RUBEK (*indifferently*) No, no, I only meant did I promise to show you –?
MAIA All the glory of the world? Yes, you did. And all that glory should be mine and yours, you said.
PROFESSOR RUBEK That is a sort of phrase that I was in the habit of using once upon a time.

Ibsen must have grown self-conscious by now about repeating this symbol yet again, but he found here a neater solution than the one in *The Master Builder*, of the difficulty of conveying a symbolical value. Solness appeared in the end to recognise and remember the occasion of his first meeting Hilde only as a kind of fantasy, or a necessary illusion which he had to treat as real. Rubek keeps the suggestion open, that he has a kind of world-dominion at his disposal, while at the same time the whole phrase is pooh-poohed as a lover's fanciful promise.

Irony of a kind continues with the entrance of the Baths Inspector. Seeing what Irene and the Sister of Mercy are going to imply, later on, it is a strange but integral part of Ibsen's purpose, we must suppose, to introduce them as humorously as possible, by making Rubek imagine that the figure he saw walking about the grounds at night was wearing a bathing costume. The Inspector is able to put him right about that, but the startled way in which he begins to tell Rubek the true facts is a first introduction to the ostensibly mysterious part of the play. Irene and the Sister pass across the rear of the stage before the Inspector can say more, but their brief appearance gives a glimpse of the hieratic, mythical mood which is going to envelop the action before long. At the same time, there is again an incongruously comical note. The eeriness which was touched on earlier now comes in much more strongly, and 'eerie' is the right word, with the right Romantic and somewhat hackneyed associations. Irene's statuesque appearance and movements, her arms crossed on her breast and her eyes staring into nothingness, with the Sister's almost identical gait, following behind her and fixing her piercing eyes on her all the time, are items from the stage instructions which a modern producer is almost bound to want to modify, if the supernatural is not to be made intrusively obvious, not to say ludicrous, in this hitherto realistic world. The spirit of the Gothic novel does not belong here.

The ghostly women disappear, without Rubek's having recognised in the leading one his former model, Irene, and the mood returns as though by over-compensation to one of rollicking assertive bonhomie. Ulfheim the hunter, who now enters, is a gross caricature of the Norwegian sportsman, a figure of fun, though the kind of comedy he seems to require is preposterous. His first words to his servant are an order to 'look well after your fellow-creatures, Lars', meaning the dogs, after which he specifies fresh meat-bones, reeking raw, and bloody, and aims a kick at the servant as he is making off. He has soon introduced himself to Rubek and his wife, in terms which again seem meant to arouse a more or less tolerant laugh at his expense:

ULFHEIM ...I hunt bears for preference, madam. But otherwise I make the
best of any sort of game that comes in my way – eagles, and wolves, and

women, and elks, and reindeer – if only it's fresh and juicy and has plenty of blood in it. (*Drinks from his pocket-flask.*)   (Act 1)

Maia, however, who seemed to take Rubek with a pinch of salt, is bowled over by this Dracula, even when he claims to have a penchant for fighting with bears hand-to-hand.

It begins to grow obvious, however, that Ulfheim is not meant as a part for the Comic Man. His rôle is to represent for Maia the call of Life, of Nature red in tooth and claw, in contrast to the increasing attachment to the Spirit which Rubek has been beginning to show. It is not out of the question for Ibsen to have thought of Ulfheim in terms like those Nietzsche used in summing up the 'blond beast'. But the barbaric theme which had formed so important a strand in Ibsen's work from Catiline's Furia onwards is given an embarrassing portentousness, while being simultaneously ridiculed. We understand this much of the symbolism, the Life–Spirit dichotomy, well enough, but are surprised by its crassness. There is an incongruousness about the whole treatment of Ulfheim, which even stringent toning-down might, in production, be unable to put right.

This makes particularly difficult the entrance of Irene a few moments later, since there is a strong streak of the Ulfheim in her too. It may be necessary for Ibsen's purposes that this should be so. Robert Brustein agrees that in realistic terms Irene appears to be a homicidal maniac, but sees in her symbolic role a justification, since she is intended as an 'allegorical spirit of Nemesis' (p. 80). We may doubt, on the other hand, whether symbolism of this kind, which was conceivably intended, can compensate for the gross insouciance with which Irene speaks, a cheerful indifference to her first husband's fate which looks rather like insanity:

IRENE (*looks straight in front of her with a fixed smile*) *Him* I managed to drive quite out of his mind; mad – incurably mad; inexorably mad. It was great sport, I can tell you – while it was on. I could still laugh within myself – if I *had* anything within myself.

PROFESSOR RUBEK And where is he living now?

IRENE Oh, deep down in a churchyard somewhere or other. With a fine handsome monument over him. And with a bullet rattling in his skull.

PROFESSOR RUBEK Did he kill himself?

IRENE Yes, he was so kind as to take that off my hands.   (Act 1)

Most of this Act needs to be acted fast, if the audience are not to take it in a Tod Slaughter vein. There is certainly no need to take Irene in solemn earnest. After she has gone on to claim she killed her second husband too, with a dagger she always keeps in her bed, as well as all her children, it is no surprise when Rubek intervenes with the familiar Ibsen remark, 'There is something hidden behind everything you say.' Perhaps Irene never killed anybody, perhaps she is meant rather to represent a kind of scepticism derived from excessive idealisation, which destroyed the children of Rubek's or Ibsen's imagination. For Nemesis, though, her language has too much of the penny dreadful.

The climax of the Act arrives when Rubek reminisces over what Irene once meant to him. She was to have been his model for a sculpture entitled 'Resurrection Day', showing a pure woman awakening after death to a realisation that she was in fact unchanged, that her nature in life had already been so consummated as to need no transformation in Heaven. This was, it is true, an impossible aim for any sculptor: the idea is literary, and could not be conveyed in spatial form. (One would not know from the sculpture and without words that the woman's present, heavenly shape was unchanged from the one she had had on earth, but as in *The Lady from the Sea* Ibsen does not think in sculptural terms.) As a result, Rubek's claim that he was prevented from making any human contact with Irene − from making love to her − by the demands of great art, looks hollow. He seems to have created not a masterpiece, as he asserts, but an unrealisable allegory.

Equally, Irene's account of their earlier life together makes no sense in terms of normal sane behaviour. She says, in a bitterly joking mood, that she gave Rubek 'something rather indispensable...something one ought never to part with', but it was not her naked body, which she certainly let him see, or the three or four years of her youth that they spent with each other. As the curtain falls, she explains:

I gave you my young, living soul. And that gift left me empty within − soulless. (*looking at him with a fixed stare.*) It was *that* I died of, Arnold.   (Act 1)

Her meaning is obscure, though echoes of Borkman's pact with the devil are present. Irene speaks of a soul as though it could be

parted with at will (Borkman, similarly, spoke of voluntarily
ceasing to love), as though her ruthlessness, cruelty, vindictiveness
were due to Rubek's having looked at her naked, without making
love to her, or to his having used her for his art and then abandoned her. One can only suppose that Ibsen's familiarity with the
idea of selling a soul allowed him to attribute such a sale to Irene
without considering the real, psychological processes that would
need to be involved. Nothing that Rubek is said to have done leads
to such a consequence, and 'selling' is used loosely, as part of a
cliché.

By the end of Act One, the basic contrast between Maia, love of
life, and carnal desire, over against Irene, spirituality, and the ideal,
is established. Act Two is needed to show Maia separating from
Rubek in order to follow Ulfheim, which she does, painlessly.
The first half of the Act also affords space to a discussion of Art and
Life of a kind that was fashionable in the 1890s – the stories of
Thomas Mann and of many other writers of this period use much
the same categories. Rubek comes to a surprisingly platitudinous
conclusion:

PROFESSOR RUBEK Yes, is not life in sunshine and in beauty a hundred times
    more worth while than hanging about to the end of your days in a raw, damp
    hole, wearing yourself out in a perpetual struggle with lumps of clay and
    blocks of stone?   (Act 2)

Maia replies with a little sigh that she has always thought so, and,
as far as the terms of comparison go, she could not be anything
but right. No one in the play is allowed to remind Rubek that he
is here seeing life in a rosy light – a thing he does not usually do –
and excluding from an artist's existence the achievements that
could reward his struggle. On the other hand, though Rubek
admits he has made enough money to live in sunshine and beauty,
he goes on to say that he is not happy in such surroundings and
needs to go on with his art. In short, his objections are so phrased
as to make all enjoyment impossible. It is not a high level of
debate.

The conclusion is, however, that Maia is no longer satisfying to
Rubek and, since she is, unaccountably, attracted to Ulfheim, they
agree to part, so that Rubek may be free for Irene.

Rubek's wanting Irene again, after her performance in Act One, takes some accounting for. In so far as she is the Ideal, it is automatic, but she does nothing in Act Two to persuade him that she has any ideal quality left. Though he seems unconcerned, there are more reasons for thinking she is not wholly sane. (She does speak later of her companion, the Sister of Mercy, coming with a straitjacket for her.) It turns out, for instance, that what she said earlier about carrying a dagger with her wherever she went is true: she has it in her corsage, like any opera-heroine, and is toying with it all the while Rubek is describing how he altered the statue 'Resurrection Day' to include not only her but all the animal faces of his later portraits. Fortunately for him, she relents, but at the point when he confesses that he 'moved' the figure modelled from her a little into the background (again Ibsen ignores the limitations of a sculptor), she whispers hoarsely that he has uttered his own doom, and is about to strike. It is only when he hears her say 'doom' that he turns round – she was going to stab him from behind – and thus makes any further action impossible, since she can hardly be expected to kill him if he knows what she is up to.

But Rubek's blissful ignorance also fails to observe that she is looking at him after this 'with a lurking evil smile', 'with malign eyes', 'with an evil gleam of hatred in her eyes', 'with a wild expression', and that she is still groping in her bosom for the dagger even at the moment when he is agreeing to spend a night on the upper part of the mountain with her. If Ibsen's stage instructions are adhered to, the part of Irene has to be played with an intensity usually associated only with old German Expressionist films.

It remains for Act Three to show Maia going off with Ulfheim – 'downwards' – while Rubek and Irene make for the heights. Maia, for her part, makes as little objection to Ulfheim's masterful ways as Rubek does to Irene's, though Ulfheim talks about tying her up with a dog's leash and then tries to rape her. That is Life, we understand, but brutal and Dionysian, not sunny and beautiful. The opposites rotate again as happens to be convenient. True, Ulfheim proves to be soft-centred after all:

MAIA Have you gone quite mad? Would you tie me?

ULFHEIM If I *am* to be a demon, let me *be* a demon! So that's the way of it!
You can see the horns, can you?
MAIA (*soothingly*) There, there, there! Now try to behave nicely, Mr Ulfheim.
(Act 3)

and he forgets all about the dog's leash. The sudden volte-face of
the Stranger in *The Lady from the Sea* is a close parallel, though less
comic. Still, the implication is clear, when Maia goes down the
mountain with Ulfheim, singing about her freedom, that Freedom
only means Life, and that means violence and he-men. Maia is
no more likely to be satisfied than Erhart Borkman is, when he
goes off to his freedom with the probably unscrupulous Mrs
Wilton. Life-affirmation has its defects.

The sudden deflation of Ulfheim brings to mind the essay by
Jens Kruuse on the humorous elements in Ibsen's later plays.
Professor Kruuse argues, in fact, that the 'many funny episodes or
ridiculous minor characters are not all that there is to Ibsen's
sense of humour' (p. 59); he goes on to maintain that this humour
is 'an active power in the lives of the great protagonists', and
though his examples are nearly all drawn from *Hedda Gabler* and
Rosmersholm, he suggests that many more can be found in *The
Wild Duck*, *Ghosts,* and *The Master Builder*, and goes on to say that
to understand the humour in the later plays is important for 'the
understanding of Ibsen's distinction as a *modern* writer of tragedies'. He might well have in mind here some such theory of
modern drama as is represented by Martin Esslin's interpretation
of the 'Theatre of the Absurd': 'The dignity of man lies in his
ability to face reality in all its senselessness; to accept it freely,
without fear, without illusions – and to laugh at it' (p. 419). No-
one, it is true, has managed to raise a laugh about senseless realities
like Auschwitz and Hiroshima, but that is the kind of thing that is
being said.

The modernity of a writer is not necessarily a valuable quality.
A variety of things are called modern, from naturalistic television
drama to *Oh! Calcutta!*, from Brecht to Artaud. The fact that
Ibsen does not take his tragic endings in solemn earnest is clear,
however, from the close of *Hedda Gabler*, as Kruuse rightly argues,
and other moments ridiculous to some degree have been noticed:
Gregers Werle's 'vasty deep', uttered at the instant of Hedvig's

death being announced, the tam o'shanter and red beard of the Stranger, the scepticism with which Mrs Stockmann greets her husband's final discovery of wisdom – these, though not conclusive, all look like pointers towards some such conclusion as Kruuse draws. That Ibsen did not aim at presenting unmitigated tragedies is also hinted at, perhaps, by the habit to which Mc-Farlane draws attention, of referring to his plays throughout his life as 'monkey tricks'.

There is a difference, though, between including comedy within a tragedy, and making the tragedy itself comic, as the Absurdists do. The Fool disappears well before the end of *Lear*, Osric plays no part in Hamlet's funeral, and the Pandarus who speaks the epilogue of *Troilus* has ceased being funny altogether. There is also a difference between the mocking by the Fool of a man of Lear's stature, and the self-mockery of Hedda. If Hedda had ever done anything to deserve our respect or admiration, there would be some point in bringing out the weakness of her strength. As it is, when she makes her brief, farcical reappearance she is merely adding one more heartless trick to the pile. Similarly, Gregers' suggestion that Hedvig should kill herself is based on too naïve a misinterpretation of Hjalmar's chance remark for his 'vasty deep' to do more than add one more naivety.

The comicality of Ulfheim, though it may be meant to present Life and Nature-in-the-Raw with irony, is crude in much the same way. On the other hand the final episode, in which Rubek and Irene climb the mountain, has all the appearance of a serious ending, apart from one or two features. The usual pattern is still present: instead of Solness climbing the steeple alone, Rubek now climbs with Irene; instead of Rosmer and Rebecca finding their consummation in suicide, Rubek and Irene find theirs in virtual suicide (they are warned of the storm), and the avalanche destroys them as an earlier one destroyed Brand. If this standard situation is mocked at all by Ibsen it could well be because he felt it to be too obviously repetitive.

Yet one cannot be certain about the irony, there is too much that looks like straightforward naivety and mishandling. When Rubek and Irene appear, they are supposed to have just completed an ascent so difficult that, as Ulfheim tells them, it will be beyond

their powers to descend again. Irene, however, is said to have 'a
fur cloak thrown loosely over her white dress', which sounds
more as though she were waiting for a taxi, while her hood is said
to be of swansdown – no doubt in allusion to her earlier conversation in which she spoke of being the swan to Rubek's Lohengrin,
(any symbolism intended is obscure). Whatever may be meant, the
kind of down used for the hood will not be distinguishable, in the
theatre, from that of several other birds. Ibsen's mind is so little on
the stage, in these stage directions, that we may doubt how
detached he felt from what he was writing, whether he really had
at this point the capacity for irony.

From here on, the dialogue is certainly portentous: for a while
nothing is said without generous indications of the symbolism.
Ulf heim is so heavily symbolical about reaching positions from
which one can neither go forward nor back that Rubek has no
need to draw attention to his mode of speech, though he does.
Rubek himself then says of the wind that it sounds 'like the prelude
to Resurrection Day', to which Ulf heim replies that this is a
genuine storm which will soon be 'all round us like a winding-
sheet', and Irene adds, with a shiver, 'I know that sheet!' The
purport of all this is more than clear enough; what is not clear is
its relation to the personalities on stage. In what sense is Irene
'dead'? Has she undergone a mystic's self-annihilation (surely not)
or is she inanely callous? What has this talk of resurrection to do
with anything that has been happening? Does Rubek believe in an
after-life? One has the impression that Ibsen is using words with
no real backing, stock metaphors in verbal form rather than in
dramatised representations.

Ulf heim now insists that Rubek and Irene take refuge in a
nearby hut while he goes down with Maia to fetch help. But though
he says ropes will be needed to effect the rescue, he himself
'climbs hastily but warily down with Maia in his arms'. A descent
so easily managed seems unlikely to offer such difficulties as he
forecast, and again one wonders whether Ibsen was not more
concerned with presenting Ulf heim quite naïvely as a strong man,
than with visualising the situation concretely. To ask this is not to
demand a crude literalism, it is rather to become aware how little
the situation can make the symbolism meaningful.

The same holds true of the ascent. Clearly Rubek and Irene expect some great consummation on the peaks. Their qualification for this is, as they now reaffirm, that they are in some sense 'dead'. Rubek has betrayed Irene, betrayed the Ideal, by not making love to her when she stood before him naked, as his model. He has failed, we might say, to make the synthesis of the real and the ideal. Irene has perished because of his failure, though this does not mean she no longer experiences evil emotions.

Suddenly, as Irene is reproaching Rubek with his lack of sensual desire for her, he announces that that is precisely what he now feels. 'Do you know', he asks 'passionately' (but that opening question shows up his pretence) 'that just that love [the love which is the life of the world] – it is burning and seething in me as hotly as ever before?' This is surprising, for Rubek has shown no sign of it till this instant. Ibsen's manipulation is nowhere more in evidence. Yet Rubek goes on in such a hackneyed way that one scarcely knows whether to speak of irony as still even remotely possible. 'Both in us and around us Life is fermenting and throbbing as fiercely as ever', and 'Then let us two, dead, live life for once to the uttermost, before we go down to our graves again!' Irene replies in kind: 'Up in the light and in all the glittering glory!' And to ensure that the synthesis is not omitted Rubek adds 'All the powers of light may freely look upon us. And all the powers of darkness too.' They will pass through the mists and climb to the top of a tower shining in the sunrise. But what is meant by the powers 'looking upon' them remains as vague as everything else. Just as Rebecca and Rosmer are satisfied that they will be dying 'together', so the joining of light and darkness is sufficient here.

If Ibsen does mean these clichés to be taken ironically we must suppose him to mean that the Hegelian tradition is one long series of clichés of this kind, Rubek and Irene being the most recent of the poor fools to have been deluded by it. The difficulty about finding any answer to such problems is that the Hegelian tradition itself includes irony, as in the irony defined by Friedrich Schlegel (see p. 112), whereby perfection is produced through ironical self-distancing from what has been portrayed. To say that Ibsen is ironical in this sense would not be to say that he was aware of the triviality of his characters – especially of Rubek and Irene in their final scene – or of the platitudinousness of their language. It would be rather to say that he meant to combine a positive and a negative where he produced only a plain triviality.

A few further dialectical devices complete the play. Though Irene and Rubek disappear from view, attempting their 'ideal' consummation, Maia is heard up to the final curtain, singing her trite ditty:

> I am free! I am free! I am free!
> No more life in the prison for me!
> I am free as a bird! I am free!

as she goes downhill in the arms of Ulfheim. In the pattern she represents a complementary opposite, a 'real' consummation in contrast to that of the other pair, though she is also treated with irony, we may suppose, since Ulfheim is her lot. Presumably she is not herself carried away by the avalanche which sweeps away Rubek and Irene. ('They', the stage directions read, can be 'dimly descried as they are whirled down in the midst of the masses of snow and buried by them' – another occasion when Ibsen is not thinking in stage terms.) But the avalanche is an arbitrary ending. Ibsen will have it so, that the pair cannot consummate their love, yet the avalanche has no connection with their ascent, and nothing in the fact of their seeking consummation leads to this catastrophe.

Yet more arbitrary is the final appearance of the Sister of Mercy, who has hitherto seemed like a malignant Fate, staring out of the bushes at Irene, following her with piercing eyes. (The word 'Mercy' is not in the Norwegian *Diakonissen*, which means simply a nun belonging to a nursing order.) Though the Sister is evidently a Christian, there has been little merciful about her, and Christianity has played no part in the play as a whole. Now, as she witnesses Irene's death, the Sister gives a shriek, stretches out her arms, calls out 'Irene!' and makes the sign of the Cross as she speaks the words 'Pax vobiscum!' This, as the final visible gesture of the play (dialectically juxtaposed with the sound of Maia's life-affirmation, off-stage) is a last inconsequential pretence at piety. If Ibsen had wanted to make the sign of the Cross meaningful he would have needed to do more about it earlier on. As it is, the gesture has all the air of a piece of showmanship. The public might be expected to take to such a solemnity. Ibsen was prepared to offer it, for what it was worth. Together with the other arbitrary moments in the final scene it makes a slapdash end to his career as a dramatist.

Speculating, one might see in the avalanche something more inwardly important to Ibsen himself. The desire for sexual union, whether or not the base, carnal lusts have been sent down where they belong, and only the purest ideal love is intended, is savagely and unaccountably repressed by some kind of authority, paternal or divine. In this sense, *When We Dead Awaken* repeats the idea of *The Master Builder*, when an unseen hand, presumably, sends Solness to his death just as he is crowning his new erection. A good deal of Ibsen's work would answer to that kind of interpretation, but it was not offered by him in that spirit, and it is only as a playwright that Ibsen concerns us here. The collapse of his powers in these last three plays is sad enough, without investigating the states of mind that gave rise to it. As plays, they fail in coherence, dramatic movement, psychological insight, even in ordinary perceptiveness about human behaviour. The increasingly crude caricatures and comic treatment indicate a lack of self-possession, a need to assert strongly where no real strength was felt. And always Ibsen draws on the one source of his inspiration, his preoccupation with his own identity. If that identity could be shown to be infinitely greater than it really was, he would be satisfied, and the feeling of inferiority which went with his youthful experiences in remote and humble Skien, with his early failures as a dramatist, and with his shyness and preference for his own company would be shown to be unjustified. Yet in the very act of proving himself a man, and a great man, he felt a sense of hubris. His ambition had to be called diabolical, it had to have the taint of Lucifer about it, if it was to be an ambition worth having. But that, once realised, afforded a continual series of dialectical progressions. If the self could be hugely wicked, as Peer Gynt wanted to be, it could also have the satisfaction of a huge downfall and a corresponding resurrection, leading to yet further impious revolts. There was always the fear, as Peer saw, that the impiety would not be big enough to count, especially as it was imaginary anyway, and chiefly confined to the plays. But that fear could be countered by making the Ideal look as ludicrous as it does in Irene – the challenge, it could be implied, was not meant seriously, but was part of the dialectical pattern all along.

In real life Ibsen was timid and irresolute. In the fantasy world, the pattern of rise and fall and renewed rise could go on indefinitely, and it was merely a matter of devising new illustrations for it. Few of Ibsen's plays are essentially anything but variations on a basic pattern, and he was too taken up with that to have time for much observation of the outside world. This is why his characters react to one another as draughtsmen rather than chessmen. They are not expected by him to have complex emotions of their own, only definite reactions of fear, hatred, ambition, jealousy, and to behave as though that one reaction were sufficient explanation of their conduct. Tesman dances completely to Ibsen's tune, not Hedda's, so that everything may seem to compel her to suicide. Rosmer leaps into the millstream with Rebecca despite the fact that her death is to make life possible for him, since the lovers must come to a disastrous end like almost all the other lovers in Ibsen. Over and over again the simple pattern is echoed, and each time the field remains clear for yet one more variation, since the goal is never reached, and the contraries always contain within themselves yet further contraries. At the same time, by allowing them to repeat themselves, Ibsen was, wittingly or not, fulfilling the Hegelian precept of expressing his own self as an essential manifestation of the Spirit underlying all things. In this sense, though each new effort at climbing the mountain or the steeple was doomed to failure through the intervention of some club-footed enemy, the whole process of challenge and defeat was itself a manifestation of the Spirit *in extenso*. Such ideas were staple items of nineteenth-century philosophies, and Ibsen would not have needed to know much of them in order to make use of them. What he failed to do was to give dramatic flavour to them that would bear any relationship to reality. His world was solipsistic, bounded in a nutshell, never the conquest it appeared to be, and it depended for its continued existence on being confined to his imaginings. Like Hedda, Ibsen never looked for a freedom that was not in itself ambiguous, restricted to the very world which he was at the same time condemning.

II
Conclusion

Considering the violence of the opposition, Ibsen's reputation in England was established with surprising speed, and not much more slowly in America. His plays came to the English-speaking world with a triumphant progress in Germany and Scandinavia, as well as a scandalous notoriety, already achieved. *Pillars of Society* had been performed in Berlin in 1878 at five different theatres within a few months of publication of the Norwegian text. *A Doll's House*, not properly performed in London till 1889, had by that time been translated into six languages and was the talk of the town in several European capitals, while Ibsen himself had received an honorary degree from Uppsala, been honoured by the theatrically prominent Duke of Saxe-Meiningen, and fêted in Berlin and Weimar. He came in on a wave of enthusiasm for Scandinavian writing which is characterised by the decision of Arno Holz and Johannes Schlaf, the German Naturalists, to publish their early work under a Norwegian pseudonym.

In the 1880s, no country in Europe yet had a lively contemporary theatre of serious drama, or had had one for the best part of a century, despite a few isolated figures. Melodrama, historical pageants, the *pièce bien faite* were the rule before Naturalism got under way. On the other hand, opera had established itself through Wagner and Verdi with a power that showed managers what a potential theatre-audience existed, and Ibsen was able to provide exciting treatments of topics of the moment, topics which the spread of popular education made all the more attractive. Ibsen appealed in Germany partly because of his self-evident affinity with German tradition: *Peer Gynt* at once recalled *Faust*, Stockmann was compared with Schiller's *William Tell*, and *Emperor and Galilean* clearly had links with the main stream of German philosophy. His plays were crisper than Bjørnson's, less turgid than Hebbel's, and being a Norwegian, he was claimed to have 'sprung from Germanic soil'. By comparison with Wildenbruch and Bendix, he was vividly real in his treatment of contemporary society.

In France, he became known even later than in England. The first performance there of an Ibsen play was that of *Ghosts*, in 1890. Though Wagner had been celebrated since Baudelaire's time, the Nordic quality in Ibsen made less appeal, and perhaps the whole scandalousness of Nora's door-slamming was *vieux jeu* since George Sand had declared the rights of women so passionately sixty years before. At all events it was not through France that Ibsen came to England, but rather, as Havelock Ellis put it, 'as the chief figure of European significance that has appeared in the Teutonic world of art since Goethe'. This association, whether approved by Norwegians or not, lent Ibsen a European stature which was upheld by the comparisons which could be made between him and Marx, Nietzsche, or Schopenhauer. Socialists like Keir Hardie and John Burns welcomed Stockmann as though he stood for something akin to their own ideals, while one critic maliciously saw in Solness a parallel to Mr Gladstone. Shaw spoke of Ibsen as though he were concerned with Supermen. There were sufficient broad similarities with main trends in European thought for Brandes to champion him as their epitome.

The first advocate in England was Edmund Gosse, in 1872, followed shortly by William Archer and after seventeen years by a host of critics of all opinions, aroused by the performance of *A Doll's House*. Gosse was a sincerely convinced pioneer who had come across Ibsen's work when it was still almost unknown outside Scandinavia, and been deeply moved by it. One of his first arguments was in praise of Ibsen's seriousness, and it is understandable that the absence of any wish to divert or titillate was a powerful attraction in itself. But the Ibsen whom Gosse went on to defend was not seen as later generations came to see him. The frequent comparisons with Tolstoy, who by that time was becoming a great exemplar of the simple life and of Christian self-denial, ignore the almost total absence of such themes in Ibsen (Gosse was no doubt thinking of *Brand*), as well as the contrast between such characters as Pierre and Levine, and the single-minded ruthlessness of so many of Ibsen's. Gosse misread the ending of *Pillars of Society*, supposing that Consul Bernick finally makes 'a clean breast of all his rogueries' – which, if Tolstoy had created him, he probably would have done – and representing *Ghosts* not as an insoluble dilemma but as a solemn and poignant appeal to conscience. His account of Rebecca West is surprising: though Gosse compared her for unscrupulousness with Becky Sharp, he found her 'intellectually and spiritually...a very much finer creature'. Her instincts, he added, evidently meaning her instinct to kill Beate Rosmer, 'are certainly distinguished, and even splendid... She sees that Beate is past helping, and she therefore sweeps her away into the milldam as fast as she can...' This surprising admiration is out of keeping not only with Gosse's general defence of Ibsen but with the tenor of his writing in other works, and we can only suppose he was unprepared for such developments in Ibsen after he first came across him. His reading of the earlier plays can hardly have prepared him for the later ones, and as the controversy in England approached he was already withdrawing a little. Of the seven plays he championed in 1889 he was content to let two go with very faint praise, even modestly to admit that better-equipped critics than himself might find Ibsen 'occasionally provincial, sometimes obscure, often fantastic and enigmatical' – all phrases that sound like concessions to his friend Henry James, who was still far from convinced. Yet Gosse was a reasonable and unimpassioned protagonist, whose moderate tone must have contributed to his influence. It was James, in fact, who changed sides.

Arthur Symons read far more into Ibsen than Gosse did. He too thought that Bernick was 'manly enough to rise through confession to a spiritual victory' (Egan p. 96), though Gosse had had some doubts about how long the victory was likely to last. Symons was altogether more emphatic, seeing in Ibsen a demand that men should live according to nature, and an offer of shrewd advice about doing so: 'he is directly and steadily practical, full of common sense, shrewdness, attention to fact, to detail'. Like W. D. Howells, considered in his time the pre-eminent American man of letters, Symons was able to draw guidance from the slimmest hints: 'for clear light upon difficult ways...for satire which is cruel and healing…for the qualities that make social drama helpful and illuminating' Ibsen was pre-eminent (Egan p. 97). It was precisely this supposed helpfulness which put some of Ibsen's critics off, though it accorded well with the Naturalist programmes, and with the kind of drama Zola had been asking for.

Yet whatever the strength with which the case for Ibsen was presented, the case against him was severely damaged by its shrillness. By 1891 William Archer was able to score heavily, merely by quoting the vituperations poured out over Ibsen by newspaper critics. 'An open drain: a loathsome sore unbandaged, a dirty act done publicly; a lazar-house with all its doors and windows open'; 'naked loathsomeness', 'revoltingly suggestive and blasphemous', 'lugubrious diagnosis of sordid impropriety', 'maunderings of nookshotten Norwegians', 'educated and muck-ferreting dogs' – the virulence of such cullings from reviews put playgoers on Archer's side by pure instinct. Archer provided more: he argued, contrary to Symons, that Ibsen was not writing in general terms about the need for ill-treated wives to leave their husbands, but for Nora to leave hers, that Ibsen intended only to arouse people to see and think for themselves, that he was not a propounder of nostrums but essentially one of the great poets of the world. Yet though no defender was more prolific than Archer, a large part of his writing consisted of showing up the opposition, denouncing poor translations, demonstrating the bad faith of reviewers, and this did much towards making the opposition ashamed of itself. Within a few years it had completely changed its attitude.

This was largely due also to the publication by Henry James in 1891 of a long article 'On the Occasion of *Hedda Gabler*', a play he had seen performed just over a month earlier. Michael Egan, in his account of Ibsen's reception, regards this as a landmark, signifying the emergence on Ibsen's side of a formidable and widely respected champion; it 'effectively silenced all opposition' (p. 16). No literary figure of such standing in England had yet spoken on Ibsen's behalf.

James was not altogether whole-hearted, though this may merely have increased the respect accorded to him. There is a vagueness at times and a note of withdrawing irony quite unlike Gosse's straightforward admiration. Though the tone is on the whole favourable, James begins by noting in *Hedda* 'the absence of humour, the absence of free imagination,' and – surely, a grave fault in James's eyes – 'the absence of style'. He goes on to speak of a 'recurrent ugliness of surface', of Ibsen's 'charmless fascination', and observes that 'he has as little as possible to say to our taste'. Yet the parochial or suburban stamp which James finds is presented as 'a sort of substitute – a little clumsy if you like – for charm'. There is a good deal to suggest less than enthusiastic recognition of a major dramatist, and his account of *Hedda*, some of whose inconsistencies have been discussed (p. 131), implies that the play was lucky to find such a superlative actress as Miss Robins. Ibsen, he remarks, is clearly 'destined to be adored by the "profession"'.

Yet the conclusion, still shaded with ironical strokes from time to time, is rounded off with the suggestion that if only England possessed a truly artistic and disinterested theatre 'it would simply be a point of honour in such a temple to sacrifice sometimes to Henrik Ibsen'. At least a minor deity has been recognised.

The article does not reveal the private feelings voiced by James in a letter to Gosse only a few weeks earlier, just after seeing Elizabeth Robins play Hedda. Gosse, so James thought shortly before, had made Ibsen out to be a 'richer phenomenon' than he really was:

The perusal of the dreary *Rosmersholm* and even the reperusal of *Ghosts* has been rather a shock to me – they have let me down, down. Surely the former isn't *good*? Any more than the tedious *Lady from the Sea* is? *Must* I think these things works of skill? If I must I will, save to you alone: to whom I confide that they seem to be of a grey mediocrity – in the case of *Rosmersholm jusqu'à être bête*.

James allowed his low estimate of *Lady from the Sea* to be publicly apparent, but not his severe criticism of any other play, or his earlier view of Ibsen in general, revealed in the letter in these terms:

they come off so little, in general, as plays; & I can't think that a man who is at odds with his form is ever a first-rate man.

But this was an opinion James was not willing to uphold in public. The letter ends with an appeal to Gosse: 'and at any rate, don't *tell* it of yours tremulously. . .'. The adopted stance soon became a conviction and within a few years James was openly preferring Ibsen to Shakespeare.

After this the walls tumbled fast. Shaw's *Quintessence of Ibsenism* of 1891, though more about Shaw than about Ibsen, was one of the trumpet-blasts that helped. Despite the screams of outrage in 1889, by 1893 *An Enemy of the People* was almost universally acclaimed in the Press, and four years later Queen Victoria herself, accompanied by the Archbishop of Canterbury, attended a performance of *Ghosts* as part of her Golden Jubilee celebrations. In that same year, 1897, after the production of *John Gabriel Borkman*, despite some vigorous dissent, the dispute about Ibsen was virtually over. It flickered on in America for some years, with New England Puritans on one side and immigrant Norwegians on the other, but by the time of Ibsen's death in 1906 respectful and even adulatory obituaries were the order of the day. From the turn of the century onwards, the new production of an Ibsen play was no longer a subject for scandalised protest but for a demonstration of cultural concern.

Biographical and critical studies began to flow, though opposition still remained. Arnold Bennett was surprised to find, in 1906, that *The Wild Duck* was so deplorably symbolical, and marvelled at the change in his own views, which in the early 1890s had made him convinced of Ibsen's superiority: 'Yet now I am pretty well convinced that Ibsen is not a writer of masterpieces'. He had gone with the tide and yet found a necessity to go back against it. Yeats had also experienced something of the same compulsion: 'neither I nor my generation could escape [Ibsen] because, though we and he had not the same friends, we had the same enemies'. The need to oppose the Philistinism represented by the Press outweighed other considerations, but not for long, and Yeats made his complete distaste for Ibsen unmistakable, as did Synge. Eliot was never so outspoken, and yet felt Yeats's point deeply enough to advance the view that Ibsen's inadequacy as a poet meant he would not last as long as Cyril Tourneur. Lawrence, after his enthusiasm in early youth, wrote (in *Twilight in Italy*) of 'a certain intolerable nastiness in the real Ibsen', whom he now saw, in 1912, as 'exciting, nervously sensational', 'impertinent, irreverent, nasty'.

So much dissent from poets and novelists is not negligible, particularly when the private wavering or half-hearted alignments of some of Ibsen's admirers is recalled.

The vast bulk of writing about Ibsen in the last seventy years is of course favourable, or at any rate assumes that so established a reputation can be taken for granted. To characterise it in a short space would be impossible, even for anyone who had managed to read it all. It contains the familiar features of academic study, tracings of influence, linkings of symbols, political and philosophical charges and counter-charges, examination of sources and drafts, accounts of its own progress and achievements, but it also contains matter of critical substance which can only be treated at length in its own terms. Some of this matter has been discussed here as it seemed relevant, though inevitably with much less than a comprehensive survey.

Yet some special causes of difficulty in Ibsen criticism can be advanced. Because of the inherent ambiguity in almost every character or situation, it is possible to defend Ibsen in contradictory ways with at first sight equal justification. Mrs Alving is both guilty of causing Oswald's suffering and innocent of it. Hedda both desires to control Løvborg and to free him. Solness's death is caused both by something like divine intervention and by Miss Wangel. This in itself gives rise to constant renewals of inquiry, as each unambiguous account proves less than adequate.

The situation is further bedevilled by the common assumption since William Empson published *Seven Types of Ambiguity*, that ambiguity is the hallmark of creative writing. It is an assumption from which Empson explicitly dissociated himself, when he came, in his final chapter, to discuss 'the conditions under which ambiguity is proper'. 'An ambiguity', he went on, 'is not satisfying in itself, nor is it, considered as a device on its own, a thing to be attempted... Thus the practice of "trying not to be ambiguous" has a great deal to be said for it.' But in a critical world where dialectical philosophies are esteemed, self-contradiction is positively admired, and Ibsen's position is the more assured. Even his implied criticisms of his own mode of writing – as in *The Wild Duck* – become further evidence of his superior awareness, his ability to affirm and deny simultaneously, and thus achieve that totality of human self-realisation which in the Hegelian tradition passes for mastery.

The frequent absence of any specific reference in Ibsen's symbols lends him yet more universal potentialities. *An Enemy of the People* can be billed in the 1970s as a play about world-pollution, regardless of its dramatic value. *A Doll's House* now appears, as it has often done before, as an attack in the fashion of the moment on the institution of marriage, despite Ibsen's own disclaimers, while *Ghosts* can be offered as demonstrating the evil effects of repression, especially to audiences under the mistaken notion that Freud declared all repression to be disastrous. Dramatic moments like the tarantella, the clutching of the phial of morphine, the riot at Stockmann's meeting lend emotional weight to these attractions, though the suggestivity of the symbols is more for-tuitous than poetic. Some of Ibsen's continuing success on the stage can be attributed to this, though dutiful respect plays a part, as well as the amiable conspiracy of actors and actresses to provide an evening's entertainment, which is not always doggedly faithful to every nuance of the text. As James Joyce said, 'it is just to pre-vent excessive pondering that Ibsen requires to be acted', and it is true that a play is essentially something that happens on a stage. It is when plays stand up to so little pondering as Ibsen's do that the defence no longer holds.

The dramatic quality in the plays, and the great pruning and economising of effort which made those written in his fifties and early sixties so much more impressive in that respect than anything else he wrote, are evidence not only of his tenacity but also of the lively impulse that made him persist in the face of disastrous early failures. There was a serious core to all his work, which, like Goethe, he might have called fragments of a great confession, though his themes were far fewer than Goethe's. A handful of deeply felt experiences in his early days drove Ibsen to one drama after another: his suspicion that he was illegitimate, the illegitimacy of his own first child, his early alcoholism, the bankruptcy and degradation of his father, the poverty which followed, the hostility of other boys and his seclusiveness in a society where he felt an outsider, always dogged his thoughts. At the same time he had the conviction of his own mission. Guilt was inescapable, but there was an imaginable world in which the self could be realised in complete freedom from guilt. The fullest expansion of his powers must be possible, without anyone else being the worse for it. A figure like Faust, though it need not have occupied his thoughts continually, was well suited to this ambition, in so far as Faust expects to overcome his isolation by the device of identifying his own self with all other selves, whether they assent to the symbiosis or not.

From the late 1870s onwards these early experiences constantly recur, though they had not been quite absent before. The guilty secret must be revealed, whether by Bernick or Nora; it must be possible for this to happen without total disaster. Freedom in sexual relations need not have the disastrous consequences it had had for himself (he was responsible for payments towards the upkeep of his illegitimate son for fourteen years): like Captain Alving he should not pay so heavily for kicking over the traces. But together with such assertions came the realisation of the contrary: the urchins who jeered at Ibsen as a schoolboy had left their mark. The secret could not be revealed, illegitimacy was an ineradicable blot; worst of all, the chain from father to son was unbreakable.

The writing of plays based on these realisations and counter-realisations subtly intertwined itself with his own life. *Ghosts* was not only in itself about his own fate and frustration, it was proof of the continued hostility of society to what he wanted to reveal. Stockmann was, up to a point, right: they deserved nothing but extermination, though reflection showed that this could only be said with tongue half in cheek. From the mid 80s onwards, the themes of the plays come more and more to treat of artists of one kind or another, whether sculptors or architects or writers of books. Through such figures he could set down his chagrin as well as his continuing aspirations in terms of what had now become his life's work, since he was not so much concerned by this time with the realisation of total freedom – that had been countered by his own irony too often – as with the possibility of making successful plays. Success in drama, which did not involve a breakthrough but only a statement of the insoluble contradictions, was taking the place of the earlier hope for success in rising above them.

The international fame of the 1880s sustained this trend. The unbearable personal suffering was meaningful to other people ignorant of his circumstances; a bond could be created even if he could only reveal the hurt without curing it. It was at this time, however, that the symbols began to become more intrusive. They asserted themselves, from *Ghosts* onwards, with increasing strength because he could now more confidently assert for his own condition a more universal significance, such as he had suspected it possessed even at the time of creating Earl Skule. 'We are all ghosts'. With that declaration of a comprehensive philosophy, he broke the ice. Stockmann widened the gap: not only were we all ghosts, we were all hypocrites. After that the symbols proper began to take over, the wild duck, the white horses, the tall steeple. They seemed to add a dimension to his personal condition, though in fact they merely supplied false buttressing. The situation in the plays, however much they might reflect his own, were not helped by these portentous additions, which led to further ironical thoughts about their own absurdity. The self-reflections turned more and more to their own substance for their continuing life.

Underneath, he recognised that. Nothing had been achieved, no values asserted, fame was a will o' the wisp, popular success despicable, and the tug-of-war of affirmations and negations led nowhere. The knowledge is reflected in the peculiar form of his humour, which is thin and carping, sardonic, bleak, a black humour that grotesquely reflected his awareness of dissatisfaction, and registered that too, as a further degree of self-knowledge, though without ever letting it become a self-acceptance. It is a humour that defends him against a possible critical reaction, rather than one that goes out to enjoy the situation with a spectator whose own perceptiveness is admitted: there is nothing genial about it. Like his careful provision of explanatory speeches covering all the points to which a hard-line Scribean critic might object, his humour was really another line of fortification.

The attractiveness of a conventional life was still strong. He could break loose from the pessimistic compulsion with a sentimentally conceived victory for Ellida Wangel, in which the odds were heavily weighted on her side, and the elemental forces were thinned down. But *Hedda Gabler* is like a fierce rejection of that acclimatisation, all the more virulent against convention because of the concession which the preceding play had made. The fact of his emptiness was inescapable, and so was the fact that there was nothing left but to write about it, to lay bare the stranglehold which destroyed his aspirations as Hedda destroyed Løvborg's. The necessity to dramatise the inner conflict went on. But where Nora still had some faint prospect of winning, and even Stockmann went on in the face of overwhelming odds, none of his characters now stood a chance, unless by another sentimentally devised victory like Allmers'. Hedda held out nothing but a hope of freedom that was vitiated as she pronounced it, in the very terms in which she pronounced it: Dionysian revelry in pseudo-respectable Christiania. Her romantically conceived suicide had also a positive element, in so far as it was a courageous, 'noble' gesture that Løvborg had failed to make, but that too was bitterly undermined by her doll-like head popping out between the curtains just before the fatal shot. Only a mood of self-laceration remained, but the last laugh was still against the Bracks: 'People don't do such things.'

The fact of *Hedda Gabler*'s success is a sign of the times. Baudelaire's 'hypocrite lecteur' was beginning to admit that he did know what Boredom was, and saw his reflection in Hedda. Dispirited spectators might even see a grand gesture in that bullet-shot through the temple. The overwhelmingly strong inertia of Büchner's Danton was beginning to be recognised, in the 1890s, as of the moment, and Wedekind's desolate world of cruelty was establishing itself. The world of Samuel Beckett was still fifty years off, but *Hedda* foreshadowed it. Yet despite this chiming-in with leading notes of the day, the last four plays of Ibsen's career show an increasing withdrawal from reality, a fundamental retreat into Narcissistic self-regard and self-rejection. The change is marked by the difference between Rosmer and Solness. Rosmer's inspiration had clearly come from outside, through Rebecca. Solness's comes from Hilde, but Hilde is much less distinct from his own desires, almost a projection of them. The earlier ambitions are being transferred to a solipsistic world, and *The Master Builder* is as much concerned with whether Ibsen himself can go on writing plays with a religious or spiritual meaning as it is with the overt problems of Solness the architect. Borkman has even less access to the world outside. He has nothing left but a determination to do something or other, and though the old Faustian theme is still in evidence the real issue remains obscure, and neither Ella nor Gunhild can penetrate the isolation. Only the benediction they pronounce at the end asserts against all likelihood that a great man, though at the end of his tether, deserves recognition at least for the magnitude of his ambition. Ambition without substance is all that remains.

Ibsen is confessing to himself, not wholly despairingly, his own failure. When Rubek appears, in the last play of all, and dismisses all his former sculptures as worthless caricatures, it is not impossible to hear the voice of Ibsen magnifying his own one-dimensional boobies and villains into grotesque animal-headed monsters. The reasons for Rubek's dissatisfaction remain as unclear as Ibsen's – since they are not expressed through any criticisms valid for sculpture, they have no transferable significance for drama either. But precisely because they are unclear, the possibility of paradox is still present. The victory is gained by admitting defeat, 'to be oneself is to slay oneself', to have worked through all the cycle of positives and negatives that can be experienced in a lifetime is enough. The statement about Ibsen's life has been made, during half a century, and it amounts to nothing; but the Naught is the All, the shredding down of the layers of the onion to its central nothingness at the same time displays the process of shredding, and the two statements, the nothingness and the process, suffice.

There is never any end to the dialectical process, any more than there is in it any end to the extremes of black and white, booby and villain, simultaneous success and failure. The more rigidly drawn of Ibsen's characters are as much the result of his attachment to systems akin to Hegel's as they are of his personal frustrations and inabilities to perceive more subtly. Yet so long as paradoxes are accepted not as mysteries to be resolved but as natural and inevitable facts of existence, to be accepted and multiplied rather than reduced, his reputation need not suffer, and statements about him can go on glistering this way and that, like shot silk.

One final unambiguous claim is still made on his behalf: the claim that what he wrote was, despite its prosaic form, essentially poetry, as he maintained it would be. There is something suspiciously paradoxical about the claim, it is true, and perhaps in the long run it can only be tested through intimate knowledge of his own native language. Criticism of Ibsen-in-English will always be precisely that and no more. Yet judging what English-speaking critics with a knowledge of Norwegian tell us about the poetic values of the original is not an impossible task, and though it seems too technical to include in the body of this work, it has a place in an appendix.

The upshot is, it is true, that the case for Ibsen as a poet has still to be made. There is no more foundation for it than there is for the value placed on his plays on other grounds. But the juggernaut has been rolling for a good many years now, and is likely to go on by its own inertia indefinitely. Only deliberate effort will reverse the movement.

Appendix
The poetry and the prose

The most serious criticism of Ibsen has always been concerned with the quality of his writing. Yeats had him in mind when he spoke, in a preface to a play of Synge's, of the 'writers of our modern dramatic movement, our scientific dramatists, our naturalists on the stage' who wrote 'in the impersonal language that has come, not out of individual life, nor out of life at all...' Synge was equally opposed to what he called Ibsen's 'joyless and pallid words', to which he contrasted his own desire for plays in which 'every speech should be as fully flavoured as a nut or apple'. The memory of those criticisms still haunts the defenders of Ibsen today, when knowledge of his own language is more widespread among critics than it used to be. Since the protests were made against Ibsen as he appeared in translation, it may still be possible to show that in the original tongue he remains the poet he always claimed to be.

Ibsen began both as a lyric poet and as a dramatist, and his early plays used both verse and prose. When he decided to abandon verse altogether he did so because 'all the many ordinary and insignificant characters would have been blurred and mixed up with each other if I had let them all talk together in measured rhythms'. He did not see verse as a peculiarly subtle means of revealing depths of character. He was also influenced by the Naturalist vogue: 'what I wanted to portray was people, and it was precisely for that reason that I did not allow them to speak with the "tongues of angels"'. He might still have chosen to write verse-plays, even in the epoch of Naturalism; there were still many dramatists interested in neo-Romantic verse-drama, and Wagner had shown how little Naturalism need be the theatrical style of the age. But Ibsen advanced the Naturalist ideal as a reason for not letting bank-managers and clergymen speak in verse. It was only after this that he came back to the paradoxical claim, shared by none of the Naturalists themselves, that he was in fact still writing in poetry.

Or rather, that is what is said on his behalf. The occasion of the paradoxical claim was a request from the actress Lucie Wolf in May 1883 for a prologue in verse. In declining to provide this, Ibsen replied that he was devoting himself now to the 'very much more difficult art of writing poetry in straightforward, realistic, everyday language.' But though this is usually taken as a basis for the counter-attack on the criticisms of Yeats and Synge and others, the translation of his words can be misleading. What is rendered as 'writing poetry' is in fact *digte*, which, like the German *dichten*, need not imply anything remotely like poetry, but rather a certain literary quality above the ordinary level. *Digte* is equally possible as a description of the work of a certain kind of novelist as of that of a poet or dramatist. Ibsen's sentence in his letter could have been rendered almost as well with 'writing in straightforward, realistic, everyday language', so long as it was understood that he was continuing to make a claim to be taken as a serious writer. 'Writing poetry' seems to introduce an element of deliberate paradox which need not have been in his mind at all. He was simply saying to Lucie Wolf 'I will not write you a prologue in verse, because I find it difficult enough to write good plain prose.'

The misunderstanding of *digte* has led all the same to a lot of attempts at showing Ibsen truly wearing vine-leaves in his hair, while making use of the ordinary speech of his day. The myth once established, any prose Ibsen wrote qualifies for a demonstration that it carries the power of poetry. There is the case of Rebecca West's account of her plot against Beate Rosmer, originally raised by R. G. Cox in *Scrutiny*. Could it be, Cox asked, merely the translation which sets Rebecca's speech on such a completely different plane from any comparable speech in Shakespeare?

REBECCA And yet I *could* not stop. I had to venture just the least little bit further. Only one hairsbreadth more. And then one more – and always one more – and then it happened – . That is the way such things come about.   (Act 3)

As it stands, there is no disputing: this is language without life or emotion, with no particular distinction of any kind. In comparison with the passage Cox suggested, from *Macbeth*, it is lacking in the very thing Ibsen hoped to achieve by writing prose – character. Here Macbeth plans to murder Duncan as Rebecca in effect planned to murder Beate:

> My thought, whose murder yet is but fantastical,
> Shakes so my single state of man that function
> Is smother'd in surmise, and nothing is
> But what is not.

The whole effect of this is of an entirely different order. Ibsen's language suits, it is true, the rather nonchalant way in which Rebecca regards the whole affair – her remark at the end, that murders generally do happen after such a piecemeal progression, does suit the theoretical, detached feeling about murder which she says she had. The question remains, whether such language is typical of Ibsen, and it can only be answered by looking again and again. On his single instance, Cox carried initial conviction.

With a knowledge of Norwegian, however, this same passage can, with sufficient faith, be shown to be one of the most telling in the whole play. Inga-Stina Ewbank draws particular attention to the ordinary enough phrase, 'and then it happened', in order to demonstrate its quite different power in the original. The four syllables *og så* kom *det* ('and so *came* it') are at the climax of several staccato sentences, 'quick, low jerks which give the sense of the suppression of enormous nervous force and lead us to anticipate a breaking-point'. In the original, which does have one syllable less than the English, the phrase has 'a dull finality', like the sound of a body hitting the water – in short, Ibsen is poetically expressing the feeling of Rebecca's own body hitting the millstream. Also to be noticed is the stress on the verb, and the vagueness of *det*, providing 'a kind of depersonalisation so that what is happening is seen as a process outside human control'. The same four words also convey, but by evoking rather than stating, something of the 'mysterious forces at work in the world of the play' – in short they are a hint at the white horses. Ibsen could never have hoped for such an obliging imagination.

As much obligingness is shown by critics who claim no knowledge of the language at all. The rapture of F. L. Lucas, which he did not tie to any particular passage, has already been mentioned

(p. 24 above). Francis Fergusson singles out for special commenda-
tion the speech by Mrs Alving in which she talks to Pastor Manders
about the reasons for her lack of courage, in not opposing the
possible marriage between her son Oswald and his half-sister
Regine.

MRS ALVING I am half inclined to think we are all ghosts, Mr Manders. It is
not only what we have inherited from our fathers and mothers that exists
again in us, but all sorts of dead ideas and all kinds of old dead beliefs and
things of that kind. They are not actually alive in us; but they are dormant all
the same, and we can never be rid of them. Whenever I take up a newspaper
and read it, I fancy I see ghosts creeping between the lines. There must be
ghosts all over the world. They must be as countless as the grains of sand, it
seems to me. And we are so miserably afraid of the light, all of us.*   (Act 2)

Fergusson comments that the scene is ostensibly concerned only
with the 'gossipy facts', the threatened scandal of Oswald falling
in love with his half-sister, but that this is only the literal surface:
in the speech just quoted, Mrs Alving suffers the blow of having
seen the two together, in courage and faith, and is rewarded with
her deepest insight:

This passage, in the fumbling phrases of Ibsen's provincial lady, and in William
Archer's translation, is not by itself the poetry of the great dramatic poets. It
does not have the verbal music of Racine, nor the freedom and sophistication of
Hamlet, nor the scope of the Sophoclean chorus, with its use of the full comple-
ment of poetic and musical and theatrical resources. But in the total situation in
the Alving parlor which Ibsen has so carefully established, and in terms of Mrs
Alving's uninstructed but profoundly developing awareness, it has its own
hidden poetry: a poetry not of words but of theater, a poetry of the histrionic
sensibility. From the point of view of the underlying form of the play − the
form as the 'soul' of the tragedy − this scene completes the sequence which began
with the debate in Act I: it is the pathos-and-epiphany following that agon.

(p. 155)

One would have to agree that any poetry the translated lines
contain is hidden. As far as it goes, Mrs Alving's speech is clear

---

* Men jeg tror naesten, vi er gengangere allesammen, pastor Manders. Det er
  ikke bare det, vi har arvet fra far og mor, som går igen i os. Det er alleslags
  gamle afdøde meninger og alskens gammel afdød tro og sligt noget. Det er
  ikke levende i os; men det sidder i alligevel og vi kan ikke bli' det kvit. Bare jeg
  tar en avis og laeser i, er det ligesom jeg så gengangere smyge imellem linjerne.
  Der må leve gengangere hele landet udover. Der må vaere så tykt af dem som
  sand, synes jeg. Og så er vi så gudsjammerlig lysraedde allesammen.

prose, with little other distinction. What Archer did not bring
out was the repetitive beginnings: 'It is not...It is...It is not', and
'There must live...There must be', which give a certain rhythmic
cohesion. But why did Fergusson use Archer's version at all, if he
wanted to make a point about the poetry: if it is not in Archer,
how do we find it? Why speak of 'fumbling phrases' (which does
not seem appropriate anyway: there is nothing fumbling about
them), why make so many concessions in comparing Ibsen with
other established dramatists, and yet do nothing to indicate where
the hidden poetry lies? Why, most of all, end by speaking of a
'poetry of the histrionic sensibility', without offering any clue to
what that unusual category might sound like? Fergusson does us
no useful service here.

The critic who has faced the issue most squarely, however, is
John Northam, and his claim on Ibsen's behalf is very large
indeed. 'All of Ibsen's books', Northam contends, 'early or late,
in verse or in modern prose, are a form of poetry' (p. 1). If this can
be established, then clearly the Yeatsian objections must be over-
ridden, and even though there might remain room for disagreement about the handling of character, plot and incident,
Ibsen's reputation would still stand very high. Being aware of this,
Northam goes to some length to define his position. He is not willing to settle for a mere intention or ambition on Ibsen's part to write
poetry, or for a mere attempt at expressing intensity of experience
beyond the normal. He refers rather to several definitions of
poetry, relying on 'the commonplace...that a good play, any
good play whether in verse or prose, is more than the sum of its
words' (p. 7) and building up from this to the statement that 'a
play [by Ibsen] contains imagery that is not only verbal but visual;
that is to say not merely words which by association and controlled
expansion of meaning help to enrich the significance of parti-
culars, but also effects that work through the eye in performance
...' As his argument progresses, however, it becomes evident
that, like Fergusson, Northam is not always strictly concerned
with poetry as a matter of words. 'When [Ibsen] enters upon his
series of modern prose plays,' Northam continues, 'the emphasis
moves away from the verbal to the visual as more and more is
left unsaid because unsayable.' It begins to appear that the claim

will not be made in terms of words at all: 'In the plays of this later period of his life, Ibsen may have adjusted the elements of his dramatic poetry but he has not ceased to write poetry' (p. 7) – in other words, it is the imagery of a wild duck, or of a steeple, or of 'burning the child', the visual element, that constitutes the poetry, rather than the verbal element, the words used.

It has been part of the purpose of this present study to show how at least a great deal of this visual imagery is other than poetic: how the ambiguity of the wild duck is confusing, and ironically intended to appear confusing, rather than ambiguous with the life of poetry, how the steeple attached to Solness's lowly domestic buildings is incongruous in its realistic setting, how the white horses of Rosmersholm are used to create a superstitious and thus melodramatic climax. The supposedly unsayable element in *Little Eyolf* has also been discussed, and there is no occasion to repeat these arguments now. The issue at present is a matter of poetry in words, and Northam does not draw back from stating his position plainly in this case either. Though the emphasis has moved away from the verbal, by his account, he does not maintain that the verbal ceases to play its part. On the contrary, he provides many examples of Ibsen's prose, analysing the rhetorical devices, exploring the rhythms, and linking the prose to his general statement that the 'modern prose plays are, even more decisively than the earlier plays, works whose essential experience is conveyed not through plot or character study but through complex and, by now, highly structured patterns of unified dramatic imagery' (p. 7). It is not absolutely clear at this point, it must be confessed, whether he is lending weight to Ibsen's statement that even his prose was poetry, or whether he is speaking of Ibsen's *poésie de théâtre*. Later on, however, his argument is explicit: there is a kind of poetry in Ibsen's characters which is prevented from emerging with its full power, a 'deep poetry at bottom', to use Ibsen's own phrase about Hedda, which is stunted from the outset:

Brand, though more fully committed [than Falk] to the society he must live in, remains free to articulate his moral poetry in words and in actions; even though Ibsen now recognises that his very power must make his achievement irreconcilable with actual living he, too, can resist contamination by society; moral poetry also can remain inviolable even when it is mistaken. Mrs Alving is the first character whose very poetry is infected by the social conditions it is directed against; her moral poetry is tethered by a social habit of thought so that her vision expresses itself in the cadences of social rhetoric and in actions that are at best ambiguously free.   (p. 180)

The fuller sense here is that Mrs Alving's mode of speech is curiously close to that of Pastor Manders. Northam shows how Manders has a predilection for a sort of rhyme effect, how, in a single passage, several of his 'lines' have identical or similar beginnings, and identical word-terminations ('recklessness', 'lawlessness', 'heedlessness', 'unscrupulousness'), and a fondness for doublets like 'house and home', for alliteration and cliché (pp. 82–83). When Mrs Alving replies to Manders, Northam observes, it is remarkable 'that a woman so unlike Manders in personality should speak in forms so similar.' They both, he concludes, speak as society has educated them to speak. Yet Mrs Alving is also very different from Manders, even in her speech. Unlike him, she does not speak for a conventionally rhetorical effect, her 'rhymes' are not flourishes, but registers of emotional preoccupation, she uses no word-play, no doublets, no alliteration, in short she is expressing her own experience, but 'sufficiently under the domination of society still to control her thoughts and her language into conformity with the social demand for a neat shape to things' (p. 86).

The two speeches which Northam offers as most clearly showing a similarity in patterning are these, the first by Pastor Manders, the second by Mrs Alving (as divided by Northam into verse-like lines):

MANDERS   You have been governed by a fatal spirit of self-will throughout
           all your days.
           All your bent has been turned towards recklessness and lawless-
           ness.
           Always you have refused to acknowledge any tie upon you.
           All encumbrances on your life you have thrown off with
           heedlessness and unscrupulousness,
           like a burden that could be disposed of by you yourself at will.
           It did not suit you any longer to be a wife
           and you parted from your husband.
           It became irksome to you to be a mother,
           and you put your child forth amongst strangers.   (p. 83)

MRS ALVING I would never have survived if I hadn't had my work.
           Yes, I think I can say that I have worked.
              All those extensions to the estate,
              all the improvements,
              all the useful developments Alving got the praise
                 and credit for...
              I was the one who drove him on
                 when he had his more lucid intervals;
              I was the one who had to carry the full load
                 when he relapsed into debauchery
                 or sank into whimpering spinelessness.   (p. 85)

Mrs Alving's speech shows in fact rather more similarity with
Manders' than Northam allows, for she uses both alliteration and
doublets in the original of the passage. But the vital question is
whether one can properly speak here of any deep poetry at
bottom, a poetry infected by society or by any other contamination. Did Ibsen mean no more than that some of his prose was
spoken with the rhythms of passionate utterance (it is certainly
not all passionate)? And is there a vital difference, so far as poetry
is concerned, between the personal protest that Mrs Alving is
making and the impersonal yet almost Biblical phrasing of
Mander's speech? Where are the signs that Mrs Alving has any
poetry in her to be stifled? Where is the latent poetry which she
would express if she were not prevented by the society in which
she lives? If the argument holds at all, it must hold not only for
Ibsen, but for other writers also. Yet there would be small cause
for finding a stifled poetry in Jane Austen, despite the fact that
when Emma speaks to Harriet Smith, congratulating her on her
supposed success in winning the love of Mr Elton, she too has
rhyme effects, several similar beginnings of sentences, and identical
word-terminations, as well as doublets and a certain rhetorical
flourish:

              There is so *pointed* and so *particular* a meaning in
                 this compliment,
              that I cannot have a doubt as to Mr Elton's intentions.
              You are his object
              – and you will soon see the completest proof of it.
              I thought it must be so.
              I thought I could not be so deceived...

Yes, Harriet, just so long have I been wanting
   the very circumstance to happen
which has happened.
I could never tell whether an attachment between
   you and Mr Elton
were *most desirable* or *most natural*.
Its *probability* and its *eligibility*
have really so equalled each other!
I am very happy.
I congratulate you, my dear Harriet, with
   all my heart.
This is an attachment which a woman may
   feel pride in creating.
This is a connection which offers nothing but good.
It will give you everything that you want –
consideration, independence, a good home –
it will fix you in the centre of all your real friends,
close to Hartfield and to me,
and confirm our intimacy for ever.
This, Harriet, is an alliance which can never
   raise a blush in either of us.   (Ch. 9)

The speech of Hedda Gabler's analysed by Northam is more passionate than Emma's, though still essentially prose. Dividing up her several short speeches welcoming Løvborg's suicide as though they were verses does little more than bring out the natural rhetorical units, as Northam calls them. They then run:

                      At last an achievement!
                      I tell you there's beauty in this.
       Eilert Løvborg has had a reckoning with himself.
            He has had the courage to do – what had to be done...
                 What a release it is,
this thing of Eilert Løvborg's...
                    A release to know
that something really can happen in this world that shows courage and free-will.
Something with a touch of spontaneous beauty to it...
                  ...I only know
that Eilert Løvborg has had the courage to live his life after his own fashion.
                 And now –
this great thing.
   This thing with beauty to it.
     That he had the strength and the will to take leave of life's feast –
                so early.   (p. 174)

There is no denying that a certain repetition, of a kind associated with both verse and prose, is apparent in this arrangement. The case is weakened, indeed totally destroyed, by the fact that, in the play, this is not one single speech but many. The lines printed in sequence here are separated at intervals by equally long speeches by other characters, and there are not only omissions from two of the speeches by Hedda, seriously affecting any apparent rhythm in them, but a gap of some twenty speeches by others intervening between the first and second half of what she says in the whole of the passage quoted. In short, the audience in the theatre cannot experience Hedda's words in the form to which they are reduced for this analysis. The formal qualities which might just conceivably approximate to poetry, if the general argument were conceded at all, exist only in the compressed and shortened version presented in Northam's book, not in any possible stage performance.

The analysis does not at first claim to find anything poetic even in the form of the speeches as they are presented, only that Hedda 'speaks from the centre of her personality', and that her obsession 'has content, serious content'. As it continues, however, the same frankness of presentation allows the claim on Ibsen's behalf to diminish, if that claim is to be understood as 'writing poetry in straightforward, realistic, everyday language'. Hedda begins, Northam agrees, with an air of certainty, with clear statements. Soon, however, a 'significant vagueness begins to creep in':

Within each rhetorical unit, the element that is meant to define fails to do so. The 'beauty' of what Løvborg has done is defined by a vague figure of speech – 'has had a reckoning with himself'. Hedda herself seems to find it hard to define his 'courage' – there is that significant little pause between 'to do' and 'what had...'; and when she finds the words they are vague. Indeed she returns for a second attempt at definition with 'the courage to live his life after his own fashion' but that is no clearer. She tries three times to define her sense of release, and each time falls back on 'something'. 'Thing' leads to the climax of her definition: 'this great thing. This thing...', but the climax itself, her most strenuous attempt to be specific, emerges as another vague figure of speech: 'to take leave of life's feast'; poetical and sentimental.   (p. 175)

After so many concessions, it is surprising to find the analysis concluding that Hedda's vision 'cannot be dismissed as an empty one when it has such content'. The analysis shows only that no significant content becomes apparent, and it is leaning too far backwards to say that 'the vagueness of her rhetoric shows that Hedda is gesturing towards values that she cannot give full definition to,' if by that is meant 'the unsayable', with all its grandiose association, rather than that Hedda simply does not know what she did expect of Løvborg. Even less can one move from such a demonstration of vagueness, poeticality and sentimentality to saying that 'However deep Hedda's poetry may be driven by her social conditioning, she remains a poet' (p. 183). There has been nothing in the demonstration to show that poetry comes into the question at all. A woman who reaches the height of her praise for a supposedly noble suicide with such a cliché as the one about taking leave of life's feast remains only inauthentic. What feast did Hedda Gabler ever see in life? She throws in the cliché because words mean as little to her as everything else does.

The justification of Ibsen's reputation on the strength of his language still remains to be done, if it can be done at all. What he is like in Norwegian can, it is true, only be fully experienced by those to whom Norwegian is or is like a native language, but unless that knowledge can be brought convincingly to the rest of the world, the presumption that a dramatist crude in so many other ways would be unlikely to achieve great heights in language must be allowed to stand. The instinct of Synge and Yeats seems to have been right.

A list of
critical works referred to

Some passages quoted will be found in James McFarlane's collection *Henrik Ibsen, A Critical Anthology*, Harmondsworth 1970. Reference may also be made to *Ibsen, The Critical Heritage*, edited by Michael Egan, London 1972. The following list cites editions used for other passages discussed or referred to in the present text.

Bentley, Eric, *In Search of Theatre*, London 1950

Bradbrook, Muriel C., *Ibsen the Norwegian*, new edn., London 1966

Brustein, Robert, 'Henrik Ibsen' in *The Theatre of Revolt*, London 1965

Cox, R. G., 'Rehabilitating Ibsen' in *Scrutiny*, vol. XIV, Cambridge 1947

Esslin, Martin, *The Theatre of the Absurd*, London 1969

Ewbank, Inga-Stina, 'Ibsen and the "Far more difficult Art" of Prose' in *Contemporary Approaches to Ibsen* (ed. Daniel Haakonsen), Oslo 1971

Fergusson, Francis, '*Ghosts* and *The Cherry Orchard*' in *The Idea of a Theater*, Princeton University Press 1949 and (paperback) 1968

Gosse, Edmund, 'Ibsen's Social Dramas' in *Fortnightly Review* Vol. 65, 1889

Granville-Barker, Harley, 'The Coming of Ibsen' in *The Eighteen Eighties* (ed. Walter de la Mare), London 1930

James, Henry, 'On the Occasion of *Hedda Gabler*', *New Review*, June 1891, and letter of 25 November 1894, quoted from James McFarlane's *Anthology*

James, Henry, *The Scenic Art* (ed. Alan Wade), Harmondsworth 1968

Kruuse, Jens, 'The Function of Humour in the Later Plays of Ibsen' in *Contemporary Approaches to Ibsen* (ed. Daniel Haakonsen), Oslo 1971

Lucas, F. L., *The Dramas of Ibsen and Strindberg*, London 1962

McCarthy, Mary, 'The Will and Testament of Ibsen' in *Sights and Spectacles 1937–1958*, London 1959

McFarlane, James, Introductions to the volumes of *The Oxford Ibsen* (1960–77)

Muir, Kenneth, *The Last Periods of Shakespeare, Racine and Ibsen*, Liverpool 1962

Northam, John, *Ibsen. A Critical Study*, Cambridge 1973

Peacock, Ronald, *The Poet in the Theatre*, London 1946

Robins, Elizabeth, *Theatre and Friendship*, 1932

Shaw, George Bernard, *The Quintessence of Ibsenism*, London 1891, second edn. 1913

Steiner, George, *The Death of Tragedy*, London 1961

Synge, John Millington, Preface to *The Playboy of the Western World* in *Collected Works*, vol. IV, Oxford 1962–8

Tennant, P. F. D., *Ibsen's Dramatic Technique*, Cambridge 1948, reissued New York 1965

Weightman, John, 'Ibsen and the Absurd' in *Encounter*, October 1975

Williams, Raymond, *Drama from Ibsen to Brecht*, London 1968

Yeats, William Butler, Preface to Synge's *The Well of the Saints* in Synge's *Collected Works*, see above

A chronological list of all the plays

(1828 Ibsen born at Skien)
1850 *Catiline* (published)
1850 *The Burial Mound* (= The Warrior's Barrow) (performed)
1853 *St John's Night* (performed)
1855 *Lady Inger of Østraat* (performed)
1856 *The Feast at Solhaug* (performed)
1857 *Olaf Liljekrans* (performed)
1858 *The Vikings at Helgeland* (published)
1862 *Love's Comedy* (published)
1863 *The Pretenders* (published)
1866 *Brand* (published)
1867 *Peer Gynt* (published)
1869 *The League of Youth* (published)
1873 *Emperor and Galilean* (published)
1877 *Pillars of Society* (published)
1879 *A Doll's House* (published)
1881 *Ghosts* (published)
1882 *An Enemy of the People* (published)
1884 *The Wild Duck* (published)
1886 *Rosmersholm* (published)
1888 *The Lady from the Sea* (published)
1890 *Hedda Gabler* (published)
1892 *The Master Builder* (published)
1894 *Little Eyolf* (published)
1896 *John Gabriel Borkman* (published)
1899 *When We Dead Awaken* (published)
(1906 Ibsen died)

Index

A. IBSEN

This section may simplify reference to the main points in the critical argument, by grouping together instances of Ibsen's dramatic technique and thus enabling the cumulative force of the criticisms to be more plainly seen, also by showing how his concern with dialectical philosophies (however little systematic or deliberate) interrelates a number of his themes and symbols.

i. *Dramatic technique*

CHARACTERISATION: naivety, 31, 34, 55, 65, 69, 79, 80, 90, 101, 102, 115, 135, 142; 'mere cyphers', 21; manipulation of characters for desired ending, 142–4; grotesques or caricatures, 43, 47, 135, 192; unmotivated volte-face in the interests of dramatic action, 50, 70, 80, 88, 89, 93, 96, 116–17, 122, 128, 130, 138, 139, 142, 167, 193; simplification of motives, 21, 28, 36, 79, 142; lack of differentiation in speech, 23, 30

DRAMATIC DEVICES AND MODES OF TREATMENT: expositions, 2, 43, 63–4, 99–102, 114–15, 126, 151; curtain-falls, 2, 35, 69–70, 76, 123; blackmail, 44, 65, 141–2; 'appropriate coincidences', 109–10, 151; congruity between events and theme, 78, 88, 124, 138; stage-directions, 160–1, 195, 197; poetic justice, 121; irony, 28, 36, 90, 98, 107–9, 159, 161, 165, 187–8, 194, 196; black humour, 144, 147, 192, 193–4, 209; melodrama, 35, 43, 44, 48, 49, 52, 55, 57, 70, 97, 143, 173, 218

SYMBOLS: devils (see also Faustian echoes in section A.ii.), 10, 18, 64, 75, 110, 155, 156–7, 158, 178, 190, 198; loss of children, 39, 56, 79, 108, 138, 155–7, 165, 167, 172; fire, 66, 74–5, 155–6; symbolism in plays before *The Wild Duck*, 105; duck, 105–9; Christ/Judas, 110; Ibsen's critique of symbols but continued use of them, 113; white horses, 123; sea, 125; sculptural metaphors, 126, 190, 192; Stranger as elemental power, 128–9; wound in the temple, 143; claim that in Ibsen verbal and visual imagery co-operate: steeple, 153–4; brutal Nature, also Nemesis, 189; Lohengrin's swan, also Resurrection Day, 195

USE OF LANGUAGE: 23, 30, 210, 213–23

ii. *Themes connected with dialectical philosophies*

alternation of themes of plays, 42, 51, 99, 112, 124, 173
ambiguity, 13, 14, 49, 67–8, 82, 106, 110, 113, 136–8, 140, 170, 171, 181, 199, 218

Christianity, 2, 7, 10, 15, 17, 18, 61–2, 72, 75, 119, 120, 163, 171, 197, 201
Faustian echoes (see also Goethe in section B), 3–6, 9–11, 13–16, 18–19, 42, 62, 156, 163, 169, 178–9, 184, 200, 207, 211
incest, 70–1, 74, 81, 118, 169, 172, 183
joy in living (see also Nietzsche in section B), 12, 17, 62, 73, 76, 77, 81, 135–6, 181, 196
Kingship, 6, 7, 39, 91, 152–3, 158–9, 178, 181, 187
pairs of women, 18, 179
synthesis (see also Hegel in section B), 15, 17, 112, 122, 196
universal significance claimed, 62, 91, 109, 111, 209

iii. *Works* (see also p. 226)

Brand, 11–15, 18, 19, 21, 22, 61, 72, 82, 201
The Burial Mound (The Warrior's Barrow), 72
Catiline, 5, 14, 119
A Doll's House, 5, 41–58, 62, 79, 80, 149, 200, 207
Emperor and Galilean, 2, 15–18, 26, 74, 112, 184, 200
An Enemy of the People, 71, 84–98, 149, 205, 207
The Feast at Solhaug, 8
Ghosts, 3, 26, 46, 47, 59–83, 137, 149, 156, 174, 181, 184, 193, 201–2, 204, 205, 207–9, 216, 219
Hedda Gabler, 23, 26, 46, 58, 66, 131–48, 161, 193–4, 204, 210, 221–3
John Gabriel Borkman, 10, 18, 39, 42, 163, 173–99
The Lady from the Sea, 124–30, 163, 193, 204
Lady Inger of Østraat, 6, 149
Little Eyolf, 163–73
Love's Comedy, 14, 72
The Master Builder, 7, 17, 42, 149–62, 187, 193, 198, 210
Peer Gynt, 5, 14, 15, 18, 19, 61, 163, 200
Pillars of Society, 20, 26–40, 41, 51, 55, 200, 202
Poems, 2
The Pretenders, 8, 14, 38, 39, 42, 64, 91, 154, 181, 184
Rosmersholm, 77, 114–24, 149, 193, 202, 204
The Vikings at Helgeland, 7, 17, 119
The Wild Duck, 32, 99–113, 193, 205
When We Dead Awaken, 20, 163, 173, 182, 184–98

B. GENERAL

Absurd, Theatre of the, 193
Agnes Bernauer, 111–12
Anna Karenina, 55, 56, 135
Archer, William, i, 23, 201, 203, 217
Ashcroft, Peggy, 134
Augier, Émile, 45
Austen, Jane, 220–1
Avariés, Les, 82–3

Baudelaire, 210
Beckett, Samuel, 186, 210
Beethoven, 184–5
Bendix, Roderich, 201
Bennett, Arnold, 69, 205
Bentley, Eric, 14, 24, 224
Bergman, Ingmar, 135
Bjørnson, Bjørnstjerne, 8, 39, 93, 98, 154, 200
Bradbrook, Muriel, 23, 161, 163, 165, 224
Brandes Georg, 61, 93, 201
Breaking a Butterfly, 57
Brecht, 53, 99
Brieux, Eugène, 82–3
Brontë, Emily, 130
Brustein, Robert, 184–5, 189, 224
Büchner, Georg, 30, 210
Burckhardt, Jakob, 4
Burns, John, 201

Chekhov, 135, 146–8
Cox, R. G., 185, 214–15, 224

Damaged Goods, 82–3
Dame aux Camélias, La, 52
Davis, Derek Russell, 68
Dumas *fils*, Alexandre, 51

East Lynne, 52–3
Egan, Michael, 203
Egmont, 99
Eliot, T. S., 1, 123, 205
Ellis, Havelock, 201
Empson, William, 206
Esslin, Martin, 193, 224
Ewbank, I.-S., 215, 224

Father, The, 154–5
Fergusson, Francis, 24, 216–17, 224
Flaubert, 144–5
Freud, 118, 125, 207

Goethe, 3, 4, 5, 10, 11, 13, 15, 16, 18, 19, 32, 41, 99, 112, 164, 178, 207
Gosse, Edmund, 20, 98, 201–2, 204, 224
Granville-Barker, Harley, 57, 71, 175, 224
Grene, David, 164
Grillparzer, Franz, 8, 9, 156

Halévy, Ludovic, 2
Hamlet, 5, 6, 194
Hamsun, Knut, 21, 155
Hardie, Keir, 201
Hebbel, Friedrich, 45, 52, 56, 111, 201
Hegel, Hegelian, 4, 15, 20, 59, 60, 111, 112, 119, 122, 196, 199, 207, 211
Heiberg, Johan, 4
Heller, Erich, 112
Herman, Henry, 57
Herodes und Mariamne, 45
He Who Said No, 99
Holz, Arno, 200
Howells, W. D., 202

Ibsen, Hedvig (sister), 169
insanity, 7, 93, 104, 149–50, 165, 189, 192
Iphigenie auf Tauris, 32, 99

James, Henry, 24, 131–2, 135, 145, 165–6, 167, 169, 202, 203–5, 224
Jones, Henry Arthur, 57
Joyce, James, 207

Kafka, 152
Kieler, Laura, 43
Kierkegaard, 15, 156
King Lear, 147, 174, 180, 182, 194
King Ottokar, 8
Koht, Halvdan, 4, 140
Kruuse, Jens, 144, 193, 224

Lawrence, D. H., 1, 205
Leavis, F. R., 1
Le Gallienne, Eva, 140
Lincoln, Abraham, 94 (n)
Lohengrin, 195
Lucas, F. L., 24, 64, 215–16, 224

Macbeth, 8, 174
McCarthy, Mary, 1, 132, 224
McFarlane, James, 20, 21, 24, 61, 108, 139–40, 161, 165, 194, 224
Madame Bovary, 144–5
Manchester Guardian, 60
Mann, Thomas, 112
Mariage d'Olympe, Le, 45
Marx, Karl, 201
Mary Magdalene, 52
Medea, 132, 146
Meilhac, Henri, 2
Meyer, Michael, 23, 144
Mill, J. S., 94 (n)
Molière, 38
Muir, Kenneth, 164, 224
Munch, Edvard, 3

Nietzsche, 2, 13, 55, 72, 73, 77, 122, 189, 201
Northam, John, 23, 65, 73, 77, 82, 122, 153, 165–6, 168, 169, 171, 217–23, 224

Oedipus at Colonus, 182–3

Osborne, John, 1
Othello, 123

Peacock, Ronald, 19, 224
Phèdre, 123, 146
Plimsoll, Samuel, 33
politics, 5, 9, 29, 92–3, 94 (n), 114, 116

Quintessence of Ibsenism, The, 53, 205

Racine, 55, 164
Ring of the Nibelung, The, 182
Robins, Elizabeth, 132–3, 139, 165–6, 169, 204, 224
Romeo and Juliet, 123

St John, Gospel of, 122 (n)
Sardou, Victorien, 2
Saxe-Meiningen, Duke of, 200
Schiller, 10, 11, 30, 98
schizophrenia, 68
Schlaf, Johannes, 200
Schlegel, Friedrich, 112, 196
Schopenhauer, 60, 125, 153, 201
Scribe, Eugène, 2, 101
Scrutiny, 1, 185, 214
Seven Types of Ambiguity, 206
Shakespeare, 20, 30, 36, 41, 108, 147, 163, 164, 173–4, 182, 205, 214–15
Shaw, 1, 22, 53, 60, 83, 201, 205, 224
Smith, Maggie, 141
Sophocles, 164, 173–4, 182
Steiner, George, 20, 224
Stephens, James, 165
Strindberg, 55, 154–5
Symons, Arthur, 202–3
Synge, 1, 20, 205, 213, 214, 223, 224
syphilis, 68

Tennant, P. F. D., 21, 23, 100, 224
Threepenny Opera, The, 53
Tocqueville, de, Alexis, 54–5
Tolstoy, 36, 55, 147, 201, 202
Tourneur, Cyril, 205
Traviata, La, 52
Trial, The, 152
Tristan und Isolde, 122–3
Troilus and Cressida, 194

Uncle Vanya, 135, 146–8

Uppsala, 200

Verdi, 200
Victoria, Queen, 205
Voysey Inheritance, The, 175–6

Wagner, Richard, 123, 182, 200, 213
Waste, 71
Wedekind, Frank, 210
Weightman, John, 1, 224
Wildenbruch, Ernst, 201

Wilhelm Meister, 15, 112
Williams, Raymond, 19, 224
Wolf, Lucie, 214
Wood, Mrs Henry, 52
Wuthering Heights, 128, 130

Yeats, W. B., 1, 20, 21, 205, 213, 214, 223, 224

Zola, 203

WITHDRAWN
MOUNT ST. MARY'S
COLLEGE
EMMITSBURG, MARYLAND
142743

WITHDRAWN

JUL 2 3 1980